SUCCESS IN THE CLEAN BEDROOM

A Path to Optimal Health

SUCCESS IN THE CLEAN BEDROOM

A Path to Optimal Health

By

Natalie Golos

William J. Rea, M.D.

Foreword by Doris Rapp, M.D.
author of the Best Seller "Is This Your Child"

Note that the word "he" is used throughout this book as shorthand for "he and she" and is not meant to imply gender discrimination, male superiority, or the authors' laziness.

Pinnacle Publishers
Rochester, New York

Library of Congress Cataloging in Publication Data

Golos, Natalie; Rea, William J., M.D.
Success in the clean bedroom: a path to optimal health
Bibliography; p.
Includes index
1. Environmentally-triggered illness. Popular works. 2. Multiple chemical
sensitivities. Popular works. I. Title.
February 1992
Library of Congress Catalog Card No. 92-060164
ISBN 0-9632308-0-8 Pbk.

DEDICATION

To Jane and David

without whom this book would never have been possible

— and to all who suffer from chemical sensitivities

(both those who know it and those who don't.)

PREFACE

Forget the gloom and doom. Forget the panic. Forget the disasters, the toxic waste dumps, the sick building syndrome. Forget the bizarre interviews with people presented as freaks because they have environmentally triggered illness.

The news media is filled with these.

Concentrate on the SUCCESS STORIES. That's the thrust of "Success in the Clean Bedroom."

Although some of the book is written in first person, it is the combined effort of two pinoeers, William Rea, M.D. and Natalie Golos. We have joined forces to share what we have learned, first as victims of the disease and then as professionals, learning and teaching others the way back to health.

This book can help you educate yourself and find answers about restoring and maintaining optimal health.

FOREWORD

If you have environmental illness and don't know why, *Success in the Clean Bedroom* will provide many answers gently sprinkled with sensible but necessary precautions. The authors emphasize many unsuspected problems that perplex, bother, and incapacitate many adults who have been unsuccessfully seeking answers for years. They explain that it is no longer necessary to learn to live with many environmentally-related medical and emotional problems. Page after page of practical tips explain what you can do for yourself to figure out why you don't feel up to par and are unable to reach your full potential as a person, parent, or spouse.

The chapter about Home Testing, for example, can help you detect exactly what in your home can be causing you or your family to feel unwell or act in an inappropriate manner. It can also help you figure out what is best to buy from a health standpoint.

If you suspect that you have any food allergies, Part V, "Allergy Free Cooking" and Part VI "Allergy Free Cook Book can help you.

This is the best book on food allergies and there is no second best. *Success in the Clean Bedroom* tells how to recognize offending foods and how to enjoy a varied diet so you can retain your good health or restore your previous feeling of well-being. This book anticipates the daily problems busy people face when attempting diets and realistically offers many choices and compromises, i.e., how to handle the desire to break or change a diet. The greatest asset of this book, however, is the simplicity and variety which it offers. The authors have used their imagination and wealth of knowledge to outline the essential recipes which will make the rotary diet workable and usable on a long term basis. The suggestions make the diet not only tolerable but more pleasant.

In essence, this book simplifies and expands the rotary diet so that it is possible to enjoy a wide variety of foods. The authors will be revered by those who have found previous rotary diets a dreary, impossible challenge which robs them of the joy of eating. It can no longer be said that one does not know what to eat or that there is not enough to eat.

Success in the Clean Bedroom will also be helpful to many who may not associate their health problems with allergies. This includes the many people who are exhausted to the point of being unable to do their housework, nervous to the point of being unable to hold a job, irritable to the point of divorce, foggy-headed to the point of being unable to complete their education, and depressed to the point of suicide. Vast numbers of people are plagued with daily or intermittent unexplained muscle pain, joint aches, arthritis, abdominal pain, diarrhea, constipation, hypertension, heart disease, bizarre weakness, paralysis, and seizures. Mothers feel inadequate and unworthy because no matter how hard they try, their children are always ill and no cause can be found. Amazing numbers of children are made to feel unloved, unwanted, bad, and stupid at home and at school, because parents, teachers, and physicians have failed to recognize the role foods and chemicals play in intolerable behavior, extreme fatigue, hyperactivity, and inability to concentrate. Many children are embarrassed and punished daily because of passing gas, wetting the bed, or soiling their underwear.

The manifestations of illness which I have just enumerated, of course, have multiple causes—but the one which is frequently overlooked is environmental illness. In some patients, the above medical problems stop when they find the role that unsuspected food or chemical offenders play in their illness.

This book has something to offer almost everyone. It will enable those with mild illness to stand alone. Those who have severely debilitating food and chemical illness do not just need this book—they must have it. In addition, they need the personal care of an environmental medicine specialist. The authors offer a way out when you are between a rock and a hard place. Once their method is mastered, you will have more time, more money, and—most important—better health.

Doris J. Rapp, M.D., FAAA, FAAP
Assistant Clinical Professor of Pediatrics at the State University of New York at Buffalo

Author of *Is This Your Child*, *The Impossible Child*, *Allergies and the Hyperactive Child* and *Allergies and Your Family* xi

ACKNOWLEDGEMENTS

SPECIAL GRATITUDE

To the authors and writers who granted permission to quote their papers and books: Dr. James Cox; Dr. Patrick Donavan; Carolyn P. Gorman, M.A., H.E.E.D.; Russell Jaffe, M.D., Ph.D.; Marjorie Hurt Jones, R.N.; Wayne H. Konetzki, M.D.; George Miller, M.D.; Joseph Miller, M.D.; Doris Rapp, M.D., Jane Roller, M.Sc.; and Francis Silver, P.E.

To the dieticians who furnished nutritional assistance: Stephanie Bauer, R.D., L.D.; Linda Carlisle, R.D., L.D.; Kelly Daniel, R.D.; Louise Gilmer, R.D., L.D.; Karee Grier, M.A., R.D., L.D.; Maryann Lazer, M.A., R.D.; and Barbara Maynard, R.D., L.D.

To those who helped with the manuscript: Maryann Lazer, M.A., R.D.; Glyn Nelson, B.A.; and Marjorie Rosenfeld, M.A.

A special thanks to the two assistant editors: Violet A. Houser, B.A., and Ellen J. Shenk, M.Ed.

Table of Contents

PART I

INTRODUCTION

1

HOW TO USE THIS BOOK

My co-author, Bill Rea, and other doctors who have used my earlier books encouraged me to tell how I changed my life-style and returned from life-threatening illness to a healthy, happy, normal, and productive life again. Hopefully, this book will encourage you chronically ill people and teach you how to do this yourself. It will also inform you healthy people who feel that this illness could not possibly happen to you. I held this same view when I was a healthy and athletic person.

My story and the other success stories will not be in chronological order but will be introduced in appropriate sections as they illustrate the way to success over environmentally-triggered illness.

As you read through this book you will notice that several different kinds of type are used. We have done this because the book has many different messages to give and each one will be in a different type.

"Basic Type." This first main print represents the culmination of 15 years of co-operation between the two co-authors and presents the main message of the book including success stories.

It will help you, once you have finished reading the book, to go back and use it as a reference work. It will be used for helpful tips and procedures that you will want to look up at various points in your journey toward health.

"Natalie's Story." This type will be used to tell my own experiences. Hopefully these experiences will

help you understand the illness, learn how to
recognize it, know how to get help and where to go
for it, assume responsibility for your own health,
regain your health, or remain healthy if you are now
healthy.

"Instructions." This is the type that gives instructions for many
kinds of exercises, and suggestions for relaxation techniques and
testing methods.

*"Products". This fourth type, in this typeface, will be used
throughout the book for suggested products.* I must say that strange as it
may seem, I need to use my books every day because I can't possibly
remember all the details, addresses, and sources. But all the information
is there for me—and for you—when we need it. Although the products
favorably mentioned in this book have been tolerated by at least 10 or
more very sensitive patients, no product is safe for everyone. This is an
individual process and you must still test each product for yourself.

Everyone, even people without allergies or chemical sensitivities,
should test products while they can still be returned. For example, one
woman who had no problem with allergies bought a shower curtain but
found that she could not stand the smell when it was hung.

*You will find this print used in the text to lead you to Appendix E for
products that have been found to be fairly safe for most people. In
Appendix E, names, addresses, and phone numbers of companies that
supply relatively safe products will be in this print as well as helpful
organizations.*

2

SUCCESS STORIES

Years ago at the onset of my illness I had to convince trades people, service people, and doctors such as gynecologists, ophthalmologists, and otolaryngologists that mine was not an isolated case. Because of the great interest in my first two books, I had learned that many others also had this problem.

Now I have to convince people that I am not alone in my triumph over environmentally-triggered illness. There are thousands of other chemically-sensitive people who have now regained control of their lives as I have done. Many of them have changed professions while others have learned to accommodate their illness in their professions.

Illness. Before we give their stories it is important for you to understand two things: the nature of illness and the nature of environmentally-triggered illness. Dr. Ronald Finn, chief consultant of the Royal Liverpool Hospital in Liverpool, England and 1982 winner of the prestigious Albert Lasker Award in medicine, divides illness or disease into "congenital, degenerative and environmental. Environmental illness is subdivided into infectious and non-infectious, i.e., chemical, physical... Many of the common diseases are due to interactions between these groups. Thus a very common cause of disease is due to the interaction of an environmental agent in a genetically susceptible individual." [Anyone in a family prone to allergies.] "Congenital and degenerative disease is difficult to treat but the removal of an environmental cause is theoretically much easier and effective, providing irrevocable damage has not already occurred."

Environmentally-triggered Illness is described by Dr. Doris Rapp in her book *Is This Your Child* as an illness that is caused by anything you eat, drink, smell, or touch."

All stresses whether they are caused by a food, chemical, toxin, or an interpersonal problem, place a load on our body which can weaken our immune system. When we have too many stresses our immune system overloads and cannot handle even the ordinary stresses that we encounter in everyday living.

In this book you will learn about the different types of stress, the problems they cause, and ways many people have successfully dealt with them.

ᥬ ᥬ ᥬ

Because of—not in spite of my illness—I have three new professions. I have become an author; this book is my seventh on the subject of environ- mentally-triggered illness and allergies. I have learned to be a counselor in the field of environmental medicine. And as the result of nine years of training and practice in body therapies, I have developed a new cleansing procedure called cellibration therapy. More about that later.

ᥬ ᥬ ᥬ

Many nurses and technicians have been able to accommodate their illness in their current profession and now work in the offices and centers of environmental medicine (EM) specialists, medical doctors who treat environmentally-triggered illnesses. These professionals bring to their centers not only training in nursing and medicine, but also their personal understanding of what the patient is experiencing.

Co-author, Bill Rea, is a cardiovascular surgeon who developed environmentally-triggered illness years ago. His symptoms included falling asleep while driving, dizzy spells, and bouts of flu. When he almost blacked out during surgery a colleague recommended an allergist. The allergy shots provided some relief, but Bill realized he needed to look further and he took a series of food tests. He learned, through the testing and through reading, that he was a universal food reactor. This means that he was sensitive, in varying degrees, to all foods. At first he handled this by fasting during the long working day and adhering strictly to the rotary diet, described in the chapter on food rotation; at night he ate a substantial meal. He continues to rotate his food.

Suspecting that he might also have chemical sensitivities, Bill cleaned up his home environment in Dallas, Texas, replacing the gas furnace with electric heat and rugs with hardwood floors. It was almost a year before the excitants in his house had dispersed enough so he could move back into his home. Although Bill's health began to improve with these changes to his home, substantial improvements came only after he cleaned up his work environment.

By maintaining a pure environment in his home, office, and surgery, by drinking pure water, and by rotating organic food, today Bill Rea is healthy without the use of medications.

His experiences have many ramifications. He continues to perform as a surgeon and from watching his patients has learned about the impact of the environment on cardiovascular disorders. Bill has developed one of the leading centers in EM and is the international leader in this field. His annual "International Symposium on Man and His Environment in Health and Disease" attracts doctors from all over the world. Many of these doctors also study with him in his center. (Also see inside cover about the authors.)

Gwen Roark. This is the story of a young woman who became seriously ill yet was able to enter a new profession and rise to the top. Gwen had given up teaching Home Economics when she married and had a family. When she became ill Gwen's problems included an extreme sensitivity to cold and fingers that often turned blue.

She was diagnosed as having Reynaud's disease, a circulatory disorder, and given medications to thin her blood and dilate her blood vessels. Soon after beginning this medication Gwen developed severe headaches and was given medication for these headaches so that she could continue to take the medication which dilated the blood vessels. However, nothing helped her and the finger turned black, an indication of developing gangrene. To prevent amputation of the finger the doctor suggested that some of the nerves that regulated the tone of the blood vessels should be clipped.

At this point Gwen asked for a consultation with another cardiovascular surgeon and was referred to Dr. Rea. By that time the finger was ulcerated and was so advanced that he suspected that it would have to be amputated, the procedure usually used in such advanced cases of Reynaud's disease. Having learned from clinical observation that Reynaud's disease is a vascular disorder that responds to the ecologic approach, Dr. Rea suggested that she be checked for allergies and sensitivities. After a few days in the environmentally controlled unit of the hospital Gwen's blood started circulating through the fingers, the ulcerations cleared up, and her finger was out of danger. Subsequent testing showed that the poor circulation was caused by sensitivities to certain foods and chemicals.

Gwen learned that avoiding these excitants prevented symptoms of Reynaud's disease; these symptoms returned with any exposures to the chemicals or foods to which Gwen was sensitive. Because there were so many things that made Gwen ill it was difficult for her to function normally.

Soon after leaving the hospital Gwen learned that Natalie was in Dallas teaching chemically sensitive patients the process now called cellibration therapy (described in Chapter 4) which Natalie had found reduced the severity of some of her own reactions. Gwen joined the project and after learning this process re-entered the hospital for some testing.

First her vital signs were measured; the temperature of her finger, taken by an electric thermometer, was recorded at 93 degrees. Because varnish was one of her problems, Gwen was then placed in a varnished chair. After 15 minutes her hand became cold, the finger began to turn blue, and the temperature of her finger was recorded at 73 degrees. Natalie worked with Gwen for 20 minutes and the vital signs were taken again. This time the temperature in her finger was recorded at 95 degrees, two degrees higher than her normal temperature.

Gwen still has to be careful, and whenever possible she avoids the pollutants which cause her symptoms. However, she finds cellibration therapy a valuable tool to reduce her symptoms when she is exposed to the toxins that cause her problems.

Gwen had been planning to go back to work, and she realized that she had to find employment in an environment where she would not be exposed to the things that made her ill. So she decided to work in a place where the environment would help improve her health. She began to work at the Environmental Health Center in Dallas, one of the leading centers in the field of environmental medicine, and eventually studied to become a technician.

Gwen rose to the top of her profession, becoming a supervisor. Doctors, who come from all over the world to learn about environmental medicine from Bill Rea, send their technicians to study with Gwen Roark and learn procedures in provocative neutralization and testing patients in general. She has also traveled extensively to meetings of medical societies where she talks with doctors and answers their questions about procedures for patient care.

She worked with Dr. Cyril Smith, the physicist who introduced the field of EM to the method of testing very sensitive patients for their sensitivity to the electromagnetic field (EMF). He taught Gwen the procedure for testing and treating these patients and Gwen has been able to teach others in the United States to perform the test and prepare the treatment for those who are sensitive to the EMF.

The Iriscorder, a machine which detects ophthalmologic problems by testing the autonomic system and records reactions on a computer, was recently introduced into the United States by Japanese ophthalmologists. Gwen was taught how to use this machine and was selected to go to Japan for two weeks to learn more about working with this machine.

As this goes to press Gwen is recovering from a bite by a deadly poisonous snake. She has said that she is certain she could not have survived without the knowledge acquired from her experience with EM. Her spirits are very positive and she hopes to return to work in the near future.

Electromagnetic Sensitivity (EMF). Many people are now becoming sensitive to electric fields and magnetic waves. Sensitivity to these must be considered when you are cleaning up your indoor environment and you should be aware of EMF emitters (See Chapter, *Do-It-Yourself House Call*). These include electric wiring, microwave ovens, TV sets, computers, electric hair dryers, electric blankets, fluorescent lights, and anything that has an electric motor in it.

Successful Case of EMF. M.S. is a 30 year old engineer who worked at an airport. He developed incapacitating "drop attacks"—he would suddenly fall down. These attacks became so bad that even a change from green to yellow on a traffic light would cause the problem. This, of course, kept him from driving. He also observed that when he walked by tin solder he would pass out. All electric devices caused similar symptoms.

To reduce his total load, M.S. learned how to improve his environment by avoiding the EMF emitters listed above and by following the concepts described in *Do-It-Yourself Housecall*. Combining avoidance with a proper rotary diversified diet, an excellent relaxation therapy, and injection therapy for metals, foods, and mold, M.S. was able to return to work without problems. He has been functioning at his job at the airport for the past three years without symptoms or any medication.

A World Traveler. This success story has a twist. Iris Ingram, 77 and retired, recovered from her environmentally-triggered illness and now lives a full life.

The first indication that Iris had a problem was when she developed a red rash resembling a burn on her neck. The rash eventually went away and Iris discounted her allergist's advice to test for food allergies and stop using gas in her home.

When she moved to a highrise apartment with a gas stove and frequent chemical sprays for a roach infestation, Iris had bouts with "flu," weak spells, and once hemorrhaged so badly that she had a D & C.

She next moved to a house with an oil furnace, an oil tank in the basement, and a stepson's Go-Cart which, when revved up in the basement sent gasoline fumes into the bedroom through the laundry chute. In two months Iris' red rash returned; this time all over her face, especially on her nose. When she came home from work in the evenings she would begin to burn like fire, she caught a lot of "flu," and she homorrhaged again, which meant a hysterectomy.

They moved to a new house, and within three days Iris became very dizzy and weak in her legs. Occupancy of their summer home helped until it was sprayed for carpenter ants. Then Iris went to the emergency room with rapid heartbeat and chest pains. Although she remained dizzy she was sent home diagnosed with psychological ailments. Finally she was referred to an allergist and Iris returned to Dr. Kailin, the allergist whose advice she had previously disregarded.

She and her husband Bob found a "clean" place to live — an electrically-heated townhouse with untreated natural birch floors. For three years she worked with treatment on all levels: physical—organic food and a clean indoor environment; psychological—learning bioenergetics and self-hypnosis techniques; and spiritual and psychic. She was cured of her dizziness, heart problems, and bodily weakness. These symptoms returned when she went shopping and when she was exposed to pesticide-sprayed areas or smoke filled rooms. Iris learned to relate the symptoms to exposure.

A number of years after she began to practice the techniques taught by Dr. James Cox, Iris, who loved to travel, decided to go on a cruise to Alaska. She had to exercise cautions such as avoiding cabins with new carpeting, staying above deck when the ship took on oil because the fumes penetrated below deck, and walking where the wind blew exhaust away from her. Although she encountered problems from pollution in Alaskan cities due to inversion and a trip in an oil-heated, hermetically-sealed railway car, to cope she used bed rest, breathing and relaxation techniques, and exercises she had learned from Dr. James Cox, a Pastoral Counselor in the suburban Washington, D.C. area.

A year later Iris took an eight week trip alone to South Africa and England. She learned how to handle the airplane spraying, found public accommodation which suited her specific needs, and covered new carpet and recently varnished furniture with aluminum foil, sheets, and blankets. At times she was subject to fumes that she could not control but she was able to ameliorate the reactions using the techniques described in Chapter 4, *Cellibration Therapy*.

Iris says: "I am still troubled with environmentally-triggered illness. But I *like* to travel, to go places and be with people. Now that I am a widow, I am lonely staying home alone in a clean environment so I *live with* my reactions. Everyday I do things that cause reactions and I do my best to clear them and then go on. When the reactions are *too* great then I have to give in but I have learned to COPE as long as I return to my clean environment and my proper diet."

Other success stories include people who were so handicapped they had to learn how to change their environment as described in this book. Because they had problems obtaining some environmentally safe products they have developed lucrative businesses supplying these products to other people with this illness. Examples include a leading firm which sells relatively pure, relatively safe cotton clothing, bedding, beds, and fabrics. Other successful businesses supply foods, soaps, and additional pure products.

A Safe and Effective Air Filter. "I don't know what is causing it, but you are about to collapse. Your blood work indicates that your allergy load is thirteen times the normal load." Gil Burnett was 38 when his doctor gave him this report. An executive with Southwestern Bell, Gil encountered daily stress, several hours of commuter traffic each day, and long hours of work in a newly constructed office building. He lived in an energy efficient suburban home.

As a child Gil had had asthma and other allergies. Now all the chemicals he was breathing, the fast-paced lifestyle, and his tendency to allergic reactions had overloaded his immune system and caused serious health problems. Dr. Rea diagnosed Gil as a "universal reactor" who was unable to tolerate most foods, airborne pollutants, and various chemicals. After being released from three weeks of intensive care and treatment in the hospital, Gil set out to change the environment in his home. In doing so he discovered a leaky valve in the central air system which had been distributing natural gas throughout the home for an indefinite period of time. Gil's doctors believed that this low-level chemical exposure had slowly poisoned him and his entire family.

The environmental changes Gil made to his home included removing the gas appliances and bedroom carpets. All the air cleaner systems that Gil found made his symptoms worse so necessity became the mother of invention. Using his engineering background Gil made a filter that was so effective that Dr. Rea's associate, Dr. Donald Sprague, began to refer other patients to him for a similar product.

Soon Gil and his wife, Jane, incorporated *Dust Free*^{TM}, Inc. and began marketing a self-charging electrostatic air filter. Gil's own design was marketed the next year and he continued to improve the product throughout the years. Dust Free^{TM}, Inc. now employs over 50 people and distributes air quality control products throughout the United States and several foreign countries. *(See Appendix E)*

Pure and Natural Products. This next success story illustrates how one individual turned her health nightmare into a profitable business and controlled her health problems at the same time.

Janice Swack, a 63 year-old woman, had a work history dating back to her teens when, at the age of 14, she began baby sitting and working in the local candy store. Janice was an over-achiever and continued working through high school, college, and graduate school. She went from her teenage menial jobs to teaching, being a speech and hearing therapist, school administrator, and college teacher. Her final position was that of a hearing officer (judge, adjudicator).

At the peak of her career Janice developed strange symptoms. She became dizzy when she went into department stores, developed migraine headaches, severe arthritis, Reynaud's disease, and narcolepsy so severe she had to stop for naps on the side of the road going to and from work. Her concentration and memory were impaired, fluorescent lighting bothered her thinking and vision, and she developed a Hiatus hernia and severe indigestion. Other physical symptoms included vaginal yeast infections, rashes, bodily itching, and dandruff. Additionally, she became very depressed — it was as if her entire physical and mental states had been altered.

When Janice heard on the radio about environmentally-triggered illness she was amazed at the similarity between her symptoms and the description given. She called the recommended physician and began treatment. In testing she was sensitive to almost everything for which she was tested and she was put on a regimen of food control using the rotation diet (which will be explained later) and given large doses of medication to curb the yeast infection.

Janice began to change the environment in her house searching for natural and pure products which were uncontaminated by synthetics and other toxins. She soon discovered that few of these products were readily available on the market and she began making blankets, sheets, pillows, and cotton clothing while continuing her search for ready-made and acceptable products. Her physician began referring patients with similar needs to her for advice.

Janice realized that she had a viable business opportunity at her fingertips. Since her stressful position was taking its toll she began to plan her retirement and organize her new business. This is how the *Janice Corporation* was born. It provides pure, natural products and makes items which are not available in the marketplace. Products include custom-made mattress sets, soap, underwear, sleepwear, blankets, sheets, cotton pillows, and other difficult to locate pure and natural items. *(See Appendix E)*

People such as Gil and Janice have not only turned their own lives around with these successful new types of businesses, but, by developing a source of relatively safe products, they are performing a very important service for other people with environmentally-triggered illness.

Unfortunately, the general public seldom hears of these thousands of success stories. The media usually presents the bizarre aspects of this illness or points out people who are either at their most sensitive stage or who are the failures.

Failures. In this illness, just as in every other illness, there are people who do not respond to our treatment with the same degree of success. Reasons for this lack of success are varied:

- many persons have such badly damaged immune systems that they will always remain fragile.
- others have problems with the initial cost or with insurance companies who refuse to recognize that reduced hospital admissions and medications make this type of treatment cost effective.
- lack of self education also contributes to failure. Environmental Medicine specialists and their staff try hard to educate patients but some patients want a quick fix, expect the doctor to do it all, and refuse to exert the effort to take charge of their own lives.

&a &a &a

Natalie's Story. Because the media tends to focus on these failures, as I wrote earlier, my doctors have persuaded me to reveal the story of my trials, failures, and successes. Throughout this book, as Bill Rea and I present the dangers of the environment and give relatively safe substitutes, you will learn how through my ignorance I ignored signs that would have warned me of the illness that was coming because of toxic exposure and my own unhealthy lifestyle. Hopefully, you will learn from the mistakes that caused my illness. What is even more important is that you will be able to avoid the pitfalls that the

pioneer patients and I stumbled over while trying to
find the way back to health.

ૐ ૐ ૐ

Prevention. All of my previous books had some information about
prevention but they were mainly written to help the victims who were as
incapacitated as I had been. Ideally, prevention should begin as early as
possible.

I hope that the message in this book will also reach people who appear
to be healthy as I did, are leading productive and happy lives, and who
say, as I did, "If I have to give up smoking or eating this candy and
drinking this soda, or have to worry about my health, it's just not worth
it." Believe me, I now wish that I had been able to read a book
describing the cost of apathy.

When I first became ill I could not even locate a manual to guide me
and my fellow sufferers. You are more fortunate to have books giving
you the basic knowledge acquired by the pioneers in the field and the
additional scientific information from physicians and research scientists
now entering the field.

Contamination from Plastic Containers. In her latest book, *Is This
Your Child?*, (See Appendix F) Dr. Doris Rapp cited information she had
learned from an article by John Lassiter, Ph.D., in *Pediatrics:* "If a
mother receives blood from a plastic container just before her infant is
delivered, certain chemicals from the plastic can be found in the baby's
blood. Is this the way to begin life? When we are ill, should we be given
the drugs plus a bit of plastic intravenously, just because it is modern or
convenient and cost effective?"

Carrying that a step further, mothers should question the plastic they
feed their babies every time the infants drink milk from those soft plastic
baby bottles? Using the information about prevention in infancy could
prevent many persons from falling prey to such illnesses.

Vietnam and Desert Storm. We would also like to give a warning to
the veterans of Vietnam and Desert Storm. In both those wars the
exposure to toxic fumes was high and it would be wise to learn how to
take your health into your own hands and use the information in this book
to prevent a serious illness. Don't ignore minor symptoms as I did. Let
my experience be a warning to you.

ૐ ૐ ૐ

My Story. I was a healthy and active person quite
involved in athletics in addition to my daily work.
It took an automobile accident, a stove gas leak, and
an oil leak in my furnace to make me ill.
Additionally, as I lay in traction weakened from the

accident, I had exterminators spray my apartment every week for six weeks to prevent infestation by bugs from neighboring apartments. It still took six years during which I had many minor problems before I became totally overloaded.

(**Overloading**. My co-author defines overloading by comparing the body to a barrel. The barrel can hold only a certain amount of water and one extra drop will cause it to spill. The body responds to stress in the same way. If the body receives more stress than it can tolerate it overloads and illness results.)

If I had known about EM then I might have paid attention to the warning signs. I doubt it; I was probably too smug about how healthy I was.

With the deterioration of my condition I found that an exposure to newsprint increased my symptoms. Within five minutes of exposure to newsprint my vision deteriorated and the itching that had been confined only to my eyes spread throughout my body.

Hyperactivity in Adults. I also developed hyperactivity and learning disability. From my years teaching school I recognized that my condition was becoming like those of the hyperactive students I had taught. Now at last an adult understood how hyperactive children feel. I felt as if something were crawling inside my skin and I had to be active. As an adult, I was able to use this excess energy to write my first two books. But I finally understood the hyperactive child who disrupts a classroom, wakes up a parent in the middle of the night by jumping on the bed, or acts in other antisocial ways. The child doesn't know how to convert that excess energy into constructive action. He needs guidance, not punishment.

Short-term Memory Loss. I could also understand the children that Doris Rapp speaks about in *Is This Your Child*. Whenever I was reacting I was capable of recalling well-known facts and information but found it difficult to be able to grasp new information. Now I could understand the child who does very well on a test but does not absorb anything new. The teacher who doesn't understand short-term memory loss may say the child is daydreaming or not paying attention.

This compounds the problem because the child who is already suffering is being reprimanded and frequently punished. Treated as a disciplinary problem this child frequently misses class and falls behind the other children. The result is that education suffers and the child does not live up to his potential.

This insight helped me over very trying times and gave me an incentive to fight back and pass along what I was learning. This knowledge kept me going during the long nights when I was partially paralyzed on my left side and suffering from severe cramping on my right side.

Because I reacted to the heated plastic fumes of TV and the toxic print of books and newspapers, I diverted my thoughts from my trouble by writing my first book. Although my first reason for writing was to provide help for children, I knew that what I was learning about relatively safe indoor air quality was needed by everyone.

❧ ❧ ❧

We believe it is important to put this illness in perspective.
- Prevention is the best cure.
- Minor symptoms may be a warning to take precautions.
- Severe health problems can often be controlled by avoiding one or two things. For example, a pediatrician found that removing milk products from children's diet helped to reduce asthma.
- Critically ill patients do not have to be condemned to a life of illness but can reach success with effort and patience and return to a "normal" life.
- Do not despair if you have an illness whose cause has not yet been discovered. Physicians who understand environmentally-induced illness—sensitivity to chemicals, drugs, and foods— have been able to help many individuals who have been labeled hypochondriacs. Contact the *American Academy of Environmental Medicine* for the name of a nearby knowledgeable physician. (*A.A.E.M.*, P.O. Box 16106, Denver, CO 80216; (303) 622-9755; Fax (303) 622-4224)

Hopefully, with the help of these physicians and methods learned from *Success in the Clean Bedroom*, there will be enough formerly disabled people to fill an encyclopedia devoted entirely to "Success Stories."

PART II

THE CHALLENGE

3

DO-IT-YOURSELF HOUSE CALL

An article from the front page of *The Wall Street Journal* described at great length an illness which was finally attributed to the pesticides the man had inhaled while mowing his lawn. A very healthy individual who had never given a second thought to such a danger, said, "Now I'm afraid to go home and mow my lawn." (We might add that pesticides are even more dangerous in a house well sealed to conserve energy.)

We are not suggesting that all healthy individuals should begin tearing their houses apart and putting up porcelain steel walls and tile floors. But if every healthy reader of this book becomes aware of the contaminants which poison the indoor air, and makes a few inexpensive changes that do not affect his lifestyle, we will feel we have accomplished a very important mission.

How do you know if you are chemically sensitive? It is important to understand that everyone reacts in one way or another to toxic chemicals. The average healthy person does not have any overt signs immediately. However, if you feel uncomfortable walking through a clothing store, a beauty parlor, or the detergent section in a grocery store, these are signs warning you that you are susceptible.

Warning: Very often people who are now very chemically sensitive ignored these small signs when they first began to appear. Be wise—start taking preventive measures while you still have the choice. Turn to the "Home Testing" chapter and do some of the simple chemical tests. What you find may surprise you.

Indoor Air Quality

An example of the importance of this message is evident in the Congressional hearings on the House bill on indoor air quality which was introduced by Congressman Joseph Kennedy. Although the Environmental Protection Agency (EPA) spokesperson testified before the committee that there were enough laws on the books and a new law was unnecessary, Congressman Scheuer, chairing the hearings, disagreed. He pointed out that many of the visitors in the room were EPA employees who had become ill while working at the EPA (Waterside) headquarters, a "sick" building which has a very toxic carpet. So the EPA couldn't even protect its own employees.

Public Apathy

The irony of this story is that a huge can of very toxic paint sat uncovered just outside the hearing room. It was there before we went into the hearing, and it was still there when we returned from the hearing. No one appeared to be using it; it was just sitting there, uncovered, contaminating the air in the halls.

An important first step, then, is to make the public more aware. The second step is to clear up the apathy of people who say, "But I'm healthy; I don't have to make any changes."

Develop Sound Ecologic Habits

Now is the time to start developing healthy habits—from eating the best foods to using healthy products. Begin with your personal health care. Get adequate rest and exercise *at least* 30 minutes a day as directed by your doctor. Walking, jogging, swimming, and bicycling are good forms of exercise.

General Rules. These are beginning steps recommended for the health conscious individual. Of course, if you know you are chemically sensitive, you will already have eliminated toxic products such as fabric softeners and sprays.

Always check labels and buy the least toxic products. Avoid products with a strong odor. Do not buy aerosol cans or products labeled hypoallergenic, as this usually means synthetic.

Eat Healthy Food. Do not eat foods prepared with preservatives, additives, or artificial food coloring. Avoid sugars and junk food. Eat only fresh or frozen food rather than canned. Drink only bottled or filtered water stored in glass containers.

Use Natural Fabrics. Whenever possible, choose cotton, linen, wool, and silk. If natural fabrics are not available, use blends containing at least 60% cotton. Buy synthetics such as nylon, dacron, and polyester (in that order) only as a last resort.

Personal Care Products. Never use perfume or cologne. Choose unscented soaps, cosmetics, deodorants, and shampoos. Use a natural bristle hair brush and tooth brush and natural toothpaste. If possible, use a stainless steel or wooden comb.

Detergents and Paper Products. Use only unscented soaps, fabric softeners, and anti-static sprays. Facial tissues and toilet tissue should be white and unscented.

Setting Priorities

Now it is time to begin your house call. No one can tell you what you must do to clean up your house; it must be your decision. We can tell you what is polluting your house and suggest priorities. Then you must decide how much you can afford, how much you want to change your lifestyle, how well your family will cooperate, and if your health is worth some of the suggested expenditures.

A note to the health-minded individual. As you make your own house call, you can easily make some of the recommended changes at no expense and little inconvenience. It would be wise to refer back to this chapter before making any new home purchases.

As you read this section, consider your state of health and decide on priorities. The priorities discussed here include those for the very ill. Choose the ones you wish to use.

As you make your house call, be very thorough. Record everything as you walk through the house either on a tape recorder or by writing it down. It is easy to overlook many things that could be eliminated.

Check all fabrics, furniture, and rugs using the testing program in the "Home Testing" chapter. If the "crawly feeling" test works for you, that is the best way to detect the difference between toxic items and pure items.

Testing Your House

Because it is now established that the indoor air quality is worse than the ambient air (out of doors), we know you are the one who can do the most to clean it up. The goal of this chapter is to teach you how to do it.

While you can test many things yourself, as suggested here, some things such as mold, formaldehyde, radon, the electromagnetic field (EMF), and other problems need professional testing. You can have a professional come to your home to test these things for you, or you can obtain kits to help you do the tests yourself and perhaps find solutions on your own. *(See Appendix E for mold plates, formaldehyde kits, and radon kits.)*

A. THE BEDROOM

As you make this house call, the first room you enter is the bedroom. This room is the first priority and the reason we called this book *Success in the Clean Bedroom*. Whether you sleep six or eight hours a night, it is important that your rest period be in as pure a room as possible.

For the selected few who can build the perfect new house, the smallest bedroom in the house would be your best choice so your bedroom could be as barren as possible. Your sleeping room would have as many windows as possible and to prevent exposure to traffic fumes, they should not face the street. You would have in your room only what you consider necessities: a bed, a table, a clock, a lamp, and possibly a clock or metal radio. Even your clothes would be in an adjoining or dressing room.

However, the purpose of this chapter is not building a new house. For that, see *Appendix F, "Recommended Reading."* This chapter is designed to help you make changes in the house or apartment in which you now live.

Look in your house or apartment to see if there is a small room, perhaps a former nursery room or den, that could be converted into your sleeping room.

Caution. If you have any chemical sensitivities, never sleep in an area close to a cedar-lined closet or cedar chest. Remove a cedar chest immediately even if you have to sell it. If you can't change your bedroom, seal off the closet and don't use it. (See section on "Closets" later in this chapter.)

Nothing is more important than the bed itself.

Check Your Bed and Bedding. Your mattress should be made of untreated cotton and enclosed in a zippered mattress cover made of cotton barrier cloth. *Barrier cloth* is a closely-knitted cotton fabric used for surgical uniforms. Its very fine weave acts as a barrier which provides some protection against dust, pollen, and other foreign particles often found in pillows, mattresses, upholstery, and auto interiors. Test barrier cloth first to be sure you can tolerate it. *(See Janice Corporation or Cotton Place, Appendix E.)* Use bedding and curtains made of untreated cotton or linen and wash them with pure soap, baking soda, or Organic Green. *(See Chapter on "Keeping It Clean.")*

Replacing Your Mattress. If you are reacting to your mattress, buy one with no chemical finishes, chemical odor retardants, sizing, or layers of foam or polyurethane. Your doctor can waive the legislation requiring flameproofing. The regulation permitting the waiver is in paragraph 1632, "Standards of Flammability of Mattresses [and mattress pads] (FS 4-72 of the Consumer Product Safety Commission, Flammable Fabrics Act Regulation); the amendment is paragraph 1632.1. It can be flameproofed with borax.

Janice Corporation (see Appendix E) custom makes mattresses and box springs without fire retardant according to your physician's prescription. The company will also pretreat the ticking with vinegar and baking soda washes for further protection.

If you have a dust allergy and have been using a soft plastic cover on your mattress and springs, replace it with a barrier cloth cover. You can buy a ready-made cover or buy the barrier cloth, zipper, and instructions kit from *Cotton Place or Janice's. (See Appendix E.)* If necessary, replace the bed with a canvas army cot and get rid of the mattress. Another alternative that may sound more attractive is available from *Dona Designs. (See Appendix E.)*

Remove fabrics such as polyester, rayon, nylon, acrilan, and dacron from the room as soon as possible; their synthetic fibers are made of plastic. The purer your bedroom is, the faster your recovery will be.

ża ża ża

I experienced a problem with some of my linens—one reason I am now leery of "bargains." My friend bought them in an outlet store, and her check of the sheets, pillow cases, and towels found them labeled "all cotton face." But I couldn't use them, even after they were washed. On rechecking, I saw that the underside of the label read 10% polyester. It was only the facing that was all cotton.

Before you use anything made of fabric, wash it to remove any sizing or additive. When you buy things in quantity, pre-wash one item, test it, and use it before you wash the rest of them.

ða ða ða

Check Your Pillows. Avoid pillows filled with plastic foam, rubber, or plastic fiber-fill such as dacron, dynel, polyester, poly-foam, or polyurethane. Feather pillows and even goose down are too troublesome and usually are chemically treated.

Until you can buy a cotton pillow, fill a pillow case with turkish towels, towels torn in strips, a soft cotton receiving blanket, soft baby diapers, or white cotton batting. *(See Appendix E for Dona Designs, K.B. Cotton Pillows, Inc., Cotton Place, or Janice's.)* Put pillows in the electric dryer weekly to freshen.

Check Your Blankets. Because soft plastics frequently cause a great deal of distress, especially those that retain an odor, we advise that you steer clear of electric blankets. With the evidence of the dangers of electromagnetic fields (EMFs), it certainly is unwise to have an EMF emitter on your bed. In addition, when the plastic-coated wires of these blankets are heated, they release a rather heavy plastic-fume load, despite the fact that there is little odor. Many electric blankets and heating pads also have plastic covers. In contrast, hard plastics such as Formica or the older Bakelite are usually not a problem unless heated to a fairly high degree.

Check Your Draperies and Curtains. Before making new draperies, you will probably have to remove the sizing and dye fixatives from the fabric. Test a swatch first to see how many washings it requires and whether it needs to be treated with vinegar or baking soda. If you are working with a decorator who washes the fabrics for you, make sure you give proper instructions. As a precaution, write these instructions into the contract.

Traverse curtain rods are often plastic; use round wooden or metal decorator rods. If you are dust sensitive, use simple rods and curtains that can be removed easily for frequent washing. Complete laundering is not always necessary; to remove dust, simply rinse in plain cold water and dry thoroughly.

Check Your Floor Coverings. Carpeting is not good for anyone because carpets gather dust, become moldy, and cannot be thoroughly cleaned. Carpet cleaning causes problems by adding the toxins of the cleaning fluid and mold because the carpets cannot be thoroughly dried. Vacuuming raises dust and fluff from the carpet itself, and you inhale the formaldehyde and other toxins from the carpet.

Washable *area rugs* can be a substitute for carpeting for other rooms in the house but should be used in the bedroom only if necessary. *(See Appendix E.)*

Vacuum Cleaners. If you must keep your carpet, consider trying the *VITAL-VAC VACUUM AIR CLEANING SYSTEM, MIELE, or NILFISK* for vacuuming carpeting or furniture. Sometimes people who have no carpeting vacuum their floors and furniture with a vacuum cleaner that does not raise the dust in the air.

Before deciding to buy any of these machines, make sure the company has an arrangement whereby you can test it out yourself and return it at a small cost. *(See Appendix E.)*

Covering Carpets. If you cannot afford to get rid of the carpeting and it is presenting a serious problem, it might be wise to cover it by tacking down barrier cloth over extra heavy-duty aluminum foil, Denny Foil; if finances do not allow that, use old sheets over the foil.

In the book *Less Toxic Living*, published by the *Environmental Health Center in Dallas, Texas, Carolyn Gorman* states, "If you are unable to remove the carpeting, cover the floor with THERMOPLY STORM BRACING. Seal seams, and seal around the baseboard with SEARS ALUMINUM TAPE." Test both of these very carefully before buying in large quantities.

Replacing Carpets. When you decide to replace the carpeting, it would be safer to put down a plain, cotton rug. If you have hardwood floors, use scatter rugs that are not backed with plastic, rubber, or glue substances. Since non-skid rugs are out, you must walk carefully or anchor rugs with furniture. Whatever floor coverings you use, make sure you remove them from time to time for laundering. *(See Rugs, Appendix E.)*

Clean Your Wooden Floors. To clean your wooden floors, use three parts olive oil to one part reconstituted lemon juice. Some people use one part linseed oil to one part vinegar. Unfortunately, most linseed oil is treated, and many people are sensitive to vinegar, so use caution.

Furniture

Check Your Sofas and Chairs. Re-upholster furniture you already have with white barrier cloth as your base. It will serve as a partial buffer against mold and dust that accumulate in furniture. Choose slipcovers of untreated cotton, silk, or linen, that can be easily removed for frequent washing. If you are dust- or mold-sensitive, avoid upholstered furniture in the bedroom or any room where you spend a lot of time.

If you must replace sofas and chairs in the bedroom, buy colonial, Scandinavian, or modern styles with loose cushions. If cushions are filled with foam rubber or synthetics, have an upholsteror make new cushions with springs and white cotton batting.

Check Your Tables. Some woods, such as Philippine mahogany, are acceptable, as is wicker, glass, or stainless steel. But avoid evergreen, especially cedar and pine. When testing for sensitivity to woods, be sure to check if you are reacting to the wood or the finish. Glass-top tables may be a good choice for the bedroom.

Note: Never place an electric appliance on a wrought iron table, especially if you are electro-magnetically sensitive.

Check Your Clocks. Because heated plastic causes problems, you should consider using a travel alarm or a transistor clock. If you use a clock radio, keep it away from the bed. Electric clocks emit EMFs which, although undetectable, make many people ill. Keep them out of the bedroom.

Check Your Lamps and Lighting. Old lamps are usually not troublesome, but you may find that the wiring in new lamps bothers you. When two to four years old, they are easier to tolerate. Ceiling fixtures usually do not present problems.

Glass, metal, or pewter fixtures are good choices. Using incandescent bulbs with a metal grill reduces the need for styrofoam, fiberglass, or other synthetics. Check lamps and sockets for plastic. Plastic becomes most offensive when heated because more molecules are airborne. Avoid plastic ceiling light covers and diffusing globes on table lights.

Use 100% silk shades that are washable. Also recommended are metal or glass shades. Fluorescent lamps produce hydrocarbons and should be avoided, although protective glass shields do help. *(See Appendix E for OTT Light* which is a fluorescent light with radiation shield.)

Remove Books, Magazines, Newspapers. Keep plastic book covers and kerosene-soaked printed pages out of your sleeping area as much as possible. Air books and papers outside before reading, or let someone else read them first. Remove reading material as far as possible from the air you breathe while sleeping.

Avoid Mothproofing. A national column distributed by the Los Angeles Times syndicate quoted Dr. Eloise Kailin on the dangers of mothproofing rugs with the chemical dieldrin. She reports that "...dieldrin does not stay in the mothproofed rug. With wear, particles of the rug break off and become ordinary house dust that people breathe. When it passes over heated surfaces, it generates other toxic gases. With our chronic exposure to hard pesticides and hundreds of other mildly toxic chemicals, our ability to tolerate further exposures is breaking down."

Avoid Fresh Paint. Clean your walls with a damp cloth and *Bon-Ami cake soap. (See "Keeping It Clean.")* Avoid painting your bedroom unless the old paint is so toxic that something has to be done about it. No satisfactory substitute for paint exists. If you must paint, first test the paint on a small portable surface. *(See Appendix E for paints* less toxic than most commercial brands.) Let the paint air a few days or as long as necessary.

If you can tolerate it, ask your painter to mix one box of baking soda to one gallon of paint. Sift the baking soda to prevent an uneven finish. Tell the painter to keep adding the baking soda until the bubbling stops. Be sure he doesn't make it too thick because there is no way to thin it.

Paint walls either off-white or white, but not stark white. A little pigment protects your eyes from the bright glare of a pure white wall. Do not use tints because the dyes contain toxic fixatives.

Check Your Paneling. If you have paneling made of pressed wood, pine, or cedar in your bedroom, change bedrooms as soon as possible. If you can't do that, cover the walls with heavy duty aluminum foil, taping it down either with SEARS ALUMINUM TAPE or a surgical tape. *(See "First Aid.")*

If that doesn't help, cover the aluminum foil with a couple layers of cotton material, one of which is barrier cloth. Barrier cloth by itself won't keep out chemicals but may serve the purpose over the aluminum foil.

If you're going to replace paneling, use only pure hard wood, avoiding pine or cedar. Test each kind of wood; various batches of the same wood may be problematic. If you are sensitive to most woods, try untreated, unpainted Philippine mahogany, and use nails instead of glue.

Check Your Wallpaper. Use "that crawly feeling" to test it. (See "Home Testing.") Unfortunately, most wallpapers are treated with fungicides and other chemicals.

If necessary, cover your wallpaper as you did the paneling above. However, if you decide to change your walls, do not use wallpaper unless it is a pure aluminum wallpaper without mylar in it.

You can apply it with ELMER'S GLUE or wheat paste you can make or buy. Under no circumstances should you use wheat paste if you are sensitive to wheat.

Check Your Heat Source. If your heating system is making you ill, purchase some electric space heaters, especially for the bedroom. Be careful not to buy a heater with a fan. Aluminum or painted baseboard heaters can cause problems, especially if coated with a tar-containing product.

Hot-air heat can also cause difficulty, even if it is electric, because of oils in the fan. The fan blows dust and other particles into the air. This is bad enough when it is air conditioning, but when heat is present, the fan is spreading through the air what is known as "fried dust." Turn heat off in the bedroom and seal the vent with layers of aluminum foil taped with freezer tape or aluminum tape if tolerated.

Portable Electric Heaters. Some very sensitive people can tolerate the *POLONAS MODEL PH61-TC/VHC ELECTRIC HEATER* or a *glass and stainless steel heater made by Inter Central, Inc.* in Reading, Pennsylvania. *(See Appendix E.)* The latter is worth its high price tag; it is ecologically clean with no glue or adhesive. However, it still takes 24 hours to get rid of residues from the manufacturing process. Both floor models and wall models are available. Even in cold climates, it is possible to heat the whole house if you purchase enough units.

Some patients can even tolerate ELECTRIC INTER-THERM HEATERS which are available in appliance stores, and others sometimes can tolerate the metal radiator from Sears.

A plumber who wanted to use baseboard heating despite his sensitivity to metal discovered a solution. By putting in twice as many units as normally required, the heating is spread over a greater number of units, the fixtures do not become as hot, and the system is easier to tolerate. Steel hot water heaters are usually tolerable.

To be on the safe side, try to keep the room very warm while you are away so you can turn the unit off while you are there. Highly sensitive people may react to the EMF of an electric space heater. A room with a sunny exposure can help greatly.

Check Your Closets. If possible, remove everything from the closet, including soft plastic garment bags or other containers. If the closet and the room cannot be completely stripped, limit the contents to 100% untreated cotton fabrics. Remove shoes, purses, or dry cleaned clothes from the closet, or any paper or plastic items. This includes synthetic fabrics such as nylon, rayon, acrilan, dacron, drip-dry or permanent press clothing, or fiberglass material.

Use filters made from activated charcoal covered with cotton to control fumes in closets and dresser drawers. *(See Appendix E.)* Air woolens at least once a week to avoid moths; wash cottons frequently.

In place of shelf paper, use plain butcher paper, aluminum foil, or the more expensive stainless steel foil. Self-sticking shelf paper or decorating paper such as Con-tact contain pesticides that increase the toxicity of the plastic. Remove mothproofed shelf paper, even if it is advertised as odorless.

Remove "nonallergenic" dynel pillows, imitation leather products, floor waxes, or furniture polishes from the closet. Moth crystals, permanently mothproofed sweaters, and dry cleaning processes that include mothproofing are very toxic. If you must store irritants in the closet, protect yourself from fumes by sealing the bottom of the door with material covered with heavy-duty aluminum. Avoid plastic doors when remodeling.

When you have a large house, there is no problem removing all contaminants from the bedroom and the closet. However, when space is a problem, there are ways to get around it.

Homemade Storage. You can make a pretty dressing table by placing an attractive cotton cover over two galvanized 20-gallon garbage cans. Under the cotton, place a flat piece of metal or tolerated wood between the two handles on the lids, so it has a flat surface and looks like a dressing table.

Then devise a system. Place shoes and other items in boxes to be placed inside the cans, label the boxes, and make a list of the order in which the boxes are packed.

To locate a pair of shoes check the list, note where the pair you want is located, remove all the boxes above it, and take out the pair of shoes. Put your favorite pair of shoes in a box on the top.

Keep books and magazines out of the bedroom (don't even keep them in garbage cans) unless absolutely necessary.

By the way, garbage cans are very useful even for those who have storage space in the basement. Why contaminate the basement when you can store any toxic items in cans? Keep a bag of charcoal in the cans and replace the charcoal every three or four months.

Check Your Dresser. If you must have a dresser in your bedroom, it may be safe to have a custom-made one or a very old one. But be sure to check both old and new dressers. Old dressers may be moldy or contain residues of perfumes or other toxic substances previously stored in them. The hazards of new dressers include treated wood, insecticide treatments, and varnishes. Even if made of pure, untreated wood, new dressers usually have drawers made of pressed board treated with formaldehyde.

Line the drawers (as well as the outside, if necessary) with heavy duty aluminum foil and secure with tape. Test several kinds of tapes, using the test procedure.

Be very careful what you keep in your dresser. If you or someone in your family uses cosmetics, do not keep them in your bedroom; move them to the medicine chest or a cabinet beneath your bathroom sink. Do not store perfumes and sachets, cosmetics, sprays of any kind, scented products, deodorants, plastic jewelry, or other accessories in your dresser.

Testing Your Dresser. Temporarily remove the contents of your dresser and place them in another room. Let the drawers air for a day or two, then place them back in the dresser and keep closed for at least 48 hours. Use procedures found in the chapter on self-testing such as the sniff test and/or "that crawly feeling."

If you have no problem with the inside ot the dressei, test each item before placing it back in the dresser. If you test positive to anything that you must keep in your bedroom, "put a lid on it" to prevent odors from permeating your room. Enclose small items in glass jars or empty cans with lids: coffee cans, cookie containers, etc.

Remove plastic lamps with plastic sockets, shades, picture frames, clocks, and paper or cardboard items.

Telephone. If you are very sensitive and you must have a phone in your bedroom, buy an old metal telephone with cloth wires. Call *John Bogriski at (717) 282-5100 (See Appendix E)* to order and ask him to remove the cotton wad from the mouthpiece (it is usually toxic) but not to clean the phone. Connect the phone to a jack so that you can remove it from the bedroom when not in use.

Light Bulbs. Do not use the Permalite long-life light bulbs sold by handicapped workers over the telephone. They apparently contain some type of plastic that extends the life of the bulbs.

Air Filters. The usefulness of air filters depends a great deal on individual sensitivity. The electrical part of the filter may produce pollution which offsets the purifying advantages of the filter. When air quality in your bedroom is not good, consider buying an air filter. Investigate one of the following companies: *DUST-FREE and ALLERMED. (See Appendix E.)* These two companies are very accommodating. Make arrangements to test the filter on a trial basis, with option to buy, and an agreement to return it within a certain period of time if it is troublesome to you.

Remove Humidifiers or Dehumidifiers. Both should be avoided. Humidifiers direct mold into the air, while dehumidifiers transform the mold they collect from the air into a more concentrated form inside the machine.

At the end of this chapter is a section labeled *"Miscellaneous Toxic Problems,"* listing things that may be found in any room. Check that list carefully to see if any of them are in your bedroom.

In addition, look for some unusual conversation piece that we could not anticipate. Check that out very carefully and test it for yourself.

Check for Dust Collectors. Perhaps you have an antique vase that presents no problem, but if it's filled with plastic flowers or even silk flowers that gather dust, don't keep it in the bedroom.

Look for mementos from your childhood or stuffed toys made from synthetic fabrics. Even if made of natural fabrics, they are dust collectors; remove them from the bedroom.

Plants. This may be a touchy problem for some people who love plants; plants are beautiful, they do give off oxygen to the room, and are anti-pollutants. However, they also present a problem.

Mold that comes from dirt and dust plus other environmental factors such as natural scents can present a problem. An even worse contaminant is the vase containing mold from dried plants and dried flowers. The disadvantages of having such plants and dried flowers in the bedroom far outweigh the satisfaction and beauty they add. Keep them in another room.

Reminder. Of course, all of this information that applies to the bedroom also applies to all other rooms. It may take you longer to remove the contaminants out of the kitchen and bathroom and basement, etc., but as you read about each room, make a note that anything that should be removed from the bedroom should eventually be removed from other rooms. For example, plastic self-stick shelf or decorating paper.

B. THE KITCHEN

Now let's move into the kitchen, the second priority.

Check Your Kitchen Sink Cabinet. Use the same procedure as you did with the dresser in the bedroom. However, before using aluminum foil to line it, wash it very carefully as described in *"Keeping It Clean."* If there is still an odor, then you must line it. Otherwise, you may wish to leave it unlined.

In most homes, the worst toxic dump is under the kitchen sink. Everyone should eliminate aerosol cans and pressurized spray cans. If you were to put the purest water into an aerosol can, it would become contaminated by the propellant. Even the pump-spray versions are not totally safe.

Cleaning Solutions and Other Aromatic Products. Remove the following items and any others that have an odor from your house. If you must keep them, place them in an outdoor garage or storage bin or at least in the basement in sealed cans: paints, turpentine, solvents, lacquers, pressurized spray cans, kerosene lighter fluid and fire-starting solutions, nail polish and remover, scented soaps, hair spray, deodorants, shoe polish, furniture polish, metal polish, floor waxes, mops and rags used for waxing, detergents, ammonia, bleaches, and cleaners.

Usually you can detect a solvent by an odor; if it has an odor, avoid it. Many kitchen cleaners contain solvents to remove stubborn fats and oil films.

Remove bleaches such as Clorox and kitchen scouring powders which contain chlorine. Remove all products that have ammonias, phenols, and creosols in them. Some disinfectants such as Lysol contain these.

Remove detergents because petrochemical kerosene is used in the manufacture of most detergents.

Because pine tree resins are so troublesome to chemically sensitive people, remove all pine-scented products such as household cleaners, animal bedding, etc.

Less-Toxic Cleaning Products. If you are chemically sensitive, immediately discard *all* toxic products. Everyone else would be wise to make the changeover at least when replacing cleaning products.

You may be surprised to know how much money you spend on cleaning products. Turn to *"Keeping It Clean"* and learn how to save money as you clean your house the healthy way.

Check Your Appliances. Clinical observation indicates that one of the worst contaminants is gas. Never cook on a gas stove. If you do not have an electric stove, use only electric appliances such as electric frying pans (no Teflon), electric broilers, or hot plates to cook for the entire family as well as yourself. If you have a gas stove, turn off the pilot light, wrap the burners in aluminum foil, and seal with freezer tape. This prevents tar-like deposits on the burners from releasing molecules into the air.

If you are sensitive to metal, investigate a Corning Ware range oven, a range with a Corning glassware top. According to some patients, it is easy to clean and use. Other imitations are now available, but we have no information as to whether they are satisfactory.

Repairing Your Appliances. It may be wiser to repair old refrigerators, stoves, and dishwashers than to buy new ones because new appliances usually have plastic interiors that give off fumes for long periods of time. As this goes to press, Kitchenaid still has stainless steel interiors, but check each model before buying.

Check very carefully with service persons when arranging for repairs on appliances or anything else in your house. Let them know that you do not want anything toxic, and that you want to test anything that they will use such as appliance parts, adhesives, taping, pipes, etc.

Check to see if service people will work with you. Ask them to come to your house first to discuss the problem, to refrain from smoking before coming, and to use no perfumes or colognes. If they are unwilling to cooperate or make light of the issue, you know they will not exercise adequate caution.

Avoid Asbestos. Insulation, vinyl flooring, wiring, wallpaper, Con-tact paper, potholders, and stove mits often contain asbestos. Use it sparingly.

Check Your Countertops and Cabinets. As your awareness of pure living increases, you will spend more and more time cooking. So plan your workspace carefully. If you replace countertops, use stainless steel or ceramic tile.

Cabinets may be of a hard wood, metal, or even ceramic tile or stone. Synthetic glues and stains are major contaminants in many households. You can make an excellent less toxic stain from walnut shells. Grind up the shells, add water, and boil until the water turns dark. The only drawback is that it is difficult to clean. You can clean raw wood with reconstituted lemon juice on a cloth. Rub out scratches with a piece of walnut or pecan meat; the raw wood will absorb the stain from the nut.

We recommend Corning Ware chopping boards, especially the large 16- x 20-inch size. If you are building a new home or remodeling your kitchen, you may wish to install two or three of these boards permanently in your countertops.

Check Your Cookware. Use pots, pans, dishes, and silverware that are not made of or coated with plastic, Teflon, or aluminum. Even when cooking for others in the household, avoid these materials because they give off toxic odors when heated. Pyrex and Corning Ware are the best choices, and stainless steel is acceptable. Use stainless steel baking pans and cooking utensils.

For frying, use iron skillets or enamel-coated cast-iron. [Note: Frying is never recommended. However, if you do occasionally fry or saute foods, an iron skillet is preferred. Iron is said to permeate the food, so it is a good nutritional source of iron. If you saute primarily with water and perhaps just a bit of oil, you can steam your food in an iron skillet and thus absorb some of the iron.]

Many pots and pans have Bakelite handles, which you may not recognize as a plastic. Phenol and formaldehyde are components of Bakelite, and emit fumes when heated even slightly. The hard Bakelite in telephones is not a problem for most persons.

Plastics. By this time you are aware of the perils of plastics. Because they are so widely used and frequently are hidden inside harmless-appearing products, you must be vigilant. Problems may arise from either the toxic agents added to keep plastics soft or by small plastic molecules that break off from larger plastic polymers. Because individual sensitivities vary, you may be able to tolerate one kind of plastic molecule but not another. Even if you do not appear to be sensitive to it, avoid plastic (especially soft plastic) whenever possible to keep down your total load of toxins.

Avoid all types of plastic containers, even Tupperware. The best alternatives are wide-mouth Mason jars and glass gallon jars in which restaurants buy bulk foods. If you cannot find new jars, ask your favorite restaurant or a cafeteria to save some empty jars for you.

Wash them thoroughly with apple cider vinegar or baking soda before using and sterilize by placing them in the oven at 200° F for about 30 minutes. Wash the lids very carefully, and if they are metal, boil them for 20 minutes to make sure no residual odor can permeate your food. Line lids with *wood-derived cellophane* (not petroleum-derived). *(See Appendix E.)* Until you have obtained such cellophane, use aluminum foil.

Use stainless steel cutlery—avoid plastic-handled knives, forks, and spoons.

Cotton in the Kitchen. Paper products should be kept to a minimum since they contain many chemicals such as chlorine bleach and formaldehyde. Using old cotton rags in place of paper towels to wipe up spills can save you a lot of money. Make cotton napkins by sewing the edges of squares torn from old sheets. When you must use paper products such as paper towels, there is a product called *Today's Choice. (See Appendix E.) Note: Never dry your food with paper towels, not even Today's Choice.*

Roach Control. Because pesticides are very toxic, you must keep them out of the house at all costs. Prevention is most important to keep your kitchen clean and insect free.

Inspect all grocery bags to be sure they contain no roaches from the store. Repackage food immediately and put it in the proper storage place. Remove all dried goods from paper bags immediately and put them in glass containers or cellophane bags. Do this over the sink so nothing is spilled on a table or on the floor.

Take care of roach problems before they begin. Wash your kitchen thoroughly with Rugged Red solution. *(See "Keeping It Clean.")* After it has been rinsed, spread a thin coat of Rugged Red solution (two parts Rugged Red to eight parts water) and let it dry. Then, spread a fine mist of dry boric acid in all nooks and crannies and creases, behind stoves, refrigerators, and cupboards.

If you keep your kitchen clean, you will not have a problem with roaches. *(See "Less Toxic Pest Control.")*

C. THE BATHROOM

As you enter the bathroom remember that much of what we have already discussed will apply to the bathroom. There are some things which apply specifically to bathrooms that you will want to consider in making your house call to this room.

Check Your Fixtures. Most bathroom fixtures are now made of plastic and synthetic compositions. When making changes, buy a porcelain sink and tub and a wooden toilet seat. The base of the shower stall should be tile rather than a plasticized substitute for cement. Floor tiles in the bathroom, shower stall, and powder room should be four by four inches or larger in order to keep the amount of mortar used to a minimum. Do not install plastic shower units. Use cast-iron or galvanized piping for all plumbing, including soil lines and stacks. Don't let a plumber use lead soldering.

Towel Racks. Install enough towel racks to spread out towels so they will dry quickly. Mold develops more quickly if towels must be folded on the rack. Choose chrome towel bars and ceramic holders.

Have an extra towel rack near the shower stall to hold your bath mat and another one for large old towels you can use to dry the sides and floor of the shower after each shower. This is especially important if you are sensitive to mold. Make shower curtains from barrier cloth.

Remove all damp or wet towels, washcloths, and bath mats as soon as possible and wash them immediately if time allows. If not, put them in the dryer so mold will not accumulate. Later when there is time, wash the towels and mats and dry them again.

If you have the facilities, of course, you can line dry them outdoors. *(See also "Mold Care" in "Keeping It Clean.")*

Shower Curtains. Remove your plastic shower curtains. Try a homemade shower curtain of *barrier cloth* or terrycloth. *(See Appendix E.)* To test, throw over the bar and fasten with safety pins two or three inches apart.

Caulking. There is no safe caulking, but some sensitive people can tolerate silicone rubber after allowing it to air for a week or two. Carefully test it on a portable surface before applying. Do not use any silicone or foam caulking. An additive-free mortar is also a fairly safe caulking but requires more frequent replacement.

Check Your Medicine Cabinet. Check all pills or tablets, preparations for the scalp, hair, or skin, including mouthwash or toothpaste, and after shave lotion.

Discard all medications with expired dates, as well as anything you have not used in a couple of years. Use the same procedure to test your medicine cabinet as you did for your dresser. *(See "Bedroom.")*

Before replacing anything in the medicine cabinet, wash the cabinet very carefully (or have someone wash it for you) with Borax, baking soda, or vinegar. *(See chapter on "Keeping It Clean.")*

Seal in a jar or can with a tight lid anything that has an unpleasant odor or anything that tested positive which you wish to keep for future use or for another family member.

The worst contaminants in the bathroom usually consist of cosmetics and toiletries. Most commercial products contain formaldehyde and alcohol plus many other toxic products. For the most part, it is wise (and incidentally less expensive) to make your own. *(See "Cosmetics and Toiletries.")*

Any makeup you use should be confined to when you go out. Around the house it's a good idea just to "wear a nice clean scrubbed face."

Plastic dentures are not for the sensitive patient. Replace them with vulcanite dentures if you can tolerate these. Your dentist must request them for you.

Check the Cabinet Under Your Bathroom Sink. The same contaminants—cleaning products—that you find in the kitchen are probably also in the bathroom. Refer to "The Kitchen Sink" for items to look for that could be toxic and clear them out.

Before returning anything to the cabinet under the sink, use the same procedure you used with your dresser in the bedroom and your kitchen sink.

D. MISCELLANEOUS TOXIC PROBLEMS

As we have said previously, everything that applies to the bedroom, kitchen, or bathroom, also applies to other sections of the house.

We tried to cover things that are found in many areas in the main three sections. Other things that do not fit specifically in a particular part of the house are listed here.

Car Exhaust Fumes. Check to be sure none of these enter your house from an open window or an attached garage. If you have an attached garage, especially if it is close to your sleeping quarters, avoid keeping your car in the garage. If weather conditions make it necessary to keep it there, do not warm up the car in the garage. Start it up, pull it out of the garage as quickly as possible, and warm it up some distance from the house.

Christmas Trees. If you are sensitive to pine tree resins or the turpentine that comes from them, it would be wise to decorate your Christmas tree outside of the house or use an aluminum tree.

Where children are involved and you wish to have one indoors, you may be able to tolerate the Norfolk Island Pine, a Southern Hemisphere evergreen that can be found at nurseries or some florists. They make beautiful year-round potted plants which can be decorated for Christmas and brought into the house.

EMF Measuring Device. The *Genitron* is carried by *AEHF*. They will give you proper instructions. *(See Appendix E.)*

Furniture in Storage. Warning: If your furniture has been in storage, check it very carefully before bringing it into your home. Most storage companies and moving vans spray everything with pesticides.

When you plan to move or store any belongings, have it written in the contract that the company totally seals everything in plastic before putting them into a van or in storage.

On site near your house, have the company remove the plastic from your belongings just before bringing them back into your home.

Hexachlorophene. Check your soaps, creams, and furnace filters to be sure they do not contain hexachlorophene, which is a chlorinated hydrocarbon like DDT.

Lubrication. Check very carefully any oil used in your house to lubricate sewing machines or appliances. Graphite can often be substituted. Check first with your serviceman.

Overcoming Pesticide Treatment. If your house has been treated with pesticides, scrub the area with a detergent. If you can't tolerate detergent, try Rugged Red. Then with aluminum foil, hard wood, or ceramic tile, mechanically seal the area with Sears tape.

Remove rugs, carpets, and all inside furnishings. Clean air ducts and furnace vents with Neo-life Organic Green, Rugged Red, borax, vinegar, or all four. Use no detergent or toxic sealing. Have that written into the contract with your serviceman.

If these do not help, try using an ozonator. (See below.) **Warning:** Some pesticide-treated houses are unsalvageable. Consider this before going to great expense. You may have to move to regain your health.

Ozonator. Depending on the severity of the pollution, this machine can sometimes be useful for removing mold and toxic chemicals. Do not remain in the house while the machine is operating, especially if you are chemically sensitive, and do not return immediately after it has been turned off. Seal the room off from the rest of the house with the window open a crack. Some people have had to use the machine for a few weeks; others have had success in a matter of several hours. The same remains true for the waiting period before returning to the house. If you cannot leave the house for long periods of time, you may wish to use the ozonator more frequently for shorter periods of time. (For source, see *AEHF* in *Appendix E.*)

Removing Gas from Pipes. When switching over from central gas to electric heat, vacuum gas from pipe and vents by forcing compressed air through them. (See also above section on cleaning vents of pesticides.)

PART III

PICKING UP THE GAUNTLET

4

CELLIBRATION THERAPY

I am indebted to Margorie Rosenfeld for the name of my healing process. The name she suggested, Cellibration Therapy, delineates and combines important aspects of my two major areas of interest: environmental medicine and body therapies. What I have culled from the two different fields and combined into one process in my own search for health has resulted in healing on the cellular level once the *cells* have been *liberated* from toxins.

The purpose of the environmental control and detoxification program, discussed in detail later in this book, is to cleanse the toxins from the cells to remove the strain these toxins impose on the immune and enzyme detoxification systems.

The dietary part of the program has the same effect. Because it requires an average of 96 hours for foods to clear from the cells, a rotary diversified diet is recommended to help clear existing food sensitivities and prevent additional food sensitivities from developing. The practices I have incorporated in my cellibration therapy, from the different types of therapies I studied under the tutelage of Dr. James Cox, Pastoral Counselor, are also aimed at healing the cells.

Additionally, I appreciate Margorie Rosenfeld's play on the word *celebration* because it is an uplifting term, a jubilation so different from the somber, foreboding implications of terms like *primal scream therapy, psychotherapy, hypnotherapy,* and *psychoanalysis.*

Stress Reduction

This section on cellibration therapy includes information on stress reduction. Once you have learned how to reduce stress you can go from a state of very deep relaxation into self-healing. I will share with you how I concentrate on my cells and heal myself.

To benefit from stress reduction, you first have to understand what stress is. Many excellent books deal with the subject of stress: what its dangers are, how to reduce it, or how to avoid it. Most of us define stress as tension resulting from incidents such as a quarrel with someone we love, an unpleasant disagreement with an employer, a near-collision with another automobile, or the loss of a job. But, in fact, all of life's activities—eating, drinking, exercising, sexual intercourse—create stress. Some stress is unavoidable and can stimulate a healthy response. But the negative stresses, the ones we usually think of as "stress," can prevent healthy functioning or even endanger life.

Environmental Medicine (EM) specialists now tell us that unhealthy stress can be caused by toxic chemicals in the air we breathe, the water we drink, or the food we eat. Normal processing of food intake is a heavy load on our bodies even when we are in a healthy state. Because we are designed for this load, though, this is generally a healthy stress.

However, processing food or drink in which synthetic chemicals or natural toxins are present creates unhealthy stress. Breathing polluted air also does this. And, of course, an encounter with any food or chemical to which we have become sensitive also creates unhealthy stress. While healthy stress stimulates energy, unhealthy stress can result in illness. For mildly sensitive persons, stress reduction is desirable; for those with severe sensitivities, it is mandatory.

I agree with EM specialists that the best way to manage stress and restore the body to a healthy state is to avoid the sources of such stress by controlling the environment. However, there are no shortcuts to restored health, and it is important to use multiple approaches in attempting to improve a problem with multiple roots and manifestations. The exercise, breathing, and relaxation techniques set forth in the following pages come from my personal experience and are suggested as an addition to, and not a substitute for, environmental control and proper diet. By helping you reduce stress, these procedures will enable you to lead a more normal and effective life without curtailing activities that are important to you. It is also important to learn to control your autonomic nervous system as much as possible.

૨ล ૨ล ૨ล

Natalie's Bad Breathing Habits. "What do you mean, I don't know how to breathe?" I said indignantly. "Everyone knows how to breathe.

I was speaking to Dr. James Cox, to whom my doctor, Eloise Kalin, had referred me so I could learn to anesthetize myself. Tests had showed that I was sensitive to plastic and was reacting to the plastic caps on my teeth. However, the removal of the caps required anesthesia, which I could not take, so I needed to learn to anesthetize myself.

૨ล ૨ล ૨ล

Learning to Breathe Normally

Dr. Cox was probably the first person to recognize that people with stress disorders of all types, and environmentally-triggered illness in particular, not only breathe improperly, but also cut off their breath in a misguided attempt to breathe in fewer toxins. He developed one of the first successful stress reduction programs specifically designed for patients with chemical sensitivities. More about that later.

Giving up control of your breathing is the key to relaxation and reducing stress. To do this, drop your jaw and shoulders as you exhale, think "relax," and let your body go limp. You will find it very difficult to control your breathing when you drop your jaws and force a yawn.

Unhealthy Breathing Habits. Most people are born with the ability to breathe properly; however, we develop unhealthy breathing habits from childhood instructions to "stand up straight, pull in your tummy, throw out your chest." Before we know it, the mind begins to control the functions of the autonomic system such as the beating of the heart, circulation of the blood, and breathing.

Many therapists believe that the problems adults have in handling stress to a point result from the way they as children handled anger by holding their breath. (Remember holding your breath until you "turned blue" to frighten your mother?) A childhood pattern of restricting breathing when upset and continuing it over a period of years leads to bad breathing habits. In addition, the body may automatically breathe differently as a protective mechanism to prevent toxic substances from entering the respiratory center and to exhale toxins.

Correct Breathing. Stand up and place your hand on your abdomen; move your hand up as far as you can without touching your rib bones. The soft area just below your rib cage is your diaphragm.

Placing your hand on your diaphragm, inhale deeply and then exhale. Repeat several times. Notice the movement of your hand as you breathe. Does it move in as you inhale and out as you exhale? If so, you are breathing incorrectly.

Your diaphragm works like a balloon being filled with air. The balloon inflates as it fills up with air and deflates as it loses air. Likewise, as you inhale and your diaphragm fills up with air, it should be expanding, pushing your hand out. As you exhale, your diaphragm should be deflating and your hand should be moving back into position. This is called diaphragmatic breathing.

Test Your Breathing Habits

Now check to see if you are controlling your breathing or if it is truly spontaneous. Before beginning this test, get a paper bag and have it handy in case you hyperventilate. If you do hyperventilate, if any tetany (cramping of the fingers or lips or spasms in your hands or feet) occurs, don't be alarmed. Hold your breath or blow into the bag as if you were blowing up a balloon, so that you can rebreathe your own carbon dioxide.

Spontaneous Breathing. Now lie down and pant—loud, rapid inhaling and exhaling—like the panting of a dog. Continue to pant until your breathing automatically becomes deep diaphragmatic breathing. If you have to swallow to help the changeover from panting to diaphragmatic breathing, your breathing is controlled. As long as you control your breathing, you cannot get into a truly deep relaxed state.

To persuade your mind to relinquish control of bad breathing habits, you must do breathing exercises. Through doing the exercises, your entire autonomic or involuntary nervous system can once again take over and do its job.

Breathing Exercises

In the beginning, practice these exercises lying down. Later, practice them standing, sitting, or while walking so you can incorporated them into your daily life.

1. Relaxation Breathing. Place one hand on your diaphragm and the other on your lower abdomen. As you inhale, force your lower abdomen to swell like a balloon. As you slowly breathe out, drop your jaw and shoulders.

ða ða ða

Like many patients with environmentally-triggered problems, I had difficulty with even this simple relaxation breathing exercise. Dr. Cox and I modified it for me; later I found it helpful for patients who have the same difficulty.

⋙ ⋙ ⋙

Instead of imagining your diaphragm as the balloon, imagine your whole body as the balloon. As you breathe in, force out your lower abdomen (keeping your diaphragm and lower abdomen filled with air); fill your body with the oxygen by forcing out your chest, back, and shoulders. Bring the oxygen up through your neck pushing out your cheeks as you fill them with air. As you fill up your body, first force out your abdomen and then your diaphragm, chest, shoulders, and finally blow up your cheeks. Once your body is forced out (or filled up), don't let your abdomen or diaphragm collapse. Remember, your whole body is the balloon.

Now let go of each part. As you slowly breathe out, drop your jaw and your shoulders and force a yawn. Try to imagine the oxygen passing through each part of your body as you think, "My jaw is relaxing. My shoulders are relaxing. My arms are relaxing. My chest, my hips, my legs, my feet are relaxing." As you let go of each part, let it go limp.

If you are used to breathing into the upper chest, the following exercises may cause some dizziness or hyperventilation. This simply means that you have not been breathing deeply enough and your system is not used to it. You should practices these exercises either sitting or lying down until you have no symptoms that could cause you to lose your balance.

2. Counting Breathing (to increase lung capacity). Count to four as you inhale totally, filling your lungs; hold for another count of four and then exhale, emptying your lungs by the count of four. Repeat several times and then increase the count, gradually moving up to a count of six, eight, etc. Stop before you reach a point of strain.

3. Chest Breathing. Interlock your fingers pressing them against your chest while breathing out, emptying your lungs. Keep this pressure to make your lungs work harder on the next breath. Again, press against your chest while breathing out. Relax and take a full breath, then repeat.

4. Nostril Breathing. Breathe in through the left nostril, hold briefly, and breathe out through the right nostril. Reverse. Then breathe in through the right nostril and out both nostrils. Breathe in through the left nostril and out both.

5. Torso Breathing. Place your hands on different places on your torso and breathe into this area. Move your hands every three or four breaths until your breathing has expanded into your whole torso.

6. Pelvis Breathing. Sitting on a hard surface in either the lotus position or cross-legged, breathe so deeply that there is a movement of the "sitz-bone" along the floor.

7. Breathing Breaks. At least once every hour try to do five repeats of relaxation breathing exercise #1 to relax.

જ઼ જ઼ જ઼

I was part of a group of chemically sensitive patients Dr. Cox trained in self-relaxation, meditation, massage, yoga, and other exercises from both Eastern and Western cultures to find new ways of reducing stress. All disciplines offered some help and combining features from each of these techniques gave us a new form of relaxation by self-suggestion. We learned how to reach a level of relaxation so deep that it affected the autonomic system: the pulse was slowed, blood pressure was lowered or raised, circulation was increased, heartbeat was regulated, and so on. We were able to raise or lower the temperature in affected parts of the body, relieve or eliminate migraine headaches, lower the respiration rate, and reduce or eliminate edema. This new procedure was a great help in reducing stress.

Incidentally, once I reached a deep level of relaxation, I learned to apply it specifically for environmentally-induced illness. More about that later.

જ઼ જ઼ જ઼

In working by myself and with other patients, I discovered that other relaxation techniques were sometimes counterproductive. For example, patients are often encouraged to concentrate on directing warmth to an arm or leg by repeating the phrase, "My right arm is heavy and warm, my right arm is heavy and warm." Many patients do not feel the warmth initially; those who do not feel it may become frustrated and experience greater stress. It is inaccurate to assume that everyone in a relaxed state experiences the same sensations.

Stress Reduction Therapy. The following program, developed under the guidance of Dr. Cox, will help you find your own state of relaxation.

The program consists of three phases. As you progress from one phase to the next, you will become increasingly able to reduce the effects of stress.

PRACTICE! Don't try too hard! And don't take yourself too seriously as you begin the relaxation program. Getting upset while trying to learn an exercise for reducing stress defeats the purpose. Approach each session as a practice session instead of a session to accomplish something.

Don't practice the procedure until you understand its purpose and goal. Read the whole chapter for a description of the process—more than once if necessary. Once you understand the procedure, begin to practice it. Proceed at your own pace. You may wish to practice all of Phase I on your first day or you may prefer doing only a few steps the first time. If you practice a few steps a day, always repeat the steps you know before moving on to new steps. Keep on practicing until you reach the desired effect.

If it takes longer than you expect don't be discouraged but make sure you give it a fair chance. You may be encouraged to know that others who have reached total relaxation find that the process can be as healing as medication—without the side effects. Stress reduction therapy has speeded the healing of open wounds, healed broken bones more quickly, and prevented blistering from burns.

The procedures may seem difficult at first but if you follow the instructions carefully, the exercise will no longer seem difficult. We have divided the process into three phases to make it easier for you. Until you have gone through the whole process, we recommend that you do each step separately. We will guide you through each step gradually until you understand that particular step and are ready to move on to the next.

PHASE 1

How To Achieve the Relaxed Feeling

Lie down in a quiet place. Close your eyes to shut out visual distractions. Loosen any tight clothing. If your neck is uncomfortable do not use a pillow; instead fold a towel several times and place it under your head or roll up a towel and place it under your neck.

Step 1. Panting. As described earlier, panting is audible, rapid inhaling and exhaling like the panting of a dog.

Place your hand on your diaphragm (the soft place below your rib cage). As you inhale, make sure that your hand rises up; as you exhale, your hand falls back.

Continue to pant until your breathing becomes automatic diaphragmatic breathing. If this does not happen spontaneously while you're learning, swallowing can help produce the change to diaphragmatic breathing. With practice, your body will perform this function automatically but this could take weeks or months. Until then, practice relaxing by coordinating it with exhaling.

Stretch Your Legs. Lie flat with your legs stretched out full length. Without moving your leg (make sure that it stays flat against the mattress or floor) stretch the toes of your right foot toward your head, pushing the heel of your foot away from you while pulling the toes toward your head. Make sure that the heel of your right foot touches the mattress or floor and is not raised.

As you push out your heel and bring your toes forward, tighten up your leg. Feel the tension moving up through the calf, the knee, and up to the hip. Hold it for awhile and then release it very, very slowly to avoid straining the muscle. Let your leg go limp and feel the heel and your toes relaxing as they go back to the norm. This is the way to relax your leg. Practice this several times.

Synchronize Breathing With Stretching. As you tighten up your right leg, breathe in, using the relaxation breathing described earlier. As you tense your leg, pulling your toes toward your head as you push out your heel, breathe in, and when you are ready to relax, breathe out so that your breathing is synchronized with your movements.

Breathe in when you tense, out when you relax. Remember to relax your muscle slowly to avoid strain. Practice synchronizing your breathing with your stretching several times.

Compare Your Legs. Become aware of your legs. Compare them to each other. How do they feel? Does one leg feel better than the other? In what way? How do they feel against the mattress or floor? Make a mental note of any sensations you have in your legs.

Now, as you breathe in and out, tense your right leg as you have learned, but this time compare the feeling in your right leg with that in your left leg. See how long you must tense up your right leg before you notice a distinct difference between the two legs. Hold your breath as long as you can while holding the tension in your right leg. Breathe out slowly and relax, releasing the tension in your leg slowly to avoid straining your muscles.

Monitor Your Sensations. Notice at what point the right leg again feels like the left leg (which is not tensed up) and, more importantly, at what point the right leg feels better and more relaxed as a result of the exercise.

Repeat the procedure two or three times.

Give It a Name. Now it is time to name your feeling. Forget the word "relaxed" and develop a new, very personal language to define your relaxed state. Be very specific. Do you feel warm or cool, heavy or light? Does your right leg feel longer or shorter? Does it feel as if it is sinking or floating? Does it feel weightless or have a tingling sensation? Is it energizing?

These are some of the sensations people have experienced. You may feel a combination of these or none of them. You can get very creative with your description as did the man who reported that his legs felt like huge watermelons. What is important is not to be influenced by what others feel but to use the examples as an idea of what to expect.

A word of encouragement for those who cannot detect any change at this point. Some of the people who have benefited most from this process felt nothing at first. Now they can become so deeply relaxed that they can anesthetize themselves at will, stop bleeding, or speed up the healing of wounds. So follow the instructions and complete the rest of the exercise. Eventually you will be able to notice a change.

<u>Left Leg</u>. Follow the same procedure as with the right leg.

<u>Both Legs</u>. Now tighten both legs at the same time, following the procedure you used with each leg individually. Note the continuing changes in sensations.

Now that you have learned Step 1, here is an incentive for you to practice it until you have perfected it and to go on with other steps.

ᚹ ᚹ ᚹ

At one time I had frequent bouts of temporary partial paralysis on my left side when I could not move my arm or leg. By using this program, this cellibration therapy, I was able to relax and use Step 1 with my right foot and right leg, along with imagery (which we shall discuss later) and some of the other steps. This enabled me to shorten the periods of paralysis.

After a long time I reached a point where I could prevent the paralysis. But in the beginning the

process was very useful because my right leg and
right arm, and frequently other parts of my body,
would develop very severe cramps.

Have you ever had a toothache in your leg? Yes, it
sounds funny, but sometimes the cramping in my legs
was so intense it felt like a toothache. When I had
that feeling, I was able to use this process to
relieve the pain. It has now reached the stage where,
when I am exposed to something that used to cause the
pain or paralysis, I can usually ward it off by using
this process.

ra ra ra

Step 2. Arms. Practice the breathing relaxation three times.
Now tense your arms as you did your legs and create the tension
by making a fist with each hand.

Breathe in, make two fists, tense your arms as tightly as you
can, creating enough tension so that it moves into your shoulders.
Breathe out very, very slowly and relax. Repeat several times until
your arms are as relaxed as your legs.

After you have practiced Step 2 and feel comfortable with it,
combine it with Step 1.

Step 3. Jaws and Face. Practice the breathing relaxation
three times. Then pretend there is a pencil between your teeth.
Bite down hard as if biting on this pencil, leaving a quarter-inch of
space between your upper and lower teeth. As you breathe in,
tighten your face, screw up your nose, and thrust your lower jaw
forward, tensing all the muscles in your face, neck, and head.
Slowly breathe out and relax. With this step you can't blow up
your cheeks.

This step is especially important for those who grind their teeth
when sleeping and those with jaws so tight their dentist must use
appliances to release the jaws.

After you have practiced Step 3 and feel comfortable with it,
combine it with Steps 1 and 2.

Step 4. Torso. Practice breathing relaxation three times. Now
as you breathe in, tighten your torso, the muscles in your
abdomen, back, and buttocks. Tense your sphincter muscles.
Slowly breathe out and relax.

You may want to practice Step 4 frequently by itself if exposure
to chemicals or foods causes diarrhea and/or constipation.

Later in this section we will tell you how to use visualization and deep breathing along with Step 4 to facilitate and clear up your digestive tract.

Step 5. All Parts Together. Practice breathing relaxation three times and combine all the steps. Breathe in, tighten your whole body:

Pull toes toward head; tighten legs.

Make a fist; tighten arms and shoulders.

Bite down; tighten face, head, and neck.

Tighten abdomen, pelvis, buttocks.

Breathe out slowly...relax slowly...enjoy the release.

Abbreviated Instructions

Before beginning to practice the entire Phase 1 process, copy the following abbreviated instructions onto a 3" by 5" card to keep close at hand beside your bed:

Inhale for tensing, exhale for relaxing.

Check body sensations between steps.

l. Lie down; close eyes; compare legs.

2. Tighten and relax:

right leg, left leg, both legs;

right arm, left arm, both arms;

jaws, face, head, neck;

upper and lower torso;

whole body.

Enjoy the relaxed state. Be aware of your body, your breathing, your surroundings. You deserve the feeling of well-being that now floods throughout.

You will know you have mastered Phase 1 when you experience a new sensation which we will call the feeling. No one can describe it for you. It's a little like being in love. When it happens, you will know.

To help you recognize the feeling at the end of Phase 1, be aware of your total sensation as you lie on the mattress, how your arms or legs feel—if you can feel them at all. Note the sensation you most enjoy and of which you are most aware. Give it a name. For example, you might call it a " weightless feeling," "a floating feeling," "a heavy feeling," "a tingling feeling," "an energizing feeling," or perhaps "a lack of feeling."

Be sure you are describing your own feeling. Don't adopt labels you may have heard others use to describe their relaxed feeling.

Use the word or expression that best describes what you feel in your relaxed state.

Final Instructions

For your first attempt to go through all of Phase 1, allow an hour of quiet time, preferably before bedtime. You will gradually learn to accomplish the same results in just a few short minutes despite any noise around you.

Loosen your clothing. Place the card of abbreviated instructions on the bed beside you. Have a paper bag ready to blow into in case you hyperventilate.

Now it is time to use Phase 1 as a total technique. After you have practiced Phase 1 several times and recognize "the feeling," you are ready to do the short cut. The short cut is very similar to Step 5 with a slight difference.

The Short Cut. As you breathe in, tighten your entire body. Tense your legs as you stretch your toes toward your head. Make a fist while tensing your arms and shoulders. Bite down and tense your face, head, and neck. Also tighten the muscles in your abdomen, pelvis, and buttocks. Hold this tension as you hold your breath.

Breathing out very slowly, let your entire body go limp, thinking over and over, "My mind and my body are taking me back to My Feeling"—giving the name you call your feeling. Repeat three or four times. Practice the short cut in a sitting position at home so you can use it in your car and other places where you have to be seated.

The short cut is a very important preventive measure. Use it, for example, when driving and you are in an area where they are resurfacing the street, caught behind a diesel truck, stuck in a line of traffic behind a car with a polluting exhaust pipe, or when a careless driver pulls out in front of you, causing a near accident. Immediately begin to work with some of the breathing exercises and open your windows as soon as you are in an area where there is relatively clean air.

It is difficult to do the tensing while driving a car so just do the deep breathing exercise. When you stop at a red light or can pull off to the side, do the short cut, in a sitting position naturally.

Of course, if you are environmentally sensitive and are exposed to smoke, it is best to move away from the area thus reducing your pollutant load. If you are exposed to perfume or cologne, move away from the individual who has doused himself with the perfumed product. However, there are times when you cannot leave or may wish to stay in the area.

Caution. You may pay the price by interjecting your relaxation method for immediate results to enable you to remain in this area. However, later it is extremely important that you decrease your load at home.

If you consciously decide that it is worth the price to stay in a room where there is constant exposure to smoke, perfumed products, and formaldehyde in clothing use the short cut. Every 15 minutes or half hour, take a break and go to a smoke- and perfume-free area to do breathing exercises. If you can find a small private area, do the whole short cut, with Step 5 and the breathing relaxation.

Use your own ingenuity. You will find times when you can use the short cut on your own.

Invent your own ways. Do it as a challenge, not a chore. Consider everything you do, all of the measures you read about in this book, with a positive attitude. Don't tell yourself you are doing them because you are sick. Stop thinking of yourself as a sick person. You're not. It just happens that you react more quickly to pollutants than other people; their immune systems can tolerate pollutants for longer periods of time. You have a more acute reaction that lasts longer.

Treat it in a positive way. Laugh about it. Don't take yourself too seriously. Say it once, say it a hundred times a day, "Laughter is the best medicine." Don't worry about it. And don't let your friends treat you as an invalid. Don't think of yourself as an invalid. Think that these exercises are a healthy measure that every human being should do.

PHASE 2

To avoid confusion, do not even read this phase until you have mastered Phase 1. For best results practice Phase 1 every day.

Now that your feeling has a name, use it freely in this phase, substituting it whenever you read the words "THE FEELING." This new language is a way for you to communicate with your own body: "I feel weightless," or "I am energized," or "I'm tingling," or "I have a heavy feeling," or whatever your feeling happens to be.

Conditioning Process

Conditioning is the keystone of Phase 2. In psychology, conditioning is a process whereby a stimulus—feeling, object, or situation—begins to elicit a certain response which differs from the usual or normal response to that stimulus. In other words, if you normally react in a certain way, you can train yourself to react in the same way to a different stimulus, by constantly associating the one with the other.

Pavlov conducted the best known research in conditioning. Before he fed the research dogs, he rang a bell. The dogs were soon conditioned to salivate at the sound of the bell, even in the absence of food.

For the conditioning process to work in stress reduction, we believe you must be totally convinced that you have the ability to improve your physical condition by your thoughts. Negative thoughts seem to impede the process.

Harmful Negative Thoughts. This is not a new idea. We were born with the ability to use our thoughts positively, but often we use them negatively. For example, an infant whose mother is very disturbed picks up the mother's tension.

We believe that tensions can be transmitted to an area of one's anatomy. For example, an infant can refer that tension to his skin, resulting in eczema, or to his stomach in the form of colic if he has the underlying patho physiologic preconditioning. In an adult, the most common manifestation of such negative transmission is the tension headache.

If negative thoughts can cause headaches, why can't positive thoughts erase them? The answer is, they can. Working from this premise, we have developed the following conditioning process to reinforce positive thoughts by repetition.

Caution. Again we must emphasize that if you use conditioning to treat environmentally-triggered problems, it works only to a point. In the long run total pollutant reduction must be achieved. If it isn't, the patient will remain ill and, in fact, will get sicker with more conditioning and requiring more environmental control.

Procedure for Phase 2. Read all the instructions first, as you did in Phase 1. Do not begin to practice until you have read all the instructions.

Step 1. You are now ready to condition your body to reach the deepest level of relaxation achieved in Phase 1, which you now call "THE FEELING."

Each time you practice this, you will attain a different level of relaxation. Sometimes pressures and tensions will slow down the state of relaxation. This is particularly true if you are having a hay fever kind of reaction or a reaction from chemical exposure, the worst type of stress. The level of relaxation you achieve is largely determined by the level of tension at which you begin. So the fact that you do not achieve a deeper level of relaxation each time you do the process does not mean that you are not progressing or improving your technique.

The conditioning consists of the short cut, followed by relaxation breathing exercises accompanied by specific thoughts. You breathe in as you count, and breathe out as you relax.

Then as you breathe out, think "Relax into 'THE FEELING.'" At the same time call up the feeling. Give your body time to respond, and continue talking to yourself something like this:

"As I lie here, if I really wish to return to this level of relaxation in a matter of seconds, I must concentrate on 'THE FEELING.' I am letting my body soak in 'THE FEELING.' I am aware of 'THE FEELING' penetrating my mind, my body, the very core of my being."

"I am saying to my body, 'My arms and legs are aware of 'THE FEELING'...my torso is aware of 'THE FEELING'...I sense 'THE FEELING' in my head...I sense 'THE FEELING' in my organs. 'THE FEELING' penetrates every nerve in my body...every muscle in my body...every cell in my body."

"As I go deeper and deeper into relaxation, my body is conditioning itself to return to this state by using the formula."

Formula for Phase 2.

       Breathing in Deeply .... Breathing out Slowly
       Think "one" .... Relax into "THE FEELING"
       Think "two" .... Relax into "THE FEELING"
       Think "three" .... Relax into "THE FEELING"

As you practice the formula two or three times, consciously let your body soak up "THE FEELING" so you can return to it at will.

Breathe in deeply, feeling the air expand your abdomen, then your diaphragm, and go all the way up into your chest, your back, your shoulders, and your cheeks. Then breathe out very slowly, relaxing into "THE FEELING" you experienced during your deepest state of relaxation.

The formula directs you to "think" "THE FEELING." Obviously you can't "think" a feeling—more is involved than just being aware of it. You are really training your body and mind to register "THE FEELING" so that the next time you can begin where you left off.

Each day you begin where you left off the previous day, and each day you relax more deeply while conditioning yourself to begin tomorrow where you left off today.

The progression is not always obvious. People report that once they reach a very deep level they are unaware of a daily change. But suddenly one day they are aware of an entirely new tranquillity and peace of mind.

We and those we have trained use Phase 1 for half an hour a day to deepen the level so the body conditions itself to be relaxed and tenses only during traumas.

From time to time during the day apply the formula for Phase 2 for a three-minute period. It is a powerful way to eliminate unnecessary tensions, allowing you to handle stress without jeopardizing your health. Even unavoidable stresses caused by pollution can be reduced in this way.

Continue the conditioning by thinking something like this:

"When I count back from three to zero, I shall be wide awake and alert and so completely relaxed that the conditioning will have taken effect, and both my body and my mind have absorbed 'THE FEELING.'"

Now think to yourself:

"Three, I am now awake and alert, leaving all fantasies behind."

"Two, I am so completely relaxed that my mind, my body, and my inner core are absorbed in 'THE FEELING.'"

"One, I am conditioned to return to 'THE FEELING' by using the formula.

"Zero, I am wide awake and alert, yet completely relaxed.

Notice that the instructions say, "Continue the conditioning by thinking something like this." Ironically, we have found that many patients become so involved with the wording and trying to do the process exactly right, that rather than relaxing, they become more tense.

None of this is set in concrete—these are only suggestions. The more you use your own words, your own ideas, the more quickly they become a part of you, and the more effective they are for you.

PHASE 3

Do not begin Phase 3 until you have practiced and mastered Phase 2. When you are ready to begin Phase 3, you will do so five or 10 minutes after Phase 2 has been completed. Remember that "THE FEELING" was established in Phase 1. Phase 2 began with "THE FEELING," conditioning you to return to it using the formula. Phase 3 helps you learn to recapture "THE FEELING" using the formula.

Instant Relaxation. That's the beauty of Phase 3. It's as simple as that. Phase 1 teaches you to reach "THE FEELING." Phase 2 teaches you to condition yourself to reach "THE FEELING" using the Formula. Phase 3 teaches you that the conditioning has been accomplished.

Don't be discouraged if it doesn't come easily after several practices; practice it again after a good night's rest. After all, we are all individuals and some people need more conditioning than others or may be under more stress.

It is ironic that persons who do not have extra time are the ones who seem to need more time for the process. It is worth taking the time now to learn Phase 3 because in the long run it will improve your health and save you time. Because your sleep will be more restful you will require less sleep, wake more refreshed, and have more energy.

Combining Techniques

The relaxation breathing exercise, the first breathing exercise you learned, should be used for a few minutes every hour. It will help reduce the stress of tar or diesel fumes in traffic, emotional stress from sudden shocking news or a quarrel with a spouse, or when you have unintentionally eaten a food to which you are allergic.

Stress Reduction Therapy will go a step further and provide permanent change. For maximum benefit in dealing with a lifelong buildup of tension and stress patterns, you need 30 minutes of deep relaxation every morning to keep you relaxed during the day and 30 minutes at night to help your body heal itself during sleep. If you are unable to take 30 full minutes you should do as much as you can — even 10 minutes will help. Even after you have mastered the techniques and are on the road to good health, your immune system still needs the healing power relaxation generates to defend against the toxins in today's environment.

Relaxation is the best way to minimize the effects of stress, a common ingredient in today's society, and we have described ways to attain relaxation which many people have found helpful. Other methods may work best for you. The important thing is to find what works for you and practice it regularly. The mastery of relaxation techniques will help you accomplish more in less time than ever before.

❧ ❧ ❧

The Healing Process

I stumbled on this healing process totally by
accident. Dr. Kailin had sent me to a hypnotist to be
anesthetized for dental work but I found it difficult
to give up control to someone else (a trait that
seems to be typical of high achieving, type "A"
personalities.) Dr. Kailin then sent me to Dr. James
Cox who taught me autogenics, the system of
self-suggestion, so I could anesthetize myself. Using
this method I have had extensive dental work,
including work on my gums and crowns, using no
anesthesia at all. I also had an operation on my
thumb without the use of anesthesia.

I spent nine years in Dr. Cox's training program,
studying with some of the leading psychiatrists,
psychologists, and therapists. I studied
bioenergenics, gestalt, autogenics, and several
Eastern cultures such as the akido. Additionally, I
studied art, music, and dance therapy, as well as
improvisational theater and imagery, which we shall
discuss later.

During this study I checked to see how every stress
reduction mechanism worked on my own sensitivity. In
the process I accidentally came upon the self-healing
process that forms the basis for my cellibration
therapy.

An unlikely accident illustrates how effective this
method of therapy can be. I once accidentally plunged
my arm up to the elbow into 35 quarts of hot, boiling
grease. The pain was excruciating. While my neighbor
called my doctor to tell her we were coming, I used
ice cold water to cleanse my arm. Then I remembered
that Dr. Kalin had told me of an operation performed
under hypnosis where the subject had been guided to
withdraw the blood from the area to prevent bleeding.

Using the short cut into a state of relaxation, I
spent the half-hour ride to Dr. Kalin's office
alternating between anesthetizing the arm to stop the
pain and removing the blood from the area by

imagining my arm in icy water. Later I will share
with you other images I use.

When I reached the doctor's office, Dr. Kalin was
amazed to find no evidence of the burn. Instead of
the expected first or second degree burns the arm was
not even blistered or scarred. This accident proved
to me the truth of my belief that everything happens
for the best. There is always a reason for the worst
accident. If this had not happened, I would not have
had this wonderful healing experience and been able
to share it with others.

I want to share with you the joy, the pleasure, and
the ecstasy of feeling the energy field emanating
from every cell in the body as the cells heal and
rejuvenate themselves. This may sound presumptuous
but a few examples will indicate that this is just
what we're doing.

One example is my experience with what was once
labeled hypoglycemia. We now know that for the most
part hypoglycemia (and frequently diabetes) are
symptoms of allergies—food allergies, sensitivities
to chemicals, etc. Whenever I was exposed to any type
of sugar (including honey, crystallized sugars, and
fructose) after the initial burst of energy my blood
sugar dropped, I became fatigued, had hunger pangs,
and other symptoms associated with hypoglycemia.

To overcome these symptoms I use all three phases
when I have time. When I need to clear my pancreas
immediately to slow down the flow of insulin, I use
the short cut and, with an elaborate system of
symbols, concentrate on healing my pancreas.

I have since discovered that all I need to do is
take the breathing break and the relaxation breathing
break. Then I concentrate, repeating over and over
again, "My pancreas is healing itself." I am now
able to get rid of the symptoms in a few minutes.

When I first discovered this, I used to go on
chocolate binges. One doctor who specialized in that
particular field told me that this was unwise. While
I was overcoming the reactions, there could be
further damage to the pancreas or some other
complication.

Unfortunately, the doctor's prediction came true when I developed a very serious yeast problem. While there may not have been serious damage to my pancreas, there was serious damage to my immune system and the high concentration of sugar caused an over growth of yeast. I had to go on a very strict regimen for yeast control.

(Caution. At the risk of being repetitious let me repeat what Bill, my co-author, always reminds me. This is a good tool to be used in conjunction with, not in place of, sound environmental control measures.)

I have demonstrated cellibration therapy to several psychiatrists and psychologists to find out what happens and why my patients and I have had success with it. So far, they have given no answer but say that since it seems to work I should continue using it. I do hope that research will some day discover the mechanism.

In the meantime, I can live a normal lifestyle within reason, avoiding what can be avoided, cutting down the stress load as much as possible, and using the healing process.

I have also discovered the use of visualization in the healing process. You may recall that after my arm was burned I imagined my arm being in a bucket full of ice, and that controlled the burning sensation and kept my arm from blistering.

Another way that I use visualization is to imagine a hose, or sometimes several little hoses, inside my veins, arteries, and cells of the different organs. I imagine this hose or hoses flushing through the veins, arteries, and cells with hot water when I need to heat them and with icy cold water when I need to freeze them.

An incident with a young child taught me that I do not have to go through all the processes I originally developed. My young nephew once saw me stop a gushing of blood after I was injured with a very deep cut. A few days later this eight-year-old fell off his bicycle and cut his knees badly. He came running in and said, "Aunt Nat, can you stop the blood for me the way you did for yourself?" I answered, "No, but

I can teach you how," thinking that it would calm him while his mother cleansed the wound.

I first told him to take three deep breaths as I had previously taught him and then told him to picture his knees in ice. I also suggested that he picture the little hoses of freezing water. The bleeding stopped.

I realized that while I had to teach adults ways to block out their thoughts by using symbolism, the young child who believed in his aunt could do the process successfully only because he believed in it. It saved a lot of time and training.

This is really the secret of the process. If you believe in it, it will work. That has happened with all the people who have been trained this way. If you need to do so, brainwash yourself and keep saying over and over, "If she can do it, I can do it."

Positive thinking is a very important part of the process. This was brought home to me quite graphically one time when I needed to use autogenics for a dental visit—the reason I had originally learned the system. When I arrived I learned that the dentist's office had just been painted. This upset me because paint is a serious excitant for me and usually makes me ill. However, since I had traveled so far and waited so long for my appointment I decided to stay, but I began to worry that it would be painful because my brain would not function well in the freshly painted room.

When the technician began to work on my teeth, it was indeed painful and I kept thinking, "I knew this would happen." Then I realized that I was not practicing what I was teaching and that my negative thoughts were very strong. So I asked the technician to give me five minutes. During that time I told myself: "I know the pain is bad. I know that the paint usually makes me ill. It causes my brain to be fuzzy but that's not going to prevent the system from working. I know the process. My mind is taking me back to the last time that I was thoroughly anesthetized. My mind is taking me back to the last time I was thoroughly anesthetized." Within five minutes I was anesthetized and the technician could continue the work.

I must add, in all honesty, that I experienced a disappointment that night. When I came home from the dentist, I felt proud of myself, assured that I had conquered my sensitivity to the odor of fresh paint. Not at all. I am what is known as a delayed reactor. The onset of my symptoms is frequently delayed for several hours.

That night I had a bout with diarrhea, my usual delayed reaction to fresh paint, and as usual my stool smelled of paint. So my cellibration therapy was not a panacea or cure-all. It did, however, allow me to function when I had to and it reduced the severity and the length of time of the reaction.

Again, I want to emphasize that relaxation therapy is a process which allows you to cope with acute pollutant exposures but you usually pay a price of delayed response. However, with time, this response may be minimized from a few minutes to an hour if your total pollutant load is constantly being reduced by good environmental control.

Now back to the procedure.

ха ха ха

Anesthetizing Yourself

You may use the short cut to relaxation but if your stress level is particularly high from traveling through traffic, being exposed to perfume in the dentist's office, or to smoke in the halls outside the office you may want to follow it with as many as seven relaxation breathing exercises. After you are relaxed tell yourself: "My mind is going back to the last time I was anesthetized. My finger is registering the feeling that I had when I was anesthetized. My mind is taking me back to the way I felt from the Xylocaine the last time I was anesthetized."

When your finger begins to get numb, rub your finger alongside your mouth and over your gums, saying to yourself: "My finger is anesthetizing my mouth and gums. As my fingers run over my gums my mind is taking me back to the last time I was anesthetized."

If you have never had anesthesia imagine that it would be like the numbness in your feet when they are cold or the circulation is bad.

Anesthetizing yourself is as simple as that. Imagine how you would feel if you were anesthetized, and then give yourself the suggestion that you have that feeling. With concentration and the belief that you can do it, it is possible to anesthetize yourself. Don't be impatient. It takes time to perfect the process. Keep practicing and then suddenly it's a part of you.

ża ża ża

Changing Negatives to Positives. This leads us back to positive thoughts. I have found that when I try to put negative thoughts out of my mind and forget them they become more powerful, as in the experience with the newly-painted dental office. I have since realized that it is almost impossible to get rid of very powerful negative thoughts. So I have learned to use the negative thoughts by turning them into a positive ones.

For example, when I was in the dentist's office I kept saying to myself, "The odor of the paint, which usually makes me sick, is now anesthetizing me. It is taking me into a deeper state of relaxation. I cannot shut out the smell of the paint but it will help to anesthetize myself."

I have also used this method for plane trips after my environmentally-triggered illness began. Although I have always traveled a great deal by plane I would usually be sick for at least a day after my trip and I had knots in my stomach during flight, especially when the plane would tilt or hit an air pocket. The first trip after my illness was a rough trip and my breathing exercises would help only until the plane hit another air pocket. So I began concentrating on using the dips of the plane to put me into a deeper state of relaxation. To my amazement, I began to look forward to the plane dropping and rising again because I could feel my relaxation increasing from the very thing that had previously been very stressful.

You may find that these anecdotes do not convince you of the success of cellibration therapy and the healing process. There are some objective incidents which, although isolated, will give you an indication of what could be done with a scientific research project.

Co-author Bill Rea has a very expensive machine in his clinic known as an iriscorder. He and a Japanese physician are doing research projects recording changes in the autonomic system, the way in which the eyes react to certain stimuli, of patients before and after they have been exposed to a chemical. Results from the pilot project were presented at the Ninth International Symposium on Environment and Man and His Health in February 1991 in Dallas, Texas.

I was at that conference and we conducted a partial experiment. In the test you sit for 20 minutes with a blindfold in a darkened, less polluted room. Then you look into the iriscorder and lights are flashed into your eyes at different intervals. I first had the regular examination. Then I took the same examination again right after the first examination. The second time, for the 20 minutes that my eyes were covered with the black mask, I went into my altered state and concentrated on healing my eyes and making necessary changes. The second test registered enough changes to indicate that under carefully controlled circumstances the healing process does make a difference. We do intend to test this more carefully the next time I am in Texas. Although this is not scientific proof, there is enough objective evidence to warrant further research.

Self-Healing

Another situation in which I used the process I have been describing related to the results of a routine mammogram. There was a difference from my previous mammogram and I was called back for a sonogram which indicated a cyst on my right breast. I told the doctor about my self-healing, said I wanted to minimize the cyst, if possible, and asked her if I could harm rather than help myself. She laughingly said, "Well, I doubt if it will do any good, but it certainly won't do any harm."

Six months later, having spent a few minutes each day concentrating the imagery on my breast, I went back to check it out. When Dr. Swan saw the new mammogram, she said, "I don't know what you're doing, but whatever it is, keep it up." The cyst wasn't completely gone and I am now sorry that I didn't spend more time each day working on it. Regretfully, I often neglect to use this wonderful process.

This one incident is not scientific proof but it is a clear indication that something does happen when we work with this process.

Migraine Headaches. I sometimes have vascular headaches which begin at the base of the left side of my neck and can very soon develop into a full blown headache that lasts for days. I began to experiment by using cellibration therapy to cool my head and neck and heat my hand. Today, in most cases I can prevent the headache if I start the process as soon as my neck begins to hurt. However, in some cases I cannot immediately concentrate or do not have enough advance warning and the headache does reach an extreme level. Then I find it necessary to lie down and go through the whole process of Phase 1. With a little imagery I can reduce one of those headaches to a period of about half an hour.

Tension Headaches. I have discovered a difference in my reactions when it is a tension headache as opposed to a vascular or migraine headache. In a vascular headache the back of my neck becomes very hot. In that case I know that I must drain the blood from that area and send it to my hands, heating my hands and cooling my forehead. With a tension headache I reverse the process by cooling my hands and heating my head. Neither I nor the psychiatrists to whom I have demonstrated this process understand what actually happens, but this method works for me and for the many people whom I have taught it.

Parkinson's Disease. It is quite possible that there is an element of environmental triggers in Parkinson's disease. The news media have reported some incidents that could indicate this, and doctors in environmental medicine have had success in associating foods and chemicals with Parkinson's.

Quite by accident, I stumbled on the fact that Parkinson's is at times related to personal and interpersonal stress. After my sister Fran's cancer operation, I was teaching her some new stress reduction techniques. Frances, a victim of Parkinson's, discovered two things: as she reached her altered state the pain began to subside and the tremors in her hands and feet became still.

This happened almost every time I worked with her so I tried an experiment. When she was on the bed, totally relaxed, I began to talk of her daughter who had died of cancer at the age of two. Immediately Fran's hand began to tremble and her legs shake. I then helped her return to her altered state using the short cut. The calming was immediately noticeable as her hand and leg gradually stopped trembling. Frances has been able to reduce her tremors using this method. In the middle of the night when Frances wakes up with pain and tremors and is not allowed medication, she uses the tape I prepared for her or relaxes on her own. She is able to quiet the tremors, reduce the pain, and fall back to sleep. Occasionally it doesn't work, but for the most part it gives Frances many restful nights that ordinarily would be sleepless nights.

However, since I am not a doctor, I insist that she continue to see her doctor who is a member of the Parkinson's Institute in Miami.

After this success with my sister, I was asked to work with a man who had a different type of Parkinson's and I stumbled upon something which should really be investigated through scientific research. As I worked with this man I will call Larry, I gave him the suggestion of healing first his right leg, then his left leg, his right arm, his left arm, working up through the body organs, and finally got to the left hemisphere of his brain. I concentrated on the different sides of his body to see what would happen without giving Larry an indication of what I was doing. When I came to healing the left hemisphere of his brain, Larry reported something very strange happening. The pain and trembling in his right arm were subsiding. I was looking for this because the left hemisphere controls the right side of the body; in Larry's case the right side was affected by the Parkinson's.

I have no idea if the dead cells of the brain can be rejuvenated or if the healing process of the brain will be so intense that it can at least retard the advancement of Parkinson's. A doctor at the Institute of Parkinson's in Miami has indicated an interest in a research project which would investigate the relationship between stress—both environmental and other kinds of stress—and Parkinson's disease. He has said that if this research project begins, the institute would surely accept Dr. Douglas Sandburg of the University of Miami as an appropriate chief of protocol for the project. I am hoping to get some funds to sponsor this project. Hopefully, families with Parkinson's patients will come forward to advance this project.

ᴥ ᴥ ᴥ

Ideomotor Exercises

Dr. Kailin's theory of reactions to chemicals and food is that when an excitant enters the blood stream, the target organ is usually a weak part of the body. This could be a tense area, an incision from an operation, a former injury, a system weakened by abuse, or a system or organ with a congenital weakness. This results in edema (a swelling of tissue) in the same way that a nose swells from hay fever, an incision after an operation, or an ankle when it is sprained. Improved circulation helps to reduce the swelling and the pain or distress which accompanies it.

Circulation is improved by relaxing but it is very difficult for an allergic person to relax an organ or area that has been exposed to an allergen. This is where ideomotor response exercises can be used.

Actually these are not exercises but a technique which varies from person to person. Ideomotor response exercises are a matter of concentration and deep relaxation combined. You may use the relaxation methods explained earlier in this chapter or the methods employed in bio-feedback, autogenics, yoga, meditation, etc. What is important is that the method used produces deep relaxation for you.

Remember that you should approach relaxation with the idea of practicing, not of trying to relax. Once you are successful with the relaxation procedures you can begin to practice the ideomotor technique. The ideomotor technique is also a matter of individual preference which depends on your need.

For example, if you awaken with a stuffed up nose begin by doing general relaxation exercises; at first this will take 20 to 30 minutes. I am now able to reach relaxation with three deep, long breaths, breathing out slowly with my mouth wide open, my jaw hanging loosely, my shoulders relaxed, and thinking over and over "relax."

For a stuffy nose I then start concentrating on my nose repeating over and over "My nose is healing itself." I may concentrate on a picture of myself as a tiny person spraying the inside of my nose with tiny hoses of hot water; sometimes I picture a drainage hose coming out of my nose. Some people think of warmth and one doctor to whom I taught this method pictured the actual flow of blood.

What you picture is up to your own imagination and need. The important thing is to concentrate on the problem area, clearing your mind of other thoughts, and practice. Don't push it but just practice and enjoy a clear nose, inhaling and exhaling freely.

Short-Term Memory Loss

Recently there was a news story about people who suffered short-term memory loss after eating shellfish. Scientists were baffled as to the cause, but apparently no one investigated the source of the shellfish to see if there was a possible toxin contamination. Short-term memory loss is a common symptom for people with chemical sensitivities, and it is frequently the cause of learning disabilities in children as well as adults. In fact, one physician who has environmental illness has reported that his learning disability did not manifest itself during his medical training but only after a massive chemical exposure. Many children with learning disabilities may be able to live normal lives if they could consult with a physician practicing environmental medicine. Often these physicians pinpoint exposures to environmental illness when the scientific community is baffled by problems such as the shellfish.

ða ða ða

There is a bright side to short term memory loss — it can be helped by cellibration therapy. I had frequent bouts of short-term memory loss at the most critical point in my illness. Once I could not understand why I kept receiving overdue notices for bills which I had recorded as paid in my check book until I found all the bills, ready to be mailed, in my freezer. Or I would forget where I had put things or what I had gone upstairs to do. This was particularly difficult for me on days when I was partially paralyzed and had to crawl around.

After the development of cellibration therapy, I seldom had this problem. When I misplace something or forget what I am going to say, I now stop, take three deep breathing relaxation exercises, recondition myself, and continue what I was saying. If I am in front of an audience when this happens, I turn the negative into a positive by telling the audience what has just happened. I usually explain that perfume or another toxin in the audience has caused the short-term memory loss and tell them how I have corrected it.

This ability to turn a negative into a positive has become a source of pleasure for me. In fact, it is probably the biggest and most important lesson I can leave with you. Maintaining a positive attitude, a sense of humor, and the ability to turn negatives into positives have helped me become a productive member of society again, rather than a vegetable hidden in an isolated community. This approach will help you too!

5

HOME TESTING

How often have you heard someone say, "I am perfectly healthy. I have no allergies, and chemicals do not bother me. I am not affected by pollution." Later in conversation, the same individual will make a statement like, "Oh, I can't stand her perfume!" or "Isn't that man's cigar awful?" or, "Radishes repeat on me." One woman said, "I'm not allergic to smoke. It's just that if there are too many people smoking, my eyes begin to burn. But that can happen to anyone."

That is the main point: it can happen to anyone. These toxins and foods cause reactions. To people with chemical sensitivity the reactions are more pronounced, and in some cases, people can become totally incapacitated.

The chapter on home detoxification includes a discussion of overloading. Unfortunately, no one knows when his body has reached the saturation point where it can no longer function when exposed to these toxins. So even if you think you are perfectly healthy, it is wise to test any new purchase when you can still return it, especially if it is something costly such as a carpet or sofa.

Don't skip this chapter even if you have had extensive testing by a very knowledgeable, well-qualified Environmental Medicine (EM) specialist. Testing in a doctor's office is faster, more efficient, and more accurate, but there will be times that you will want to do testing yourself. For example, you may suspect that your treatment dose needs changing because former symptoms have returned. You may want to retest something for which you are getting treatments, to see if you should go back to your doctor for retesting and new treatment doses. You may also need to test a new purchase while it can still be returned or do a simple food test on new foods now available in your area.

As we now know, chemical sensitivity is a breakdown of the immune and enzyme detoxification systems, a condition which can be improved by a thorough health program. Because the costs of medical care are skyrocketing, people have been looking for different ways to reduce medical bills. Prevention is one way to save money.

Prevention can be practiced by cutting down on things that are known to make people ill, and more importantly, eliminating the things that are now affecting the state of your health. To discover what these are, testing is necessary. If you are only mildly sensitive and are in general good health, you can do many tests at home. Even the chronically ill patient can do some home testing. First have your doctor give you a physical to rule out other organic medical problems unrelated to sensitivities. Choose a physician who knows about environmental illnesses and can supervise any testing you do at home.

If you fast for more than one day, be sure to do so only under a doctor's close supervision. The reason for fasting (aside from religious reasons) is to withdraw from the foods and chemicals in your body and it can be as serious as withdrawing from a drug addiction. If you experience headaches, dizziness, or other discomforts when fasting, you are probably sensitive and are undergoing the early stages of withdrawal.

Testing Procedure

Taking Temperature and Pulse. Before you begin to test, check your pulse and temperature each morning for a week. This will give you a comparison when you are testing because a change in temperature can indicate a reaction. Check your temperature five minutes before and 20 minutes after each test, and your pulse five minutes before and 20, 40, and 60 minutes after each test. A pulse increase or decrease of 15 or more counts per minute also usually indicates a reaction. Be sure to check your pulse for a full 60 seconds for a true reading; sometimes it will speed up or slow down sporadically.

Finding Your Pulse. If you are using your left wrist to take a pulse, place the balls of your right index and middle fingers on the left side of the inside of the wrist about one inch above the hand. You have located the pulse when you feel a throbbing. You can also find a pulse on the side of your neck under the jawbone, about halfway between the chin and the ear.

A record of your temperature changes and pulse *(see Diary below)* can help your doctor and also reduce the cost of tests. The Diary can also help you discover a pattern and sometimes detect on your own many of the causes of your reactions.

Diary. Following is a suggested way to keep your diary.

Date & Time	Food	Chemical Stress	Interpersonal Stress	Symptoms	Measures Taken T o Relieve Symptoms	Comments

Peak Flow Meter for Asthmatics. This instrument and other similar ones can be very useful in detecting asthmatic reactions. It is a plastic tube that has a numeric gauge on it to help you monitor lung spasms *(See Appendix E)*.

In *Is This Your Child* Doris Rapp gives a detailed explanation about its use and has a chart describing how to record changes *(See Appendix F)*.

Procedure. Before you begin your test, write down your symptoms, even if they're as simple as a slight headache, backache, or cough; a few sneezes; or a cramp in your toe or foot. Take your temperature and pulse and record them in comments column.

The best time to test anything—whatever it may be—is first thing in the morning after taking your pulse and temperature. Record under food or if testing a product record it under Chemical Stress.

Keep track of everything you do that day, the foods you eat, and your activities, even if they are routine such as going to the office, driving your car, stopping for gas, going shopping, or whatever. Record any change in symptoms.

Finding A Pattern. At the end of the testing period, spread out the diary pages for all 12 days (some days may have two or three pages) so you can see them all and then look for a pattern. The pattern you observe may indicate that you are reacting to something other than the items for which you are testing.

Physical Changes. Physical changes are another indicator of reactions. Before and after testing, take note of any physical changes in your appearance, especially your hands and face.

Check your skin, fingernails, and the whites of your eyes and note any changes in color.

Check your handwriting to test your coordination. Write the same piece of information (your address or something else) four different times on four different pieces of paper, labeling each page, and comparing them only after you have completed all four. Do this before the test and five minutes, 30 minutes, and six hours after the test. If the quality of your penmanship deteriorates after the test, this is an indication that the item being tested affects your coordination.

If possible have someone else observe you while you are testing; another person may observe things you fail to notice, such as restlessness, scratching, or other behavioral changes.

Spacing Your Tests. Wait three days between chemical tests. Certain substances may cause delayed reactions and this will allow you to detect which irritant is causing your problem. If you are unsure of the results of a test, wait for two weeks before testing that item again.

You can test foods more frequently. Although people may not react to a chemical for at least 72 hours after exposure to that chemical, even a person who is a delayed reactor will usually react to a food 90% within 4 hours, 9% with a small immediate reaction and a big one later, and 1% delayed over 12 hours but usually within 18 hours.

If severe reactions continue for any length of time, it is wise to suspend testing until they clear up unless, of course, they're symptoms that you recognize as having started before your testing began. You must define each individual reaction as to how long it takes and when it terminates. Otherwise, confusion will occur.

If you have chronic symptoms (symptoms you always have) that have nothing to do with testing and you cannot go to a doctor's office immediately, continue testing only after a phone consultation with the doctor. You can use the change in the severity of the reaction or of new symptoms developing as a barometer.

਺ ਺ ਺

Testing New Products. I hope that telling my own story will prevent "healthy" people from having my experience with new purchases. Looking back I can now laugh at some of the events that caused so many problems. But I laugh with a lump in my throat and a tear in my eye because at the time they were very distressing. And I say to salespeople, "Don't do me any favors. Don't try to save me any money." I was one of those people who "never had any allergies" except for a slight sensitivity to deodorants. Once when I was furnishing a new apartment, my sister suggested that since I had a mild sensitivity I should buy an acrylic carpet instead of the wool one I was planning to buy. "Besides," she said, "it will cost you less money."

Being a practical person, I decided on the acrylic. Nine months later I was diagnosed as severely sensitive and I discovered I was highly sensitive to acrylic and other synthetics, but not to wool.

For my draperies I chose beautiful antique silk shantung. The interior decorator suggested that I could save money by having them lined with a special material to protect them from sun damage. I later learned that the silk was no problem, but I was highly sensitive to the chemically treated lining.

My custom-made sleep sofa, designed for my specific needs, was treated to resist stains..."to save the cost of frequent cleaning." The product used to make the material stain-resistant was so toxic that 10 years later, I still could not sit on the sofa when I visited the relative to whom I gave it.

Now you understand my motto, "Don't do me any favors. Don't try to save me any money." But the real moral is *"Test New Products."*

ᏋᎯ ᏋᎯ ᏋᎯ

Testing Untreated Materials

Your own sensory system is the best method to test materials. You can determine your own sensitivity to such items as a piece of clothing or yard goods, draperies, a rug, or even a TV set or other appliance. This process of testing an object with your body is called "organoleptic measurement," i.e., measurement by the senses. Wine, coffee, or tea tasters and perfume testers make their living as organoleptic measurers.

The Crawly Feeling. Francis Silver, P.E., a consulting environmental engineer, believes that some people "can detect indiscreet chemicalization of a product" with their noses, while "others have learned...how to detect harmful chemicalization by touching with the palm of their hand."

Silver describes this as "that crawly feeling," which he believes is a reliable guide in knowing what to buy and what to avoid. To use this method, first place your hand on a chemically uncontaminated surface; no unusual feeling will result. Then place it on a chemically contaminated surface and you will feel a slight "crawly feeling" after a few seconds or a minute or so.

"Some persons do not get the 'crawly feeling' but may get more of a 'tingly' or perhaps a 'bad' feeling. It feels as if the surface is 'alive' and 'not right,'" says Silver.

Just rest the hand lightly (about half the hand's weight) on the surface you are testing. Don't rub, as rubbing will stimulate nerve endings and drown out the crawly feeling.

"The intensity of the feeling will be roughly proportional to the level of contamination," says Silver. "If the hand is removed from the contaminated surface, for some time afterwards a peculiar or 'not quite right' feeling will still be felt in the hand."

Silver says that by moving your hand from the control object that does not affect you to the questionable object and back again, you can determine your reaction level. By comparing several samples, you can learn that Item A is more contaminated than Item B, but less contaminated than Item C.

It is a good idea to test for the crawly feeling before buying clothing, bedding, textiles, towels, even furniture. By using noses, taste buds, or touch, Silver believes that about 50 percent of the population can train themselves to use organoleptic measurement.

You may want to think twice before parting with an old, shabby rug that is not contaminated and replacing it with a attractive new one that may ruin your health with toxic chemicals. Manufacturers now use a variety of toxic chemicals which have the potential to ruin people's health.

Your best defense against unsafe products may lie in your own hand. Following are a number of other tests for fabrics that you can perform yourself.

Bubble Test. Use this test for cotton only. Carry with you an eyedropper in a small bottle filled with water. Squeeze a drop of water onto the fabric. Water readily soaks into untreated cotton; exceptions are barrier cloth and primitive fabrics such as unbleached muslin. Primitive fabrics can be identified by a strong vegetable smell which usually washes out easily.

If the drop of water soaks in, the material is probably untreated cotton. If it remains on top, the fabric has likely been treated. The bubble test is not fail safe; back it up with another test before buying a large amount of the fabric.

Corduroy Test. Feel corduroy on the wrong side. If it is untreated the fabric will be soft while treated corduroy is hard and sticky. The safest test is to buy a small amount from each bolt to test.

Fiber Content Test. It is also important to check the fiber content listing before you purchase any fabric. Although you may not be allergic to the contents listed the fabric may have a strong smell. If this is the case, take a small sample home, wash and air it, and then check the odor. Fabrics stored near polyester or fake furs (which use strong dyes) can pick up odors from them. If the sample has a strong odor after washing and airing, do not buy the fabric.

Glass Jar Test. Place a sample of the fabric in a glass jar (at least quart sized) and close the lid tightly for 36 hours. Then open and do the sniff test below. You may react immediately with nasal congestion, nausea, sneezing, or coughing. A delayed reactor, who may not notice the problem until a few hours later, should repeat the test several times to be sure the fabric causes the discomfort.

Heat Test. If synthetics were used in constructing the material, the heat from ironing will heighten the odor. Use the sniff test while the fabric is still warm.

Sleep Test. If you are still unsure of a fabric or small object, use the sample as a pillow overnight and see how you feel after sleeping on it or near it for a night.

Sniff Test. This test is most effective if done at home where you do not have other contaminants. Follow the Test Procedure described earlier in this chapter. First thing in the morning before eating hold the material to your nose and breathe normally through it for 10 to 15 minutes. Heavily treated fabric may produce a reaction such as head pressure in a few seconds. However, not everyone can judge treated fabric using this test.

Wrinkle Test. Crush cotton in your hand. Wrinkles in an American fabric indicate that it has not been treated; however, imported fabrics may wrinkle even though treated. The general rule of thumb is that the less the fabric wrinkles, the more it has been treated.

Food Testing

Food sensitivity can sometimes be detected very easily with a simple food test; at other times it can be so complicated that it requires hospitalization in an environmentally controlled unit.

An example of a very serious problem with a very simple solution is the case of an eight-year old girl with a chronic bed wetting problem. Her parents did everything possible, including waking her up several times during the night, but she continued to wet the bed.

A medical friend of the family suggested they eliminate citrus fruit from her diet. When they did so she stopped wetting the bed. When they again fed her citrus fruit as a test, using the system that follows, she wet the bed again.

Now, this does not mean that citrus fruit always causes bed wetting nor that bed wetting cannot be caused by other foods. That is the difficulty with food testing. A lot of guesswork is involved.

Knowledge of Food Sensitivities. Before you can do any type of testing for foods, even a simple one-food elimination food test, you have to understand hidden food sensitivities, food families, and the rotation diet. So carefully read Part V, "Allergy-Free Cooking," especially the chapters on "Diet Modification" and "Food Rotation," and then turn back to this section.

In the meantime, you may be able to do a simple food-elimination test, and you can certainly do the tests on chemical products.

You should suspect a particular food if any of these four conditions exist:

- You eat it every day;
- You crave it;
- You have experienced discomfort and feel better after eating it; or
- You feel discomfort, such as a cough, headache, or other symptom, immediately after eating it.

Use the Testing Procedure and the Diary, both described earlier in this chapter.

Simple Food Elimination. For a food test to be valid, you must avoid the food long enough for the symptoms to show up, but not so long that you can readapt to the food. The average time for unmasking is four days; some people can readapt within 12 days. Although you can perform valid testing by avoiding the food from five to 11 days we suggest you stay on the safe side and avoid the food and members of that food family for seven to 10 days.

When the avoidance period is over, eat about half a cup of the food before eating anything else that day. Wait an hour. If discomfort occurs immediately, you are likely allergic to that food.

If there is no immediate reaction or symptoms are minor, and you want to check it thoroughly, eat as much of that food as possible that day. If you experience behavior changes or other problems within 18 hours of the time you stop eating this food, you will know that you are probably allergic to that food. Sometimes other allergies that you don't know about can confuse the picture and make the test inconclusive.

If you discover a food allergy, try to avoid it and related foods for three to six months. In that time, you may regain a tolerance for it. If so, eat the food no more than once every fifth day so you do not reactivate the allergy.

Trial Elimination Diet

If you suspect that there are many foods involved, a faster way to test foods is by eliminating certain groups of foods from your diet for eight days. To do this you must understand the information outlined in the section on food families. It is best not to eat prepared foods during this period because hidden ingredients could throw your test results off. We recommend that you eat only foods cooked from scratch.

Totally eliminate eight groups of food—the eight groups of foods that generally cause the greatest amount of difficulty. Even a crumb of one of these foods, such as corn, can throw off the test. In addition, if you know of one or two foods that cause you serious reactions, eliminate those, too. During the eight-day period, concentrate on eating a lot of fruits, vegetables, and animal proteins other than those on the elimination list.

Elimination List. Eliminate all of the following groups of foods from your diet for eight days:

Group 1:   Wheat and all wheat products
Group 2:   Chicken eggs
Group 3:   Corn and all corn products, including corn syrup
Group 4:   Beef and dairy products, including milk, cheese, whey, nonfat dry milk solids and calcium caseinate
Group 5:   Cane sugar, beet sugar, and molasses
Group 6:   Soy and all soy products, including tofu
Group 7:   Coffee, tea, and cocoa
Group 8:   Peanuts

Multiple Food Elimination Test. During the eight days of food elimination, carefully keep the diary presented above. Have as many pages per day as needed. Follow the instructions and the procedures for testing in the same way that you did for the simple elimination test. Begin testing on the ninth day.

The first day of testing you will test just group one, following the procedure outlined in the simple food elimination. On day two you test group two, chicken eggs, and continue in this manner for the eight days. If you have multiple food and chemical sensitivities there may be very little change in your symptom pattern. In that case it would be wise to seek the help of a physician knowledgeable in food allergies *(see Appendix E, "American Academy of Environmental Medicine")*.

The Mono Rotary Diversified Food Test. This is a less complicated and more accurate food test. To understand this test it is imperative that you carefully study "Part Five" about food and food rotation. Whether you are using the rotary diversified diet to retest foods or as a beginning of your food testing, it is advisable to check first with an EM specialist who understands the pitfalls. Do your testing under the supervision of a physician or a paraprofessional who is qualified to check it very carefully and report back to a doctor if there is a problem.

You can test either three or four foods a day for four days or more. Let us assume that you are testing on a four-day rotation. Plan your rotation so that on each day you have a different protein, a different vegetable, a different starch, and a different nut or fruit. Even your food families must be rotated. To plan such a test, turn to "Appendix C" and select each day's food from the daily charts.

From chart Day 1, 5, and 9 select the four foods that you will test the first day. For day two select foods from the food chart for day 2, 6, and 10 and continue this pattern for days three and four.

Select foods that you have never eaten or that you have not eaten in six months. If that is not possible, select foods that you do not suspect are troublesome. Do not select anything you know makes you ill. That way you may find enough safe foods to eat that test negative (no symptoms—non-allergic).

Test each food by itself, with nothing else except salt if permitted. It makes no difference whether you eat the protein in the morning or in the evening, or the vegetables whenever you wish to eat them. You must always, however, follow the same pattern. So whatever you eat on day one for breakfast, you must eat the same food for breakfast on days five and nine. Whatever you eat on day one for lunch, you must eat the same food at the same time of the day on days one, five, and nine. And so on.

Follow the routine you chose for day two for days six and ten in the same way.

Use the method listed above in procedure for testing and keep the diary as recommended. The only reason to change the exact repetition would be if you had an immediate and severe reaction that you could definitely pinpoint as being caused by a specific food. The first four days do not count at all except, as we said, if there is an immediate reaction to a food, because you could be withdrawing from any number of the foods.

After 12 days spread out your diary sheets for days one, five and nine in a row so that you can compare them. Do the same with days two, six, and ten; days three, seven, eleven; and so on. Compare your reactions. If you see a pattern of the same type of reaction, the same period of time after you have eaten, this is an indication that you are probably reacting to that specific food.

CAUTION: The first four days could be withdrawal and this could cause severe symptoms. Withdrawing from foods can sometimes be as uncomfortable and as painful as withdrawing from cigarette smoking or even drugs or chemicals. That is one of the reasons why this particular type of diet should be supervised by a professional.

At the end of 12 days, if you have had no relief by going on this diet or if you are having more reactions or symptoms than you did before starting with the rotary diversified mono food test, you can be quite certain that you have very many food sensitivities. If you cannot see a doctor immediately, you can continue testing foods for another twelve days, using exotic foods and foods that you've never eaten. However, it is advisable, under these circumstances, to see a EM specialist.

If, however, you have seen a good pattern and been able to eliminate some of the foods to which you have reacted, you can continue on a rotation plan, adding a new food each day in a test pattern and using the procedure. You can gradually move up to a rotation diet where you can combine two or three foods at every meal.

Following the rotation plan is not difficult if you understand the plan and if you know how to use the formula *(See Chapter, "The Formula")*. If you cannot figure it out by yourself, have a professional help you design your initial rotation diet. After your diet has finally been stabilized, you can change your diet and begin with recipes within a food rotation plan.

Testing for Food Additives

You may react to a certain food (or foods) to which you are not really allergic. The culprit may be additives.

For example, a woman we shall call R.M. had no problem when she ate organic apricots and peaches. She could even eat the dried ones if she bought them in certain health food stores. But on one occasion she began to itch after eating a few apricots. It took her some time to discover that those apricots had been treated with sulfur dioxide, a common situation with dried fruits.

R.M. also has no problem with foods made with some wine vinegars, but only if the wine was not treated and preserved with sulfites. Unfortunately, although sulfites have been banned from many foods, they can still be found in some wines.

An additional problem with food additives is that they are really chemicals. A chemical reaction can often be delayed 72 hours or more and last as long as five days and, in some people, even longer. With a food, 90% will react within four hours, 9% with a small immediate reaction and a larger one later, and 1% delayed over 12 hours but within 18 hours.

R.M.'s primary reaction is itching—she itches when exposed to almost any chemical. Different additives and foods cause different reactions in various people. Each person has an individual reaction and this must be kept in mind when testing.

The best way to discover the effects of additives on your health is to cook from scratch for three weeks. Read labels very carefully. Use no additives, no foods containing additives, and no prepackaged foods. This period is longer than that used for food testing because it sometimes takes longer to clear the body of chemicals.

This test can be misleading or inconclusive. If you are testing for food sensitivities, you must be aware that natural toxins in foods can also cause problems, i.e., the nightshade family of tomatoes, potatoes, green bell peppers, eggplant, and tobacco. Cabbage contains cyanogens and peppers capasian; these both trigger intestinal reactions in many people.

If health problems persist during the test, other factors may cause the problem. Removing one irritant may not be enough to show a noticeable improvement. Any condition may be caused by something other than food sensitivities and should be checked by a physician. But even a minor improvement in well-being indicates the importance of pursuing testing and using preventive measures.

Testing for Chemicals in the Atmosphere

You can perform two simple chemical tests. If you suspect your susceptibility to a particular product, avoid the chemical for two or three weeks and then test it.

Draw up a chart containing the following information: approximate date the headache or other reaction began; time and place where headache or reaction began; new purchases at that time; new activities beginning at that time; and time and place where headache or reaction seemed worse.

Sometimes it is very simple while at other times it can be very difficult to trace the cause of a reaction. Richard R. was able to trace his by using the above chart.

He remembered the exact date his headaches began because they started on a day he was scheduled to give a presentation at a meeting. He awoke that morning with a very severe headache. He had stayed in that hotel many times before and attended meetings in the same conference room with no problem. Yet, every morning of this four-day meeting, he woke up with the headache, which would clear up a few hours later.

His chart revealed that he had slept in a new pair of pajamas purchased upon arrival in the city where the meeting was held. They had not been prewashed before use, a procedure his wife always followed with any new clothing he wore.

Incidentally, it is a good idea when you purchase anything new, to wash it before wearing because it may contain additives that can be washed out.

As it happened the problem continued after the pajamas had been washed. On checking, he found they had been treated with formaldehyde to give them a permanent press finish. When he went back to wearing his usual pajamas, the headaches ceased.

You would be wise to self-test in a similar way. While you may not detect the cause as readily as R.M. did, the procedure is worth trying.

The second test involves placing a sample of the product in a tightly sealed jar for at least 48 hours or until you are ready to take the test, called the sniff test. For the next phase, go for a long brisk walk on a day when the air quality is in the good range. As soon as you return, follow the procedure outlined above in this chapter. Then open the jar and hold it under your nose for 30 minutes (unless you notice an immediate change in how you feel). If you notice no change but still suspect the chemical, close the jar. At bedtime, open it again and place it close to your bed. If it is a fabric or other soft item, place it on your pillow and sleep on it.

Minor sensitivities to specific chemicals can also be tested in other ways. You may suspect tap water because you don't like the taste or you don't feel good when drinking large quantities of it. To test your tap water, drink only pure water (spring water, distilled water, or pure well water) for a week. (Be sure it is bottled in glass or the test may indicate an allergy to plastic.) For best results, wash or rinse and cook all foods in the pure water.

On the eighth day, drink a half gallon of tap water (unless your reaction is immediate). If you experience symptoms, this may indicate a sensitivity to tap water.

Following are a few tests you can try. In each case, be sure to avoid the test substance for a week before testing. Then use the testing procedure found above in this chapter.

Acetone (nail polish remover). Put a few drops on a piece of cotton and place two feet away for 20 minutes.

Ammonia. Put one tablespoon in one cup of water; place one-half tablespoon of this mixture on a piece of cotton, four feet away, for 15 to 20 minutes' exposure.

Aspirin (Pure acetylsalicylic acid). Test corn-free aspirin as individually instructed by a doctor only if sensitivity is suspected. Reaction can be violent.

Butter. Some people who are very sensitive to milk can tolerate pure creamery butter. Do not test any ordinary commercial butter, because it could have yellow dye in it. One good way to test butter is to use GHEE, which is a purified butter. If, however, you want to test the yellow dye that is in butter, test a commercial butter. Eat one teaspoon on the first, second and third days.

Car Exhaust Fumes. Stand near a bus stop for five to 10 minutes.

Clorox or Other Bleach. Place one tablespoon in one cup water. Put one-half teaspoon of this mixture on a piece of cotton and place four feet away for 15 to 20 minutes.

Deodorant. Test on underarm.

Detergents. Rinse out face cloth in Tide, All, or other detergent, and hold near face for 15 minutes.

Fairprene (synthetic rubber dust-proofing material for mattress casings). Test as a pillowcase. Also use crawly test.

Food Dyes. Test one drop each of red, yellow, blue, and green on successive days.

Fresh Newsprint. Hold a freshly printed newspaper six to seven inches from your nose for 10 to 15 minutes.

Gasoline. Stand close to a gas station pump for five to 10 minutes.

Gas Stove. Light oven and sit in kitchen for two hours. If you have no ill effects, eat a potato or other food baked in the gas oven.

Insecticides. Use market vegetables and fruits instead of organic foods (after restricting your diet to organic foods for at least a week).

Jello (gelatin). Test with a one tablespoon serving of a different kind each day. Do not test if food dye tests were positive.

Kerosene. Place a few drops on a piece of cotton and put two feet away for 20 minutes' exposure.

Lipstick. Test each color on a separate day.

Liquids That Are Not Foods. Place a drop on the inside of your wrist where you take your pulse, using the procedure described earlier in this chapter.

Moth Balls. Place one-half teaspoon four to six feet away in a small room for 15 to 20 minutes.

Plastics. To test for food, put an oil you can tolerate into a flexible plastic food container for 24 to 48 hours. Immerse a soft plastic food bag in it. After 48 hours add one tablespoon of the oil to a salad and eat. (Do not heat the oil before testing.) To test for orlon, nylon, or dacron clothing, wear it next to your skin overnight and wear synthetics the next day.

Rubber Foam or Plastic Foam. Hold a piece under your nose for 20 to 30 minutes. If there are no ill effects, sleep on a foam pillow overnight. Also use crawly test.

Shellac and/or Turpentine. Place a few drops on a piece of cotton two feet away for 20 minutes.

Testing for Dentures

If you cannot tolerate plastic, dentures may be a problem. Vulcanite is the only available alternative we know, since porcelain and enamel dentures are no longer available. Have your dentist request vulcanite samples or a base plate from *Anderson Dental Lab in Centralia, Washington.* If testing reveals that you can tolerate vulcanite, the lab will reproduce dentures from your plastic ones, or work from your dentist's final impressions and instructions.

How to Test for Vulcanite. Check all your vital signs first thing in the morning as described earlier in this chapter. Place the vulcanite between your lip and your gums for 30 minutes. Notice whether you have any reactions or changes. (Some people can also test food this way.) If you are testing a base plate, put it in your mouth when you awaken and wear it all day unless you have a reaction. It is probably wise to repeat the test for several days.

6

HOME DETOXIFICATION

All over the United States, there are detoxification centers for alcohol, for drugs, for smoking, and very few for detoxification of the toxins we are forced to inhale.

In *Appendix E*, you will find a listing of those centers, which are recommended for those who are seriously ill, as well as for those who wish to speed up their recovery.

Patients who have had chemical exposure impact on their health and have gone through the heat chamber chemical depuration program are the first to say that it enables the body to heal. For example, Tom, a tugboat captain, was involved with the cleanup operation of the *Exxon Valdez* oil spill March 27, 1989. This exposed him to the chemicals necessary to clean the deck of the boat and barges. On August 23, 1989, he developed a fever of 100°. At this time he experienced slurred speech, sore ankles, knees, and wrists. Although his rheumatoid factor was negative, several physicians felt he was suffering from an arthritis of unknown origin. Joint pains increased, he kept getting progressively worse, walking became difficult, and in September of 1990 he had to stop work.

When Tom arrived at the *Environmental Health Center in Dallas,* he had ankle, hand, wrist pain, and numbness and tingling of the fingers. He was weak, exhibited poor endurance, and was able to walk only short distances. Because of the lab findings, the recommended treatment was heat chamber chemical depuration program. In addition to this, Tom was to minimize all chemical exposure both in his environment and in his food and water. He was put on a program of nutritional supplements and intravenous therapy to enhance the breakdown and removal of chemicals from the blood and fatty tissues. For more complete details including the results of blood tests, see *Chemical Sensitivities* by William J. Rea, M.D.

As this goes to press, Tom continues to improve and today has greater range of motion in his hands, and he can open and close them. He has less swelling and improved grip strength and dexterity. He reports decreased joint and ankle pain and can now comfortably bend his knees. He is eager to return to work.

Before we get into the home detoxification program, here is another case study, details of which are in *Chemical Sensitivities* by co-author Bill Rea. *(See Appendix F.)*

Frank was a firefighter who enjoyed good health and was dedicated to his work. However, fires can produce more than smoke. In January 1988, Frank noticed something that resembled melted plastics as he fought a fire with his usual equipment. (This did not always include the use of an oxygen-fed mask.)

Twenty minutes later Frank developed an excruciating headache in the top of his head, nausea, and elevated blood pressure, and he was removed from the scene with what was assumed to be heat exhaustion. After a few days rest he returned to work. But his headache continued daily for the next three and one-half months. The physicians felt that this fireman had suffered burned sinus mucosal membranes and lung damage while fighting the fire. Once again he returned to work. The nausea continued, his blood pressure was elevated, and his pulse rate was depressed.

Because of his continuing health problems, he was able to work only sporadically from January to April of 1988. His symptoms would improve and then get worse. For the next 13 months he continued firefighting. Finally, in the spring of 1989 his health had deteriorated so much that he felt he could not continue to function. He had severe arrhythmias and elevated blood pressure. This is not commonly seen in a 28-year-old man who has enjoyed good health.

On June 5, 1989, Frank went to the Environmental Health Center for evaluation. He was suffering from headache, nausea, irregular heart beat, elevated blood pressure, elevated bilirubin (indicating liver stress), numbness and tingling in his hands (which had a yellowish cast), and fatigue.

After careful evaluation, it was decided that Frank had suffered a serious chemical exposure while firefighting in January 1988, and this was the link to his present illness. These chemicals were now a part of

Frank, and Center physicians felt that the heat chamber chemical depuration program was the best method to reduce his body burden.

He participated in the program for the next five weeks. During this time he was given nutritional supplementation and intravenous injections to aid in detoxification. He minimized all chemical exposure and drank bottled water while eating less chemically contaminated food. At the end of this time, Frank had some symptom improvement. It was decided that the program needed to be continued, but the greatest success could be attained if he was treated at intervals. This would allow time for healing and recuperation between the rigors of heat chamber physical therapy. Frank continued to undergo detoxification in September to October 1989 and in January to February 1990. Chemical levels were drawn during these periods.

Their analyses represent the effect of the detoxification program. Chemicals mobilized from the fatty tissues are seen appearing or rising in the bloodstream. These chemicals are then detoxified by bodily enzymes and eliminated by the bowel and liver.

In September 1990, Frank was well enough to work. However, he had to continue to minimize chemical exposure. Therefore, he could not risk chemical exposure as a firefighter. He began working as a subcontractor for concrete and curb work. In March 1991, Frank was hired by the city as a fire inspector.

Frank is much better now. He employs environmental controls at home in the form of less toxic household products. He continues to drink filtered water. His blood pressure is normal. He notices a few heart palpitations if he is exposed to chemicals.

Does chemical exposure impact your health? Can heat chamber chemical depuration enable the body to heal? Frank's answer would be "yes."

No one is suggesting that the home detoxification will be as efficient, effective, and speedy in recovery as the cases represented above or the hundreds and thousands of cases that can be cited from some of the detoxification centers. However, it is a good beginning for those who are waiting to get into a center, who can't get into a center because insurance companies will not cover the expense, or for those who have already gone through these centers and wish to continue detoxification.

For years, Environmental Medicine (EM) specialists have been teaching the dangers of overload. They have been citing co-author William Rea's comparison of an overloaded body to an overfilled barrel. It eventually overflows, the spill-over being analogous to the breaking down of the body.

In her latest book, *Is This Your Child?*, Dr. Doris Rapp refers to this analogy in a new and encouraging way: as emptying the barrel, cleaning up the home, modifying the diet, and avoiding excitants. She tells us how to make the barrel larger by using injection therapy, decreasing stresses, and improving nutrition.

This chapter expands Dr. Rapp's analogy with a home detoxification plan that includes a new diet concept (the rotary diversified diet, using organic foods; combining foods in specific ways for better digestion; having a greater concentration of alkaline-forming foods).

If you are chronically ill, consult your doctor before attempting this program, and do it under supervision of a physician who understands environmentally-triggered illness.

Before attempting the diet recommended here, it is suggested that you read chapters titled "Food Rotation" and "The Formula," so that, if necessary, you can adapt the diet to your specific needs or interests.

And now a little background material.

Alkaline-Concentrated Diet

The suggested diet was first introduced by co-author Natalie Golos and Dr. Russell Jaffe in a paper at the 26th annual meeting of the American Academy of Environmental Medicine (AAEM).[1]

Dr. Jaffe suggested that during the first month of treatment the diet consist of a ratio of 80 percent alkaline-forming foods to 20 percent acid-forming foods. After four weeks, the ratio can be reduced to 60 percent alkaline-forming foods to 40 percent acid-forming foods. Setting these ratios is no easy task because the subject is not an exact science.

Note: Acid foods and acid forming foods are not synonymous. Unfortunately, when a person is trying to avoid acid-forming foods, the tendency is to avoid things like citrus fruit that seem like acid-forming foods when eaten, but when analyzed, are in fact among the highest alkaline-forming foods.

Maryann Lazer, a Maryland dietitian who has studied this aspect of the diet, says little is known and great confusion exists about which foods are acidic and which foods form acid in the system.

Another obstacle arose in preparing the diet for use by the most sensitive patients. To maintain a diet consisting of 80 percent alkaline-forming foods, it is necessary to consume a great deal of fruit. However, most patients with chemical sensitivities have a yeast problem,

---

1   Dr. Russell Jaffe, Director of the Princeton BioCenter, Skillman, New Jersey.

and yeast is believed to feed upon the sugar in the fruit, thus sometimes causing problems for these people.

However, it seemed that as sensitive people tried the diet with proper food combining and use of high alkaline-forming foods, the yeast problem remained under control. In fact, at times it seemed to improve.

The information for combining foods came from a chart in Dr. Jaffe's *Health Studies Collegium.*

To summarize it:

You may combine proteins and vegetables, as well as starches and vegetables.

Never combine proteins and starches.

Eat fruit by itself. However, you may eat the following fruits with nuts:

(lemon, lime, orange, tangerine, and grapefruit)[45]

all other citrus[45]

kiwi[56], pineapple[10,] mango[48]

all berries[40c, 66]

(apple, pear)[40a]

grape[52]

See *Appendix D* for the chart quoted from Dr. Jaffe's *Health Studies Collegium,* "Alkaline-Forming Foods and Acid-Forming Foods." It was prepared by Dr. Jaffe and Dr. Patrick M. Donavan, a doctor of naturopathic medicine in Seattle, Washington.

Dr. Donavan repeated several times that while this information is not scientifically proven, it was taken from clinical observations by many doctors. He believes clinical evidence suggests that it is so important that scientific research should be conducted on this subject.

It must be adapted specifically for people to use with the home detoxification plan.

SPECIAL DETOX MENUS*

DAY 1 MENU

Food families used: 6, 14, 28, 40b, 65, 73, 74, 75, 79, 80, 137

Breakfast

Nectarines[40b]

Almonds[40b]

Lunch

Lamb[137]

Oregano[73]

Salad

Jerusalem Artichoke[80]

Endive[80]

Dandelion Leaves[80]

Safflower Oil[80]

Raw Carrots[65]

Steamed Carrots[65]

Ñame[14]

Dinner

Millet[6]

Sesame[75]

Salad

Spinach[28]

Tomatoes[74]

Green (Bell) Peppers[74]

Cucumbers[79]

Zucchini[79]

Steamed Squash[79]

DAY 2 MENU

Food families used: 9, 11, 22, 36, 41, 44, 45, 69, 70, 106

Breakfast

Oranges[45]

Walnuts[22]

Lunch

Salmon[106]

Onion[11]

Salad

Collard Green[36]

Kale[36]

Cauliflower[36]

Bok Choy[36]

Daikon[36]

Olive Oil[69]

Steamed Rutabaga[36]

Onion[11]

Dinner

Salad

Lentil Sprouts[41]

Green Pea Sprouts[41]

Flaxseed Oil[44]

St. Sweet Potato[70]

Steamed Malanga[9]

Sweet Potato[70]

Camote[70] or

Green Pea[41]

SPECIAL DETOIX MENUS*

DAY 3 MENU

Food families used: 6, 28, 40b, 47, 48, 65, 80, 135

Breakfast	Lunch	Dinner
Mango[48]	Wild Venison[135]	Brown Rice[6]
Cashews[48]	Tarragon[80]	Gr. Pumpkin Seeds[80]

	Salad	Salad
	Celery[65]	Chard[28]
	Lettuce[80]	Beet Greens[28]
	Sp. Sunflower Seeds[80]	Gr. Pumpkin Seeds[79]
	Sunflower Oil[80]	Cucumbers[79]
	Parsley[80]	Apricot Oil[40b]

	Steamed Parsnips[65]	Steamed Beets[28]
		Yuca[47]

DAY 4 MENU

Food families used: 9, 11, 22, 23, 34, 36, 41, 45, 54, 121

Breakfast	Lunch	Dinner
Grapefruit[45]	Wild Duck[121]	**Soup**
Pecans[22]	Garlic[11]	Bean: Soy, Mung, Lima[41]
	Salad	**Salad**
	Mustard Green[36]	Alfalfa Sprouts[41]
	Cabbage[36]	Mung Bean Sprouts[41]
	Kohlrabi[36]	Avocado[34]
	Broccoli[36]	Hazelnut Oil[23]
	Canola Oil[36]	Avocado Oil[34]

	Steamed Broccoli[36]	Steamed Wax or
	Turnips[36]	Green Bean[41]
	Asparagus[11]	Taro[9]

*   *We are grateful to Russell Jaffe, M.D., for co-authoring these menus.*

Notice that the menus for breakfast make use of the organic foods that are known to be available, a rotation plan combining the foods and using the alkaline-forming, acid-forming foods.

You may not be able to follow this diet exactly as it is because you do not like certain foods, certain combinations, or because you are allergic to certain foods. For that reason, we have used the number system so you can make any type of substitution you want, as long as you know and understand the object of this diet.

Whenever possible, eat four parts of alkaline-forming foods to one part of the acid-forming foods. To repeat, because this is not an exact science, the quantities are an approximation.

(See Appendix D.)

Before you attempt any changes, note the following reasons for the selections of the foods. Day 1 has nectarines and almonds. Notice that both of them are in the same family, 40b. Because almonds could possibly fit either in low alkaline-forming or low acid-forming foods, depending on the acid/alkaline state of the individual, it will be treated as an acid-forming food. The same is true with other foods that could be classified either way.

Note that nectarines, oranges, mangoes, and grapefruit were chosen as the fruits. You may, of course, make substitutions for these, but these particular fruits were chosen because they seem to be in the classification of high alkaline-forming fruits. They are also in the lists of fruit that combine well with nuts, thereby allowing protein for breakfast if desired.

Similarly, the lunch animal proteins were chosen because they are believed to be the lowest of the acid-forming animal proteins: lamb, salmon, venison, and duck. Because of their fat content, all animal proteins are considered to be acid-forming foods.

Each day contains a salad and a cooked vegetable, both for lunch and dinner. It is difficult to incorporate into the rotation diet salads containing enough greens, with enough variety, to be able to maintain the recommended amount of alkaline-forming foods in the daily diet.

In order to consume 80 percent alkaline-forming foods, you must eat two large salads of green leafy vegetables per day. When raw vegetables are counter-indicated, the green leafy vegetables could be steamed. Wherever possible, we attempted to have no more than three, or possibly four, food families included in any meal.

Note that many choices of salad items are included in each meal so that as long as you know the object of the meal, there are choices as to what to eat.

The salads for lunch and dinner include an oil in each case because, even though oils are generally acid forming, it is necessary to include the essential fatty acids found in oils in the diet.

On day 3, note that one of the steamed vegetables suggested is parsnips because, wherever possible, you should consume a yellow vegetable once or twice a day.

At the bottom of the chart for that day, you will see yuca as a suggested steamed vegetable. The South American tubers, the ñame, taro, camote, yuca, and malanga, are recommended especially for those people who need more starchy foods in their diets. However, other vegetables are suggested as well because these South American tubers are available only in areas where there is a high concentration of Spanish-speaking people.

Although very costly, there are breads made from these vegetables. *(See Appendix E.)*

On day 4, note that members of the legume family in the form of sprouts—alfalfa and mung bean—are suggested in place of leafy green vegetables.

Now that there is a reliable source for organic sprouting seeds, use different types of sprouts as green leafy vegetables. *Sprouts* are believed to be very high alkaline-forming foods. *(See Appendix E.)*

Water in the Detox Diet

Because mineral water is alkaline-forming, it fits into the diet as well as the other components of the home detoxification program: proper physical exercises, proper breathing exercises, proper relaxation exercises, proper supplementary nutrition, and a home substitute for saunas.

Water fits into the detox program in many ways. First of all, a good mineral water with a high mineral content is alkaline forming, so it is helpful with the diet during this period. Unless, for medical reasons, mineral water with a high mineral content is contraindicated, drink more than the usual eight glasses of mineral water per day.

Since exercise that results in a great deal of perspiration is so very important in the detox program, drink two glasses of water before and after exercise. Unless medically contraindicated, add one-half to one teaspoon of potassium bicarbonate to the first glass of water after exercise.

Before as well as after aerobic exercises, perform breathing exercises and stretch exercises or isometric exercises.

Exercises

Walking is probably the best exercise if you have a good place to walk. Unfortunately, many people walk in moldy woods or along highways, where they are inhaling lead diesel fumes and benzene from gasoline.

If you do not have a pure area in which to exercise, you are better off doing some trampoline running in place in your own home. Fairly inexpensive trampolines are available in sports stores.

Or you may just choose to walk up and down the stairs, starting off with a few minutes and gradually building up to a point where you can raise your pulse. Increase it to the level that your doctor says is optimum for you.

Proper breathing exercises can be found in the chapter on Cellibration Therapy.

Ventilation Exercises. The following exercises were originally designed by body therapists to ventilate rage/hostility. Dr. James Cox refined them as exercises to clear the lungs and the whole body of toxins.

Frequently after exposure to toxins such as tar, traffic fumes, perfume, or smoke, the environmentally-sensitive person returns home with behavioral manifestations such as irritability or hostility. Salts or oxygen may help, but it is more important to rid yourself (especially your lungs and liver) of the toxins. The exercises help ventilate the hostility while ridding the body of the toxins.

Many patients have found that ventilating exercises help alleviate the gamut of behavioral manifestations—from manic behavior to depression and from hyperactivity to fatigue, as well as such problems as a foggy mind or restless legs. Systemic reactions are lessened as well.

≈ ≈ ≈

For example, after exposure to tar, I used to return home with leg pains, eye pain, and distorted vision. When I first began doing these exercises, my symptoms frequently worsened for a few minutes. My eyes and nose would begin to run, and other symptoms often occurred. Then, as the tar began leaving my system, the symptoms began to disappear. I knew I was ridding myself of the tar because as I breathed out with a large "hah" sound (as described below), I could smell the tar on my breath.

≈ ≈ ≈

Many patients report that after doing the ventilation exercises, they feel the need to eliminate and can smell the tar in their stool and/or urine.

As you practice the following ventilation exercises, remember to do your breathing exercises—breathing in as you get into position and breathing out as you follow the rest of the instructions.

As you breathe out for exercises 1 through 6, do so with a "hah" breath (a fast exhalation while making a loud "hah" sound).

1. Breathe in as you extend your arms parallel to the floor; breathe out as you thrust back with both elbows.

2. Breathe in as you thrust your arms back with both elbows parallel to the floor; breathe out as you thrust forward with both fists.

3. Breathe in as you thrust your hands under your armpits; breathe out as you thrust your fists down toward the floor.

4. Breathe in as you bend your elbows and pull your closed fists up to touch your shoulders; breathe out as you thrust your fists out to the right and left.

5. Breathe in as you bend your right knee and lift your right leg as high and as close to your body as possible; breathe out as you kick straight forward, pointing your heel toward the floor and your toes toward the ceiling.

6. Breathe in as you clasp your hands above your head; breathe out as you swing your hands between your legs in a motion similar to chopping wood.

7. Do deep knee bends with a "hah" breath.

8. Bite down as if you have something between your teeth.

Ideomotor Effect. Dr. Cox defines the term ideomotor as follows: when we think (idea), our bodies do (motor) what we think.

It is hard to believe how much positive thinking helps our autonomic system (the flow of blood, the pulse rate, and blood pressure).

ﻼ ﻼ ﻼ

In a monitored environmentally less polluted hospital unit, I have seen people lower their pulse rate and blood pressure, raise the temperature in their hands and feet, clear migraine headaches, and reduce (or totally clear) pain and other allergic symptoms by using the techniques Dr. Cox teaches.

At first I resisted them; I just was not a believer. But because I needed a substitute for anesthesia, I plugged away at them. Then when I discovered I could go to the dentist and anesthetize myself, I became totally committed to learning the techniques. Before long, when I awoke with a stuffed nose, I could clear it in a short time. It took a

great deal of practice to reduce or control more
severe symptoms but it was worth the effort. I have
learned how to overcome my bouts of paralysis. When I
feel one coming on, I can prevent it.

The techniques helped me overcome another
debilitating reaction. For two years I was unable to
drive a car because traffic fumes would cause such
cramping in my neck and feet that I could not
function. Today I can tolerate much more exposure,
and continue to increase my endurance. When I do
reach my tolerance level, I have learned to recognize
the warning signs. Using the techniques wards off
severe attack until I can retreat to a safer place.

No, I am not "cured"; my immune system is still
suppressed. But my attention to diet and a clean
environment combined with proper breathing exercises
and ideomotor techniques have helped me return to a
productive life. I keep gaining in strength,
tolerance, and health.

Whenever I become impatient for a faster recovery,
I remember how long I abused my body, how ill I was,
and how much I have improved. How lucky I was to find
an EM specialist, Dr. Kailin, and through her, Dr.
Cox, the physicians of the American Academy of
Environmental Medicine (AAEM), and my co-author Bill
Rea. Except when I am exposed to pollutants, I am
healthier now than I was as a 16-year-old athlete
earning my letter for year-round sports.

ЄА ЄА ЄА

Isometric Progressive Relaxation. Use a similar pattern for
each of the following isometric exercises and ventilation exercises.
Practice each one a few times, and choose the ones you find most
helpful. It is imperative that you do the following pattern before
you do any of the isometric exercises.

Pattern:
Take the deep, full-body relaxation breath described in Cellibration
Therapy.
- Using an isometric exercise, push or pull as strenuously as
  your muscle tone allows.
- Sense what the tension feels like.
- Breathe out as you release all tension.

- Sense what the relaxation feels like.
- Keep repeating the same exercise, taking a deep breath each time.
- Tense up less each time you repeat the exercise.
- Relax a little more each time.

- **Isometric Exercises:**
- Clasp hands and pull.
- Place hands together and push.
- Clasp right wrist with left hand and pull to the left, then reverse.
- Place hand on right side of head and push. Then do the same on left side of head.
- Pull head forward with hands interlocked behind head.
- Place palms on forehead and push backward while you push head forward.
- Pull pelvis forward, then backward.
- In seated position, cross your feet a few inches off the floor and pull in opposite directions.
- Place feet together and push.
- Place right hand on inside of left knee and left hand on inside of right knee and push outward.
- Place right hand on outside of right knee and left hand on outside of left knee and push inward.
- Clasp hands behind back and pull upward.
- Lift imaginary weight with hands.
- Make up your own isometric exercises.

Monitor your own pulse changes. Begin exercising for short periods of time, gradually increasing the exercise periods over time.

Naturally, this is a far superior program if it is a home detox program conducted under the supervision of an EM specialist who has technicians monitoring the patient's conditions.

Allergic Eyes. Even the most conventional allergist or ophthalmologist who steadfastly refuses to accept any of the concepts of environmental medicine acknowledges that eyes are a main allergy target organ. Hay fever sufferers frequently have runny, itching eyes, eye infections, and other eye problems. Dust, smoke, and mold can also cause these symptoms, according to conventional physicians.

EM specialists, however, recognize that exposure to tar, insecticides, other chemicals, and certain foods cause problems, too. They also find other symptoms such as blurred vision, loss of ability to focus the eyes on an object, pain in the eyes, and weakened eye muscles that make it difficult to open the eyes without prying them open with your hand.

Eye Exercises

Imaginary Huge Clock. Imagine the wall in front of you is a huge clock.

- Look down to the imaginary six o'clock. Roll your eyes slowly counterclockwise back to six o'clock.
- Starting again at six o'clock, reverse the movement, slowly rolling your eyes clockwise.
- Look up as high as your eyes can go to an imaginary eleven o'clock, then down to five o'clock, up to one o'clock, and down at seven o'clock.
- Repeat each of the above three times.

Focus on an Object. Find a single object in the room such as a light fixture, a small lamp, or a small picture.

- Hold a pencil at arm's length in front of you so you can see the pencil in the foreground and the object in the background. As you look at the pencil, it will appear as if there are two of the object. Slowly pull the pencil toward your nose, concentrating on the pencil and the two objects as they seem to separate further apart. Move the pencil slowly back to arm's length, watching the distance between the objects converge again. Repeat a couple of times.
- Reverse the process, looking at the object in the background until it appears as if there are two pencils. Repeat as above two or three times.
- Do not strain your eyes. Gradually build up to five minutes (but no longer) for each eye.

Hot Baths

Three times a week, take a hot bath when there is no environmentally safe sauna available. Although there is much to be said about the low-heat saunas and baths, for this program heat the bath water as high as you can comfortably manage. Before your bath do the following:

- Have someone in the house while you are taking your bath.
- Have a terry cloth robe plus several towels at hand. You will need them because you will be perspiring profusely.

- In your bedroom, cover your mattress with a big towel so you can lie down after your bath; hopefully you will continue to perspire for awhile.

Before you get into the tub, make sure you arrange a small bed of towels and a little pillow on the floor beside the bathtub so that if you become weak or dizzy, you can immediately get out of the tub and lie down in the bathroom.

When everything described above is ready, dissolve two cups of Epsom salts and one cup of baking soda in the bath water. Begin with a five-minute bath the first time and gradually build up to a 20-minute bath, with the water continuously running hot, making it hotter as long as you can tolerate it.

After the 20-minute bath, take a warm shower and soak down thoroughly with a less toxic soap or baking soda.

One patient reported that on one occasion she did not have time to shower and simply put on her robe as she got out of the hot bath. It took three washes in apple cider vinegar to clear the odor of the toxins out of her terry cloth bathrobe. Others have reported similar situations.

Note: Check with your doctor to see if you need supplementary nutrients, vitamins, and minerals.

It has been found that those people who have an environmentally safe home, or at least a clean bedroom, have had greater success with the home detoxification program.

Summary. In addition to the diet, the program includes hot epsom salts baths, the prescribed nutrients, the breathing exercises, aerobic exercises, stretch exercises, eye exercises, relaxation techniques, and a positive mental attitude.

7

SEX IN THE CLEAN BEDROOM

"Not tonight, honey, I have a headache." Wrong! Sex can be the best medicine. After reading this chapter, you may never use that line again! But first, a little background on the subject.

୨୧ ୨୧ ୨୧

When I first wrote *Coping With Your Allergies*, I jokingly said I wanted to call it *The Sterile Bedroom*, referring to the ecologically safe bedroom. The title was appropriate, and I thought the public would gravitate toward the book, thinking it was about sex, and incidentally learn about environmentally-triggered illness. I was naive to overlook the importance of sex in chemical sensitivities and should have known better.

୨୧ ୨୧ ୨୧

Hormonal Changes

In the Foreword of *Coping With Your Allergies*, Dr. Randolph listed factors "which apparently act to break or lower resistance, inducing acute reactions." He cited, "Infection, particularly viral infections, will sometimes start the train of events leading to the chemical susceptibility problem....

"Hormone changes may act similarly. Women seem to be especially vulnerable immediately after pregnancy and at the change of life, although there tends to be some increased vulnerability premenstrually each month."

Dr. Randolph wrote that in 1979. Hormonal changes are now well shown to be triggered by pollutants, i.e., male pesticide workers become sterile, and spontaneous abortions among female pesticide workers have increased.

As with many other important advances in medicine, Environmental Medicine (EM) specialists were 20 years ahead of their time in the recognition of premenstrual syndrome (PMS). Despite the criticism of academic medicine, which originally labeled PMS feminine hysteria, EM specialists forged ahead and successfully treated PMS victims with techniques similar to those used for other environmental illness victims.

Provocative Neutralization (P/N)

To appreciate the cases that follow, you will need a brief explanation of provocative/neutralization (P/N). Although most allergists do not believe in P/N testing, those who disagree often lack personal experience and base their opinions on literature poorly written and inappropriately researched by critics improperly trained in this technique. P/N testing is currently being used successfully by many doctors in America and numerous other countries.

P/N uses allergy extract solutions in the same way as allergists. However, each test is done individually so the technician or physician can watch for symptoms. But the greatest difference is that the correct weaker (more dilute) dose of the same extract can stop the provoked symptoms. This weaker, neutralizing dose can usually be administered at home by the patient (or parent) to stop symptoms whenever the patient is exposed to the food, chemical, or inhalant that caused the symptom. For a more detailed explanation, read *Chemical Sensitivities* by William Rea, M.D., *Is This Your Child?* by Doris Rapp, M.D., and/or *Relief at Last* by Joseph Miller, M.D. *(See Appendix F.)*

Headaches Related To Food Craved Premenstrually

In *Is This Your Child?*, Dr. Doris Rapp cites the case of a young women she had treated as a child:

"Valerie had two distinct types of headaches. Her first headache always occurred just before her menstrual period. She craved chocolate at that time. This suggested to us that cocoa, milk, or corn syrup might be a factor because premenstrual women often crave the very foods that cause their allergies. The other possibility was that Valerie had a hormonally related PMS headache that often responds well to P/N allergy extract dilutions of progesterone.

"Her [Valerie's] menstrual headache was intermittent and had been present since the age of 12. It was located behind her right eye and usually made her sick to her stomach. The headache would recur each morning and disappear each evening. No matter where she was this headache seemed to go with her. If it had been related to her home, she should have felt better when she left her home for several days."

Hormones and Migraine

Mary, aged 42, a patient of co-author Bill Rea, had had incapacitating, excruciating migraine headaches every month for the past 20 years. They became so severe that she couldn't function for five days prior to her period, and although she took many types of medication, was confined to her bed for those five days. None of the drugs or relaxation therapy worked.

While she had a good family life and a stable relationship with her husband, naturally she found it burdensome to be ill five days out of each month. Except for the migraines, she had no history of any sensitivities.

The next month, after neutralization by injection therapy for estrogen, progesterone, and luteinizing hormone, she was headache free for the first time in 20 years and has remained so for the last five years. She received no treatment other than the hormone mini-injections. This is not a hormone replacement; it is a balancing of the system.

Even when a woman has passed menopause, neutralizing her to these hormones helps regulate her system and is needed because the estrogen sometimes continues to be produced by the adrenal gland. If a woman is taking Premarin and/or hormones, injection therapy will also help in regulating the system.

Valerie, Mary, and others have been fortunate to find an innovative physician whose practice extends far beyond the mainstream practice of allergy.

How frustrating it is for those of us who understand the relationship between hormonal changes and chemical sensitivities to find so many physicians uninformed or refusing to accept the fact.

Environmental Medicine—An Alternative Approach

It was very rewarding to hear a segment every day of October 1991 devoted to "Healthy Woman—Taking Charge of Your Body and Mind" on the ABC program, *Good Morning, America.* As this chapter suggests, it is an area that has been sadly neglected and needs more attention.

However, it was very disappointing that so many of the areas covered such as menopause, PMS, endometriosis, and many other subjects neglected to mention, even briefly, that there were alternative approaches being used successfully by environmental medicine (EM) specialists. It is hoped that readers of this book will pass along to female friends and relatives that there are procedures that have proved very successful without the use of drugs.

While drugs are sometimes necessary, unfortunately too often the prescribed method is to use medication when other procedures have been more beneficial and have been accomplished without some of the side effects many women experience from drugs.

Premenstrual Syndrome (PMS)

Health problems caused by hormonal sensitivities are often complex because they are caused by a combination of factors. Doris Rapp's analogy to environmentally-triggered illness has frequently been quoted: "If you have five nails in your shoe and remove only one, your foot still hurts." Similarly, you cannot isolate gynecological health problems; they must be treated as part of the whole illness.

To understand how P/N can help problems caused by hormonal sensitivities, we turn to Joseph B. Miller, M.D. The world is indebted to Dr. Miller for his pioneering work in the field of provocative/neutralization (P/N) and for his leadership in using P/N for medical problems related to hormonal sensitivities, deficiencies, and/or imbalances.

PMS and Progesterone P/N

We are particularly grateful to Dr. Miller for his permission to cite cases from his book, *Relief At Last!* For example, he wrote about a patient with progesterone-related symptoms: "... I was testing a young lady with food extracts for severe headaches. One morning when she arrived at the office for testing she complained that she was having very severe menstrual cramps.

"Although she had hoped to be able to test that day, she now felt that she would have to go back home, take a pain pill and lie down with a heating pad on her abdomen. She said, 'I wish you had something in your bag of tricks for my menstrual cramps.'"

Dr. Miller knew her menstrual cramps were related to hormones and that he could neutralize symptoms with one of the hormones, insulin. He knew that at the onset of menstruation the progesterone level falls very rapidly, and he thought perhaps progesterone withdrawal might be responsible for her premenstrual symptoms.

After discussions with the patient and her gynecologist, Dr. Miller decided to try progesterone neutralization. So he made several dilutions of the standard progesterone suspension and performed the neutralizing test. Within three minutes after administration of the dilution, her cramps lessened and in half an hour they were completely gone!

Tiny doses of neutralization produce great benefits; the dose of progesterone used in this case was about 1/6,000th the dose normally used in gynecologic practice. The patient was symptom free for 18 hours and returned to his office the next day with cramps again. Dr. Miller repeated the neutralizing dose and again she was completely relieved within 30 minutes. The pain did not recur during that monthly cycle.

Only two to four injections per cycle gave her complete freedom from cramps during her next four cycles and the cramps did not return after the fourth cycle. This long-lasting relief has been confirmed in many patients by Dr. Miller and other physicians. A great majority of their patients developed almost total, long-lasting (or apparently permanent) prevention of premenstrual and menstrual symptoms after using neutralization therapy—a few tiny injections of progesterone with each monthly cycle—for three to six months.

Most of the discomforts related to the menstrual cycle (including premenstrual breast tenderness, irritability, headache, fluid retention, migraine, asthma, nasal congestion, urticaria, cyclic menstrual acne) as well as many mental and behavioral reactions appear to be helped by P/N. Relief from cramps and regulated menstrual flow are other benefits.

Influenza Neutralization

In another case, Dr. Miller relates his experience during the Hong Kong Flu epidemic in 1968. Among the patients he immunized was an 11-year-old girl whom he had previously treated successfully for multiple inhalant, food, and chemical sensitivities. The next day the girl returned with her mother who accused Dr. Miller of giving her child the flu. The child was definitely suffering from influenza-type symptoms: bleary eyes, runny nose, sore throat, foggy mind, weakness and malaise, and painful aching in back and neck muscles.

Dr. Miller explained that he had not given the child the flu, but that she was probably having an immunologic reaction to the protein of the killed viruses in the vaccine. He compared her reaction to a "neutralizing test with symptoms from the provoking dose of an allergen." Because her daughter had been tested with many allergenic extracts, the mother understood the analogy. "Then neutralize it!" she demanded.

Neutralizing a reaction to a *virus* vaccine was a new idea to Dr. Miller, but he had neutralized many allergic reactions to extracts of various food and inhalants, and the mother was quite insistent. So he prepared a serial concentration of Influenza Virus Vaccine and performed the test. In 30 minutes the neutralizing dose completely cleared all the child's symptoms. These symptoms returned on three successive days and each time one neutralizing dose cleared away the symptoms completely in 30 minutes. Over the next two weeks, Dr. Miller confirmed this 30-minute neutralizing response in 12 other patients suffering from symptoms from Influenza Virus Vaccine immunization.

P/N for Active Flu-Virus

When a 14-year-old boy, another patient, came in with active influenza virus *infection*—malaise, fever, weakness, and aching all over—Dr. Miller was able to neutralize the virus. Within 30 minutes the boy was free of the malaise, weakness, and aching, and was sitting up, chatting and alert; however, his fever was unchanged. The boy's symptoms recurred five times during the next three days and each time they were cleared in 30 minutes by a neutralizing dose. The fever disappeared after the third injection.

Dr. Miller neutralized 35 patients in the same manner that winter during a fairly large flu epidemic. Other physicians, with whom he shared these results, also provided confirmation of this therapy in treating influenza as well as herpes-caused fever blisters, shingles (herpes zoster), chickenpox (varicella), and infectious mononucleosis, and Epstein-Barr.

The one drawback of neutralizing injections is that the dose must be precise, and the body may change its dosage requirement. It may be necessary, therefore, to repeat the test at any time.

Symptoms caused by a live influenza virus *infection* persist longer, and more neutralizing doses are required. Repeating the dose each time the symptoms occur usually works out to three injections the first day, two the second day, and one the third day. After that each does usually lasts about 24 hours. Although influenza is usually considered a three-day illness, the discomforts, weakness, and secondary complications may last longer than three days. Except for the few minutes when they realize the symptoms are returning, neutralized patients do not even have to undergo the initial three days of pain.

If symptoms do persist, patients can experience relief throughout the entire time by continuing neutralizing injections. As long as complete relief is gained after each injection, the dose is correct and retesting is not necessary. But if relief is not complete, retesting can determine the optimal dose.

A relapse, with a return of symptoms after the patient is completely free of all signs of illness for several days or weeks, may occur. If this happens, complete and permanent relief usually occurs after one dose of the neutralizing injection.

Herpes Neutralization

The test procedure and neutralization process for herpes is similar to that of influenza. Pain from fever blisters, herpetic eye or ear lesions, genital herpes, or shingles is often remarkably or completely relieved within 30 minutes of the neutralizing test injection. About 90 percent of Dr. Miller's patients with herpes simplex I respond, 70 percent with herpes simplex II, and 80 percent of patients with shingles. Results are usually best if treatment begins soon after the attack starts.

One of Dr. Miller's patients was a 15-year-old girl who had many herpes blisters over her lower lip and chin every month for two years. Each painful attack lasted 10 to 14 days and was quite disfiguring. Following neutralization in Dr. Miller's office, her pain stopped in 30 minutes after each injection, and the lesions dried and healed in four days.

She had no attacks until five months later, and the next one was 18 months after that. Both were mild and brief, requiring only two or three neutralizing injections. She had no further recurrences in the following two years.

Not every patient responds so well, although this is a typical pattern.

Chickenpox Neutralization

In chickenpox patients, neutralization results in cessation of repeated crops of chickenpox blisters. New blisters do not appear, although of course the old ones take several days to heal. One of Dr. Miller's cases was a 23-year-old woman was so weak from acute chickenpox that her husband had to carry her into the office. Within 30 minutes after the neutralizing test dose of Influenza Virus Vaccine, she cleared the malaise and discomfort, was smiling and alert, and was able to leave the office without her husband's support. She used the injections twice daily for itching the first two days, then once daily for five more days. No other symptoms or new blisters occurred and the itching did not recur.

Shingles and Herpes Virus Infections

Neutralization provides rapid relief from pain for about 80 percent of shingles patients. This extremely painful disease often requires hospitalization and narcotic drugs, sedatives, and tranquilizers, but with neutralization, many patients require no other treatment and can be treated at home.

Shingles patients often experience severe pain days before any lesions appear and before the cause of the pain in known. For these individuals neutralization can prevent unnecessary exploratory abdominal surgery at the onset of the disease. It can save unnecessary diagnostic tests and x-rays, and the patient can be saved much suffering.

Herpes virus infection of the eye can be painful and is the leading cause of blindness in the United States. In this case, the injections must be given more frequently to "stay ahead of the virus" rather than waiting until the pain returns. It may be necessary to hospitalize the patient for close observation.

A single neutralizing injection is often quite effective in stopping and easing recurrent herpes attacks. When a patient has been treated by neutralization for one or two attacks, subsequent attacks are usually much less frequent.

Genital Herpes

The foregoing was presented to illustrate the progression that led to the treatment of genital herpes by provocative neutralization, i.e., P/N for symptoms from Influenza Virus Vaccine immunization; P/N to treat active influenza virus *infection*; P/N for herpes simplex I and simplex II, and finally, P/N for genital herpes.

Dr. Wayne H. Konetzki, a Waukesha, Wisconsin, allergist and EM specialist, sent a report of an 18-year-old college student who came to the office with a two-week history, following intercourse, of labial swelling which had not been too bothersome. However, two days before her office visit she developed fever, chills, and swelling with blister formation. She also had burning urination. On the day she was seen, clear drainage appeared. She was unable to sit squarely on a chair and had trouble sleeping at night.

Examination revealed the patient was upset and crying. In addition to extensive labial swelling and redness, there were two large areas of shallow ulcers characterized by marked tenderness.

She was tested and treated with provocative neutralization. She was instructed to take sitz baths and to give herself injections of the vaccine, four times on day 1, three times on day 2, two times the third day, and once daily thereafter.

The patient's mother called four days later to report. The night of her office visit, the young lady had enough pain relief that she could sleep without difficulty. By the next day, the swelling was down 50 percent and she could sit comfortably. The third day most of the swelling was gone and there was no tenderness. The lesions were not weeping. Four days after her office visit, she was back in classes and feeling well.

Not all patients respond so dramatically; however, a study like this indicates that P/N is worth investigating if you have genital herpes.

Hypersensitivity and Female Problems

We are grateful to Dr. Wayne H. Konetzki for information on the possible relationship of female problems such as Pre-Menstrual Syndrome (PMS), menstrual cramps, and endometriosis (the growth of endometrial tissue outside the uterus) to hormone hypersensitivity and/or *candida albicans* overgrowth and hypersensitivity.

Literature Search

Dr. Konetzki has made a study of literature predating present knowledge about these conditions. Among early articles he brought to our attention were Dr. Robert T. Frank's seminal 1931 article, "Hormonal Causes of Premenstrual Tension," Dr. L.A. Gray's 1941 article, "The Use of Progesterone in Nervous Tension States," and a 1953 articles by Katharina Dalton and Raymond Greene about PMS that was published in the prestigious *British Medical Journal*.

Meanwhile, Dr. Konetzki pointed out, other physicians had demonstrated that hormones could elicit positive reactions in allergy skin testing and some had begun treating dysmenorrhea (menstrual cramps) and PMS by desensitizing patients to a progesterone-like hormone.

All of this work culminated, for Dr. Konetzki, in the 1974 publication by Dr. Joseph Miller of the article, "Relief of Premenstrual Symptoms, Dysmenorrhea, and Contraceptive Tablet Intolerance," which described a technique of injecting very small amounts of progesterone (much smaller amounts than gynecologists were using) to relieve hormone-related problems. Dr. Konetzki began using Joseph Miller's method (P/N). But although he found it helpful for menstrual cramps, it was less so for other hormone-related symptoms.

Candida Albicans

A missing piece to this puzzle emerged in 1978 with the publication of Dr. C. Orion Truss's article, "Tissue Injury Induced by Candida Albicans: Mental and Neurological Manifestations." According to Truss, when *candida albicans*—a normal yeast found in the intestinal tract, on the skin, and in the vaginal tract—overgrows, it produces toxins that affect the body in various ways. Antibiotic therapy, birth control pills, pregnancy, high sugar diets, cortisone therapy, and the premenstrual state (which involves increased progesterone and a corresponding increase in the amount of sugar secreted into intestinal and vaginal mucosa) all promote *candida* growth and can lead to its overgrowth. The toxins then produced can result in the development of many hypersensitivities, including hypersensitivity to *candida albicans* itself.

Armed with this new understanding, Dr. Konetzki began testing treatment-resistant patients for *candida* hypersensitivity and, when tests were positive, treating them for *candida* overgrowth. After anti-*candida* therapy consisting of sugar and yeast avoidance, anti-*candida* drugs or supplements, and *candida* desensitization by means of drops under the tongue, many of Dr. Konetzki's PMS patients no longer needed treatment at all. Those who needed treatment responded well to very small doses of progesterone under the tongue to desensitize them to this hormone.

Dr. Konetzki, as well as some others in the environmental medicine community, are now doing hypersensitivity testing and desensitization for two other hormones as well. These are estrogen and luteinizing hormone. Just as with progesterone desensitization, only tiny amounts of these substances are employed; and results have extended to regularizing the menstrual cycle and menstrual flow as well as clearing of PMS, ovulation, and endometriosis symptoms. Some physicians using this kind of therapy have even seen ovarian cysts or infertility resolved.

In light of results like these, it is sad to contemplate the thousands of women who have been treated for hormone-related problems with massive doses of progesterone (with unknown long-term effects) or—worse still—surgery. Nonetheless, it will probably be many years before the treatment methods described by Dr. Konetzki and used by a number of EM specialists are accepted by the traditional medical community.

Dr. Konetzki shared with us some cases that support his findings.

Progesterone Sensitivity

A registered nurse, aged 35, had suffered the following symptoms for 10 days prior to each period for many years: nervousness, tension, irritability, depression, headaches, malaise, abdominal gas and bloating, insomnia, recurrent cold sores, sore throats, forgetfulness, and poor coordination. The symptoms cleared at the onset of her period.

She tested positive for sensitivity to *candida albicans* and was started on treatment. Later testing showed a positive reaction to progesterone. Sublingual desensitization therapy was not successful in treating this. Upon further testing she was found to have a low estrogen to progesterone ratio and was started on estrogen patches along with desensitization antigens with excellent results.

She recently ran out of hormone drops and had three days of severe headache, fatigue, and malaise which were relieved when the hormone treatment antigens were resumed.

Candida-Related Complex

In 1985 a 28-year-old housewife came to Dr. Konetzki with a several-year history of distressing menstrual cramps, backache, tension, irritability, and depression for 10 to 14 days prior to each period. She tested positive for sensitivity to *candida albicans* and was started on treatment. In two months she noted 50 percent to 60 percent improvement in her PMS symptoms. In May 1991 she was still having some PMS symptoms. When skin tested for hypersensitivity to hormones, she showed a significant reaction to luteinizing hormone and in August reported increased PMS symptoms. Her hormone drops were adjusted and by September her PMS symptoms had disappeared.

Luteinizing Hormone Sensitivity

This patient, a 34-year-old dental assistant, had a history of mood swings, pelvic pain, headaches, dizziness, and stomach problems dating back to the onset of her periods; they became much worse after the birth of her children. She failed routine therapies and was referred to Dr. Konetzki by her gynecologist. In November 1988 she tested positive for sensitivity to *candida albicans*, and he started her on therapy. Six months later she tested negative for sensitivity to progesterone and estrogen but reacted to luteinizing hormone and was started on sublingual desensitization therapy. She did not improve until November 1989 after the luteinizing hormone was retested and a new dose was determined. Her PMS symptoms then improved markedly, and by September 1990 they were "great."

Endometriosis

MF, a 24-year-old female campus security officer, was referred to Dr. Konetzki by the Endometriosis Association with a seven-year history of fatigue, craving for sugar, and extreme pelvic pain beginning two weeks prior to each period and extending five to eight days into each period. She was tested for sensitivity to *candida albicans,* had a positive reaction, and was started on appropriate treatment. Later a skin test for hormone sensitivity revealed positive reactions to progesterone and luteinizing hormone, and she was started on sublingual desensitization therapy to both hormones. Two months later her endometriosis symptoms had improved, and six months after that she stated she was feeling great and had no symptoms.

Asthma and Progesterone

A 16-year-old female had been treated for asthma for one year. In July 1990 she was hospitalized because of violent premenstrual episodes during which she would break furniture and threaten others. Skin tests showed a small reaction to estrogen and a much stronger reaction to progesterone and luteinizing hormone. Testing for sensitivity to *candida albicans* caused a significant reaction, and she was placed on sublingual desensitization therapy for hormones and the *candida antigen.* By January 1991 her premenstrual agitation had decreased significantly; some irritability continued during menses. The hormone drops helped a lot, and in April the dose was decreased. In October she still noted only mild premenstrual irritability and the dose was further decreased.

Asthma and Estrone

CG, a 50-year-old housewife, had severe incapacitating asthma which worsened premenstrually, with the majority of her emergency room trips and hospitalizations occurring during her premenstrual times. She reacted to *candida albicans* testing. Skin testing for hormones resulted in significant reactions to estrone and luteinizing hormone. She showed marked improvement in her asthma after being placed on therapy for the *candida* and the hormones; hospitalization and trips to the emergency room were no longer necessary.

Puberty and Hormones

Dr. Doris Rapp's book, *Is This Your Child?,* discusses the relationship between hormones and puberty. She says: "In Puerto Rico, from 1978 to

1981 there was a striking increase in precocious puberty in both boys and girls, age six months to eight years; store-bought chicken contains so much female sex hormones that some girls had menses and breast development long before they started school."

Hormonal changes may very well explain an incident in the Washington, D.C., area. Several news broadcasts reported that 16 girls at West Springfield High School had fainting spells in school. Because the involved students were girls, the problem was attributed to mass female hysteria. The real problem, glossed over by authorities, was that the building was filled with toxic fumes.

Those who are knowledgeable about the relationship between hormonal sensitivities and toxic fumes know that girls of puberty age are especially vulnerable to toxins because of major hormonal changes in their bodies. If corrections are not made in this school, many more students may be affected, some seriously.

EPA Victims

Is history repeating itself? Years ago, prior to this incident, the two co-authors independently labeled the Waterside Mall EPA headquarters building as having hazardous indoor air quality and predicted an epidemic of environmentally-triggered ill employees.

No one paid attention to our warning. After a new toxic carpet was installed, so many employees became seriously ill that EPA had to prepare alternate work space for these people. Others have had to work in their own homes.

When will people learn? Don't let this happen to students—and teachers—at West Springfield High in Virginia.

Obstetrics and Gynecology

From the viewpoint of a board certified obstetrician/gynecologist, we include portions of an interview with Dr. George C. Miller of Lewisburg, Pennsylvania. This is his partial response to the question, "What would you say is the impact of the hormonal system upon the immune system?

Dr. George Miller's Response

"....I'm beginning to think that there's a correlation between toxemia, infertility, endometriosis, and PMS. I think they all have a common immunologic denominator which is yet to be discovered.

"Many of these people respond to neutralization techniques, using a variety of combinations, including the progesterone and the estrogen in minute immunologic type doses. And I think that in the years to come it's going to lead to patients that will require surgery less often to help them live more comfortably and happier.

"Dick Mabray [C. Richard Mabray, gynecologist/obstetrician of Victoria, Texas] has some thoughts about hormones being the wave of the future of medicine in their manipulation as far as health is concerned. It wouldn't surprise me if that would be the case simply because first we blamed everything on bacteria, then we blamed it on viruses, and now the big thing is the immune system.

"If the immune system is only showing us the reason that some of these other things are important, I think that hormone manipulation, hormone stimulation, and neutralization might very well be something that will be very positive in the future, but is yet to be scientifically determined....

"One of the things that I feel very strongly about environmental medicine is that I hope our area attracts physicians from many other specialties, not that we draw them out of their specialty, but that we bring their specialty into environmental medicine, because there's lots of environmental medicine to be done in obstetrics, pediatrics, orthopedics, internal medicine, rheumatology. All of these various specialties have a place in environmental medicine."

Tampons, Condoms, and Other Hazards

So many chemicals are found in sanitary napkins, douche preparations, or prophylactics (especially condoms), that we wonder if many women who complain of severe pain during intercourse are suffering from swollen tissues in the vaginal region.

If chemicals can cause nasal passages, brain tissue, and digestive tract tissue to swell, it stands to reason that they could also cause the vaginal lining to swell.

Deficiency in Estrogen. Many chemically sensitive women cannot tolerate Premarin or estrogen in any form. Because a deficiency in estrogen has been linked to osteoporosis, the only solution we know for these women is provocative/neutralization (P/N).

Feminine Sanitary Pads. (See "First Aid.")

Tampons and Toxic Shock Syndrome. We have recommended that women avoid tampons, especially the chemicals in perfumed tampons. Nonperfumed tampons may also contain other harmful chemicals which cause toxic shock syndrome. The scientific community should study the relationship between toxic shock syndrome and environmentally-triggered illness; toxic shock syndrome victims may actually have been environmentally ill.

Sex in the Clean Bedroom

With having to curtail certain social functions, sex is one function that can always be enjoyed at home, in your bedroom haven.

Findings show that sex can be much more pleasurable in clean air. The better the air, the more active you can be, the longer you can perform, and the more enjoyment you will experience.

The opposite is also true—in polluted air, women are not stimulated and experience painful intercourse. In polluted air, men who are chemically sensitive suddenly become impotent or cannot maintain erections. For example, one patient couldn't get an erection whenever he was around perfume.

One can only wonder how many so-called "impotent" men could be restored to healthy, normal sexual activity by improving their indoor air quality.

It has been said that an employee of a large aluminum manufacturing company discovered that he could hold an erection longer in an aluminum environment. So he built a chain of "last chance motels" with aluminum rooms and aluminum wallpaper for older people who were having trouble getting erections. He was ahead of his time; the motel didn't go over very well because people did not understand the technology of keeping everything else clean. But his observation was in agreement with what we know today about clean bedrooms.

Apathy and Sex. A chemical overload or nutritional deficiency can cause apathy in sex; so can the wrong partner. Sex is not really satisfactory unless it is with a loved one and can result in many problems, especially for the chemically sensitive person.

Promiscuity. Another phenomenon is that some people get hypersexual when they're in chemical environments and become promiscuous. In this environment their sex drives increase dramatically, their libidos go wild, their judgment is impaired, and they practice unsafe sex. When their diet and environment are corrected, these people regain their equilibrium. Their judgment returns and they can control their sex drive and thus have greater satisfaction.

Infertility. A lot of people have not been able to conceive when they are having environmentally-triggered problems. Once they cleaned up their environment, their health improved, they conceived and had beautiful eco-babies.

Safe Sex. This is not intended as a discourse on the sanctity of marriage or the importance of safe sex. Both are, however, an added incentive for caution because environmentally-triggered illness adds extra problems.

How can people with environmentally-triggered illness practice safe sex if they can't tolerate condoms or diaphragm jelly? Keep searching for a condom, perhaps one made of lambskin, that you can tolerate. Boil diaphragms to make them less toxic. Beware of spermicidal jelly. Sometimes the only tolerable form of birth control for a chemically sensitive patient is a vasectomy, and the only lubricant is saliva.

Sperm Allergy. Some women become very sick when they have intercourse because they are allergic to their partner's sperm or secretion. This can be remedied by having the local EM specialist make an extract of the sperm, which the female takes to stop her reaction or pain.

The husband must be clean. If he works in a chemical lab or chemical plant, he must shower or sauna; the alternative is to abstain from sex for several days. Such precautions should eliminate problems.

Premenstrual Asthma. Premenstrual-induced asthma attacks are another problem co-author Bill Rea has observed in individuals who suffered from hormone imbalance. A few patients had severe mood swings and premenstrual asthma or migraines. Their conditions improved after Dr. Rea removed their ovaries.

Nutritional Deficiencies. Some patients have problems with calcium and magnesium imbalance; they get cramps and their bodies swell because of lack of calcium and magnesium. The treatment for the swelling is Vitamin B6, which acts as a diuretic and detoxifier. The treatment for the cramps is calcium (one to three grams a day) and magnesium (500 to 1500 milligrams a day).

People who have mineral deficiencies need a whole spectrum of minerals to function better. If you are having any of these problems, see a physician and get the prescriptions you need.

Many of the problems caused by chemical overload and nutritional deficiency can be avoided, or at least alleviated, by pesticide-free, fungicide-free rooms. That's why this chapter is called *"Sex in the Clean Bedroom."*

One woman always had had a problem with sex until she had a house call. The first change she made in her bedroom was to purchase a pure cotton pillow. When she saw that her problem eased with just that simple change, she and her husband speeded up the ecologic improvements in their bedroom. The cleaner the room became, the easier and more enjoyable sex became.

🐚 🐚 🐚

Now back to the classic line, "Not tonight, honey, I have a headache."

It was the wife of a patient who first brought this matter to my attention. She told me that when her

husband went off his diet or was exposed to an
offending chemical or inhalant, one of the things
that helped him was a good sexual encounter.

As time went on, I heard this from others,
including a couple of doctors who had also discovered
it from their patients.

On the other hand, many women complained that they
had a loss of sex drive or that sex was painful, that
they had to "endure it" to save their marriages.
These women reported that sex exacerbated their
reactions rather than helped.

I came upon one solution in the case of a couple we
shall call Mary and John Green. Mary came to me
because she had realized that her house was making
her ill. When she went away on vacation, she improved
and she became ill as soon as she returned home.
Mary's doctor asked me to help her clear up her home
and make a safe haven for her there.

Since finances prevented them from buying a new
one, we had to select priorities in clearing up their
toxic home. We first cleaned up Mary's bedroom and
then her kitchen. (See *Do-It-Yourself House Call.*)
We made other changes throughout the house and Mary's
health began to improve. Then Mary confided that she
was very tense and asked me to teach her my
"cellibration therapy."

I started with the breathing exercises and moved on
to other stress reduction techniques. She said they
helped her very much. During the second session, when
Mary became very relaxed, she began to cry and to
tell me about her problem with sex.

She had "endured" sex all her married life and had
hoped that now that they were older (her husband was
in his 70s), she would be free. But her husband
seemed to be more interested in sex now that he was
healthier, spending more time exercising, playing
tennis, working out at the gym, and doing aerobics.
Mary asked for help.

I had noticed that, although Mary was now relaxed
in many ways, her pelvic area was still very tight.
Having trained with a midwife, I knew about the
Lamaze breathing method to relax the pelvic area. I

taught her some of the techniques and suggested that she might get help from a body therapy called bioenergetics developed by Drs. Alexander Lowen and John Pierrakos, two psychiatrists who use a combination of isometric and relaxation exercises, or that she might try belly dancing, despite the fact that she was just a few years younger than her husband. Anything to open up her hips and relax them.

After our third session, I felt Mary was far enough advanced to be on her own, using the books I had recommended to clean up her home and practicing the "cellibration therapy."

A few months later I was invited to their home to see the safe haven they had developed and how they were able to entertain using the rotary diversified diet, which I had taught Mary. Mary looked absolutely radiant. John told me they had never been happier. As Mary learned the exercises and her health began to improve, John decided that perhaps he had better do his part.

He began to communicate with Mary about sex, as I had suggested. Although they had been married many, many years, they had never been comfortable discussing sex. He went to the library to find books on the subject. Together, with the help of the books, he and Mary began to explore their feelings for each other and tried new sexual techniques. In their search, they stumbled upon the best medicine Mary could have.

Mary is not cured. She still reacts when exposed to some toxic products and has to retreat to her haven, spending at least eight hours in her clear bedroom. She still has very severe symptoms at times. But Mary has found that when she is very, very sick, if they have what she calls a "total sexual encounter," her symptoms are abated. She calls her husband Dr. John. Sometimes when John is away from home, Mary will call him up and say, "Dr. John, I need you." He says he can't get home fast enough.

Mary told me that a few weeks before our dinner party, she had gone on a trip with John, where she was exposed to a diet of nonorganic food, she was off the rotation diet, and they had traveled through heavy traffic in a very polluted industrial area. When they got home, Mary's ankles were swollen beyond recognition and she was suffering from mental confusion as if her brain were swollen.

After an hour and a half of making love, the swelling in Mary's ankles had gone down. The next morning, after another hour of making love, Mary's ankles were completely normal. John said, "I went to bed with a sick old lady and woke up with a young chick—beautiful color in her face, clear eyes, and bright as could be."

The purpose here is not to write a "how-to" sex manual, but to demonstrate that sex in a clean environment can be the best medicine for sufferers of environmentally-triggered illness. And when I see these two senior citizens happier than they have ever been and acting like teenagers enjoying life to the full, it is easy to understand why.

ò ò ò

PART IV

A LESS-TOXIC LIFE STYLE

8

LESS-TOXIC CLEANING

In this chapter we will first examine cleaning aids which many sensitive individuals can tolerate. Then we will look at different cleaning problems giving the suggested less-toxic cleaning methods.

CAUTION: Because no product is safe for everyone you should test small quantities of any cleaning aid on a small surface before using it widely. While you may sell or give away items which you later discover you cannot tolerate, if an item has been used on a large area such as a floor it may be difficult to eliminate the offending odor.

A good testing procedure for some cleaners is to wash and rinse one item, such as a cotton handkerchief, and then try using it. Repeat the process of washing and using it several times. Some people become sensitive to a product, such as Borax, after using it for awhile. This may happen because some residue may remain after rinsing or because frequent use may sensitize a person to the product.

You may also test by placing a small amount on your wrist, near your pulse. If you have no reaction you will be able to use it generously. For instructions on procedures turn to "Home Testing."

Cleaning Aids

Air Fresheners. A pomander will freshen the air for months; you can make a less-toxic one by sticking as many cloves as possible into an orange and hanging it in cotton tulle netting. Peppermint sprigs in problem areas such as the garbage can and around the house generally help odors disappear naturally. (See odors.)

Apple Cider Vinegar. Apple cider vinegar is an all-purpose cleaner. If you buy white vinegar check to make certain that it has no petroleum because petroleum is used in most white vinegars. Vinegar is effective in cleaning windows, shower stalls, brass, brushes, chrome finishes, and stainless steel. It also removes the white stain on boots after they have been in snow, scorch marks on cottons, perspiration from underarms of clothing, and most important of all, it is usually effective in removing some additives and their odor from clothing.

CAUTION: Formaldehyde or kerosene can rarely be removed from material even after many washings. Unfortunately, some of the third world countries that used to furnish beautiful, clear fabrics are now using kerosene-treated fabrics.

Baking soda. This is one of the safest of all cleaning aids. Use it as a substitute for scouring pads and for cleaning and freshening baby rubber pants, thermos bottles, casseroles, ice cube trays, combs, brushes, coffee and tea pots, windshields and windshield wipers, sinks, tubs, toilets, grease stains on cars and rugs, vases, pet dishes, and yes, even your teeth. Some very sensitive people even bathe in it. (See "Home Detoxification" for procedure.)

Use baking soda instead of the more expensive and very toxic air fresheners. It removes stale odors inside and outside refrigerators and freezers, bread boxes, canisters, lunch boxes, baby's diaper pail, etc. When you remove it from your refrigerator wash it down your sink to freshen the drain. Washing your hands with baking soda will remove the unpleasant odors of onions, garlic, and fish. Even extremely sensitive people who can use no soap or detergent find that they can use baking soda as an all-purpose cleaner and for laundry. With the addition of elbow grease, baking soda can even substitute for scouring powder.

Bon Ami Bar Soap. *Bon Ami Bar Soap* is effective for washing walls and floors as well as porcelain, stainless steel, woodwork, windows, and any job for which you would normally use a cleanser. Although it may seem expensive Bon Ami Bar Soap will last a long time if you do not soak it in water and do not wet the bar of soap.

Rub a damp cloth lightly across the dry bar of soap and then over the area to be cleaned. Follow this with a slightly damp cloth and then a dry cloth. For very dirty areas dampen a pad of soap free stainless steel wool, rub it on the soap, scrub the area, and rinse. Because Bon Ami may leave a little grit the area must be thoroughly rinsed.

Bon Ami Cleaning Powder. *Bon Ami cleaning powder* is simply Bon Ami Bar Soap ground up. The powder can be used for the same cleaning jobs as the bar soap. It can also be used for cleaning ovens. In this case wet the dirty area, put some powder on the area, turn the oven on 200° F for 20 minutes, and wipe with damp paper towels or rags. While it may not be as effective as the toxic substances usually used in cleaning ovens this will be adequate if you clean your oven regularly.

While the Bon Ami bar soap and cleaning powders can be used interchangeably the powder is easier to use, especially for large areas. However, the powder leaves more grit and must be rinsed more thoroughly. CAUTION: Avoid Bon-Ami cleanser in the round can because it has chlorine in it. The powder in the original rectangular can is tolerated by most sensitive people. *(See Appendix E.)*

Borax. Borax is a natural, sweet-scented mineral that is used in many cleaning products. A natural bleach and mold retardant, pure borax can be effective as an all-purpose cleaner. In a letter to Natalie the late Dr. Lawrence D. Dickey, a pioneer in environmental medicine, wrote this about borax:

"For almost ten years, between March 1966 and December 31, 1975, I carried out a hospital comprehensive environmental control program in evaluating patients with ecologic illness. This was accomplished in rooms made as chemically clean as possible. In addition to fixtures and furnishings that were free of plastics and other materials that were known to 'gas out,' the cleaning compounds were restricted to borax and baking soda. The floors were wet-mopped with borax and filtered water. From February 15, 1972 on, the program was carried on in four especially constructed rooms with their own air-conditioning system separate from the rest of the hospital. This was the Poudre Valley Memorial Hospital Environmental Care unit. Control of chemical contaminates was much easier in this unit.

"Bacterial contamination in the past has been a problem in hospitals, and in ours, like others, the pathology department would periodically run culture checks in various areas of the hospital. The hospital pathologist found the rooms we used and the unit never failed any of their routine checks. We felt this very significant since none of the potent phenolic antiseptics were used in our area that were used in the rest of the hospital. It was a common observation that patients often had an adverse chemical reaction if they had occasion to leave the unit and enter the hospital proper.

"Borax is good deodorant, mold retardant and evidently a good bacteriostatic agent."

Lemon juice. Lemon juice is effective in cleaning brass and steel and in helping remove stains from natural fibers such as cotton and linen. It is also a natural deodorizing agent. To remove odors of fish or garlic from hands or dishes, cleanse by rubbing lemon juice on the area.

Neo-Life Products. After years of searching for cleaning products that are as effective and as cost efficient as some commercial products, we have finally discovered the *Neo-Life products. (See Appendix E.)* The products manufactured by the Neo-Life Company are reputed to be toxin-free. Three of these products—Organic Green, Rugged Red, and Neo-Life Dishwashing Detergent—are tolerated very well by most extremely sensitive persons. Some have also tolerated Mellow Yellow, Plus, and Super Plus. Organic Green and Rugged Red seem to have an even wider use than the company recommends.

Although we are enthusiastic about Neo-Life cleaning products we do not extend the same recommendation to the vitamin products distributed by the same company.

1- Neo-Life Dishwashing Detergent. Persons who can tolerate a dishwasher may also be able to use Neo-Life dishwashing detergent, which is less offensive than most commercial products.

2- Organic Green. Many people use this product for bathing, brushing teeth, shampooing hair, shaving, or washing delicate fabrics such as silk. Some use it in the washing machine for light-duty washes.

One or more applications of Organic Green will remove grease from silk fabrics. It will also help to clean perspiration marks from underarm areas of cotton clothing and other parts of garments subject to perspiration or excessive soiling. Rub garments briskly with Organic Green and then dip in water and rinse twice in clear water. For extreme soil soak the soiled area for ten minutes or longer in Organic Green and then wash the entire garment in Organic Green.

For some people it makes a good insect repellent. Before you go out into a gnat or mosquite infested area, spread it liberally on all exposed areas except around the eyes. Test it first on a small area of your skin. (See "Home Testing.")

3- Rugged Red. This heavy-duty cleaner can be used for cleaning appliances, bathroom tile, bathrooms, cars, floors, walls, windows, and woodwork. It seems to function well as a mold retardant and repels ants, silverfish, and spider mites. Spraying around windows and window screens helps prevent spider mites and flies from entering between the window and the screen.

Salt Water. This effectively cleans formica, glass, marble, and metals.

Steel Wool. When you thoroughly soap the Supreme brand it cleans well but use it only once or it will rust. Whenever you use stainless steel pads use gloves if you can tolerate gloves; when stainless steel threads penetrate the skin they can cause infections. Some sensitive people have been able to tolerate Rokeach steel wool soap pads; however, avoid all other pre-soaped pads.

Zephiran Chloride Concentrate. Zephiran Chloride Concentrate (17%), diluted as directed, is effective against mold. (For medicinal use see "First Aid.")

CAUTION: If you are extremely sensitive, do not use Zephiran Chloride in large doses. Because the odor dissipates in several hours you can probably tolerate it if someone else does the cleaning.

Cleaning Problems

Brass. Use lemon juice or vinegar with salt to clean brass. **Boots.** To remove white stains on boots after winter snows, put a mixture of vinegar and water on a clean cloth and rub lightly on boots.

Brushes. Simmer dried paint brushes for 10 minutes in a pint of vinegar.

Dishwasher. To clean periodically, run one cup of vinegar through the empty dishwasher. Because the plastic parts of the dishwater heat up when the machine is in use it is advisable to place it in a well-ventilated space and leave the room when it is running.

Drains. Pour a half cup of baking soda and a cup of vinegar into a drain pipe and cover tightly to open a stopped-up drain. Three tablespoons of sal soda (washing soda) used several times a week will keep drains from clogging.

Dry Cleaning. If you must dry clean clothes locate a dry cleaner who will use distilled Naphtha, a petroleum solvent, without added detergents and mothproofing. Sensitive individuals should avoid dry cleaning at all costs. Airing clothes after dry cleaning is helpful for some people but not for most sensitive people.

Dryer. Make sure that you have an outside vent in your home for the dryer. Although you may be told it is not absolutely necessary, lack of an outside vent may cause dampness around the dryer; this dampness causes mold.

Dust. Persons with extreme sensitivity to dust should wear a dampened surgical mask when doing work that stirs up dust. *(See face mask, Appendix E.)*

Mold and Mildew. Mold and mildew are a serious cleaning problem for everyone, especially those who live in damp, humid climates. They are particularly serious for those who are sensitive to mold.

Rugged Red used a little stronger than recommended by the manufacturer, Zephiran Chloride Concentrate diluted as instructed, Borax in water, and baking soda are all effective in retarding molds. Prevention, by wiping shower, tub, basin, and floors in the bathroom after each use, is the most effective method of control. Borax acts as a deodorant sprinkled in mold-producing places. Wiping vinegar on areas such as the rubber cushion of the refrigerator door prevents mold from forming. You may have to use a combination of these methods and many applications if the mold is very bad. It takes perseverance, but mold can be removed in a nontoxic way.

Also do not place slightly damp clothes in a closet or drawer. Having a small light on in the closet at all times was a preventive method used by one person who was highly sensitive to mold.

CAUTION: Persons highly sensitive to mold must allow extra time to make certain clothes on the line and in the dryer are thoroughly dried. Highly sensitive persons should wash pillowcases, sheets, and sleepwear after every use and cotton clothes should not be returned to the closet after being worn. (Also see the bathroom section in "Do-It-Yourself House Call.")

ᔧ ᔧ ᔧ

My Moldy Freezer. Years ago I bought a used freezer from a friend. Unfortunately, some food had been left in this unconnected freezer for several weeks and when the freezer was delivered to me the stench was very strong. Even after the food particles were removed, I couldn't go into the basement where it was stored.

A friend cleaned the freezer using Zephiran, 17% strength, and mixing one ounce to a gallon of water to give it the strength of one to 750. It took three washings with that strength and airing for a week after each washing but after three weeks I gained the use of that freezer and had it for 15 years.

ᔧ ᔧ ᔧ

Odors. Activated charcoal absorbs odors in closets, basements, storerooms, rooms with motors, and refrigerators. Baking soda is also helpful for odors in refrigerators, freezers, and sink drains.

Oven. Use Rugged Red or Bon-Ami cleaning powder and steel wool in your oven. Wipe with a damp cloth while oven is warm. Racks may be soaked in Rugged Red in hot water. To clean spills sprinkle Bon-Ami powder in warm oven, cover with absorbent towels, and sprinkle with water; the towels and steam will absorb most of the soil.

Pests. *(See "Less-Toxic Pest Control.")*

Pipes. Clogged soap and scum can be cleared from pipes using equal parts of salt and baking soda.

Pots and Pans. To clean food from pots and pans soak them in salt water before washing. Bon Ami is also effective in removing scorched food on pots and pans. While the pot is still hot pour Bon Ami Cleaning Powder liberally on the scorched food residues. Sprinkle lightly with water so that the Bon Ami is totally damp and let it stand several hours or at least until it is dry. Very often you can just lift off the scorch with a spatula. Finish the cleaning process with Bon Ami.

Refrigerator. An open box of baking soda will deodorize refrigerator for three months.

Silver. A soupy solution of baking soda and water cleans silver well. You can also use cream of tartar and water in an aluminum pan or aluminum foil; the silver must touch the aluminum to be effective.

Stainless Steel. Either borax or baking soda is effective in cleaning stainless steel sinks and appliances.

Stains. Stains on cotton or linen clothing (natural fibers) can be eliminated by wetting with lemon juice, sprinkling with salt, and placing in the sun.

Washing Machine. Adding a sprinkle of salt to the washing machine prevents colors from running. Twice a year clean machine by running two cups of apple cider vinegar in an empty washing machine.

Windows. A solution of one tablespoon of vinegar to one or two quarts of water will clean windows. One part Rugged Red to 16 parts water is also effective.

For more detailed cleaning methods see *Coping With Your Allergies* listed in Appendix F.

9

FIRST AID

If you are sensitive to drugs, be especially careful about preventive measures and preparing for emergencies. Environmental medicine (EM) specialists have great difficulty finding medicine and drugs for patients who cannot tolerate preservatives or artificial colors and flavors. However, many common-sense substitutes do exist; we will cover many of them in this chapter.

Medic Alert Record. Consult with your doctor about preparing a Medic Alert form. *(See Appendix E.)* The fee includes a bracelet or locket and a permanent record at the Medic Alert headquarters in California. In an emergency, any doctor in the country can access this information and prescribe a relatively safe treatment. Your assigned number appears on the back of the bracelet, along with a brief description of your medical problem and the Medic Alert telephone number. Doctors may call this number collect whenever emergency treatment is required.

Ask your doctor for a recommended list of drugs that you can tolerate for surgery, eye care, or dental work, including an anesthetic, pain reliever, antibiotic, and local antiseptic.

First Aid Kit

Because it is so difficult to find less toxic supplies, a first aid kit is essential for the chemically sensitive person. Remember, no product or procedure is safe for everyone, so be sure to check everything with your doctor.

Your first aid kit should contain the following items:

Acetylsalicylic Acid. If you can tolerate aspirin, order five grains of pure acetylsalicylic acid (corn-free aspirin) in a gelatin capsule. When you need aspirin, empty contents of the capsule onto a teaspoon and take orally.

Alkali Salts. Consult your doctor before using alkali salts as a laxative or a remedy to food reactions. Some doctors recommend alkali bisalts, while others prescribe trisalts. Do not use more than twice a week except on your doctor's advice. If swollen ankles or puffy eyes result, be cautious; this indicates water retention.

Your druggist can mix these salts for you, or you can order the ingredients by the pound and mix them yourself. WARNING: With some conditions such as heart or kidney problems, you must avoid sodium bicarbonate. Replace alkali salts with one to two teaspoons milk of magnesia for alkalinization.

- To make trisalts, combine three parts sodium bicarbonate; two parts potassium bicarbonate; and one part calcium carbonate.
- To make bisalts, use two of the above salts and mix in the same ratios. Purchase the salts from a pharmacist or contact The American Environmental Health Foundation (AEHF), 8345 Walnut Hill Lane, Suite 200, Dallas, TX 75231; (214) 361-9515. *(See Appendix E.)*
- Dosage is one teaspoon trisalts or bisalts in a glass of water, followed by another glass of water.

Baking Soda. Arm & Hammer brand can be tolerated by most people.

Hot Water Bottle. Use pure gum latex unless you are sensitive to nonrubber. An alternative for local heat is an infra red light bulb with holder.

Hydrogen Peroxide. Use three percent strength for surface wounds.

Ice Cubes. Freeze two trays of ice cubes and place them in a glass jar in the freezer for local application when needed. Use spring water to make ice if you are sensitive to chlorine.

Irrigation Can. For enemas or douches, use an enamel can with hard rubber attachments. Choose tubing of whatever material you tolerate best—rubber, pure gum latex, or tygon.

Medications. Ask your doctor to designate the injectable form when prescribing special drugs—these are free of hazards such as starches, dyes, and gums—and add it to distilled water to take orally. Store the preservative-free drugs in the refrigerator or freezer.

Milk of Magnesia. Use the plain liquid form, not flavored or tablets.

Surgex Tube Gauze. Because it is treated, do not place in direct contact with the body, but it is safe for most sensitive people as a layer over pure gauze. It comes in sizes to fit the head, shoulders, arms, legs, fingers, and toes. Adhesive tape is not needed because the gauze can be twisted. Plain cotton bandage may be used as a substitute.

Thermometer. Any glass thermometer is acceptable.

Triangular Bandage. Have a prewashed (to remove sizing) cotton or unbleached muslin bandage ready for use.

Zephiran Chloride. An aqueous solution 1:750 can be used as an antiseptic. Tinctured zephiran contains a dye and should be avoided. Be sure to buy the 1:750 bottle for medicinal purposes. The concentrated bottle is not sterile unless prepared by a knowledgeable professional. Use the 17 percent only for cleaning.

First Aid Treatment

Allergic Reaction. For reactions caused by a food eaten within the past hour, try to induce vomiting by putting a finger in the throat. Otherwise, take four tablespoons of milk of magnesia (laxative dose) with one pint of water. Drink another pint of water within an hour.

Other remedies for food reactions are:

- One-half teaspoon powdered vitamin C in a glass of water.
- One-half teaspoon baking soda in a glass of water, followed by another glass of water.

For reactions caused by other toxins, take prescribed medications or injection therapy. An alternative is one-half teaspoon of alkali salts. (See "Alkali Salts" above.) If suffering from nausea and vomiting, use an enema instead of oral treatment. Add one teaspoon of alkali salts or trisalts to one pint of spring water and retain as long as possible. You may use plain spring water if salts are not permitted. Take oxygen as needed. (Also see "Home Detoxification.")

Anesthetics. The least troublesome choice is pentothal, if you are not sensitive to barbiturates. Other alternatives are demerol and codeine (hypotabs or injection).

Bee Stings. Apply ice to the sting and take alkali salts. If a severe reaction is indicated by swelling or itching on areas of the body far from the sting, apply a tourniquet to retard absorption. Your physician may prescribe other preventive measures. If shock or breathing problems occur, an emergency ambulance may be necessary. Large doses of vitamin C provide great relief for some very sensitive people; your doctor can suggest proper dosage.

Blocked Sinuses. Although the *"Cellibration Therapy"* chapter presents a way to clear stuffy noses, it is not a cure-all. When infection is present or the condition is chronic, an excellent method to clear your sinuses (unless your physicians objects) is to dissolve a half teaspoon of salt in a small amount of hot water, then add more hot water to make it a cup. Pour a little of the salt water into your hand or in a saucer and inhale (but don't swallow) and the nasal passages will cleanse themselves. Sometimes you'll even taste the salt water as it passes through. Keep a washcloth handy because there may be a great deal of drainage.

Check the color of the drainage. If it is yellow, check with your doctor to see if further treatment is necessary and repeat the above procedure several times a day. If the mucus is clear or milk white, it may just be an allergic reaction.

Burns. Knowing how to recognize the seriousness of burns is important. First degree burns show redness only; second degree burns are characterized by blisters. Third degree are deep burns with severe pain and destroyed nerve endings.

Be extremely careful with second- or third-degree burns; infection is a special threat to the chemically sensitive person.

Consult your doctor. Treat burns as quickly as possible to reduce heat in the tissues. Place the burned area in cold water without delay, using ice cubes only if they are immediately available. Loosen ice cubes with cold water (use spring water if patient is sensitive) and pour the cold water into a bowl for soaking the burn. Add loosened ice cubes to keep the water chilled and soak until the burning sensation abates.

If the burning sensation continues, add bicarbonate of soda to spring water to make a soupy paste. Apply paste to burn or use cold compresses. Once dry, bandage firmly with clean cotton flannel; use gauze to hold in place.

Common Colds. To determine whether you have a cold or an allergic reaction, notice the color of nose and throat mucus. Mucus from an allergic reaction is usually clear, but when a bacterial infection is present, it usually becomes colored or dark.

By observing the usual color of your nasal mucus, you are in a better position to detect a cold. Is it clear, white, or yellow? If it is often yellow when there are no other signs of illness, it will be difficult to distinguish allergic reactions from a cold. But if your allergic reactions are usually accompanied by clear mucus, then darker colored mucus would probably indicate a cold.

The presence of fever works in a similar manner. If a high temperature accompanies your reactions, you may need a doctor to diagnose a cold. But if your temperature is usually normal during reactions, then an elevated temperature along with other symtoms would indicate a cold.

When you have a very bad allergic reaction that resembles a cold, it weakens your resistance, making you more susceptible to a bacterial infection.

To treat a cold: When throat is sore, gulp down one cup of hot water every waking hour. Also take one-half teaspoon of alkali salts with a full glass of water. Drink as much water as possible and get plenty of rest. Take vitamin C in large doses, as prescribed by your doctor.

If tolerated, you may take aspirin (pure acetylsalicylic acid) to relieve aches, fever, or discomfort. Remember, however, that a moderately high temperature can assist your defenses against infection. Be prepared to give your pulse and temperature when calling your doctor.

Constipation. Use spring water enemas. Do not take more than one enema a week over the long term unless recommended by your doctor.

Cuts. Clean with aqueous Zephiran solution 1:750 or hydrogen peroxide, then place a firm bandage on cut and fasten with cotton gauze.

Exposure to Chemicals. When exposed to heavy traffic, smoke, or perfume, shower and wash your hair as soon as you return home. Wash clothing immediately if possible or place in the basement for later laundering. (See *"Cellibration Therapy."*)

Insect Bites and Stings. Vinegar is soothing to most bites and stings, as well as sunburn. Vitamin C helps many people, but consult your doctor first on this.

Rashes and Itching. Apply milk of magnesia to affected area. Then dust with a starch powder such as potato, arrowroot, or rice starch, especially if the rash is in a moist, sweaty area.

Sore Throat. The best remedy is gulping hot water. Gargling with one teaspoon of vinegar (if tolerated) in a cup of water will also give relief. If a swollen throat makes swallowing vitamins or pills difficult, taking them with warm water sometimes helps.

Check with your doctor about taking massive doses of vitamin C. People who have reached their saturation point of vitamin C often develop diarrhea. Consult your doctor on this, too.

Sprains. Use cold applications to relieve discomfort for the first 24 hours; after that, use hot applications.

Steam Vaporizing. Place spring water in a Pyrex coffee or tea pot, boil, and inhale. Take care to avoid scalding. Some people can tolerate the hard Bakelite vaporizer units that sit in glass containers for overnight use. Use a unit that shuts off when the water is gone.

A more environmentally safe method is to use a Salton tray hot plate with an uncovered Corning Ware five-quart Dutch oven. Fill the Dutch oven with cold water and use the low heat setting to moisturize the air or for medicinal use overnight. In the daytime you can use a higher setting and hot water as long as you watch the water level to be sure it doesn't dry up. If you want more direct steam, make a tent with a towel, put it over your head, and sit with your head over the water.

Be careful of overuse resulting in a mold problem in your house. Also avoid the hot plate if you have sensitivity to the electromagnetic field (EMF).

Sunburn. If you are subject to allergies, sunbathing is not recommended. However, because it is not always possible to avoid the sun, we offer the following remedies for skin that has been overexposed to the sun.

Strain juice of two fresh tomatoes and thoroughly mix with one cup of buttermilk. Apply to the affected area. After you feel reflief, rinse in shower.

For sunburn relief, apply apple cider vinegar or make a paste of 1/2 cup baking soda, a pinch of salt, and a few drops of water. Carefully spread over affected area. After paste dries, rinse in lukewarm bath.

Other Helpful Hints

Bath Water. If you are sensitive to chlorine, a few crystals of sodium thiosulfate in your bath water will change the chlorine to chloride. Do not use internally. See Epsom Salts Bath in the chapter on "Home Detoxification."

Contraceptives. (See *"Sex in the Clean Bedroom."*)

Dental Care. If you are sensitive to chemicals, the best way to brush teeth is with pure baking soda, pure sea salt, or a combination of these two.

To make tooth powder, pulverize 3/4 cup of salt in blender and add 3/4 cup baking soda. Blend until it becomes a very fine powder.

The best materials for posterior and anterior fillings are porcelain, gold, or trans-lit. *Trans-lit* is made in Germany and is available in the United States through **Ted Moore, D.D. S.,** of Dallas, Texas. He will supply dental information on treating chemically sensitive patients to your dentist or doctor. Avoid using cavity liners for fillings.

Douches or Enemas. Use spring water.

Eyeglasses. Use glass lenses with aluminum or gold frames or no frames. Store glasses in leather cases. Avoid plastic lenses and frames, including plastic-coated aluminum frames. Do not wear plastic close to your eyes, nose, or ears. If you are sensitive even to hard plastic, gold nosepieces are available.

Oxygen Masks. If you use oxygen, you can purchase a ceramic mask with Tygon tubing from the *American Environmental Health Foundation* (AEHF). *(See Appendix E.)*

Sanitary Napkins. Use only unscented napkins. Cotton reusable pads are available for very sensitive patients from *Cycles in San Jose,* California, or *Red River Menstrual Pads* in Huntsville, Arkansas.*(See Appendix E.)*

Today's Choice feminine sanitary pads are a relatively new product on the market. *(See Appendix E.)* They have a 100% natural cotton fiber cover for softness. The pads are not bleached with elemental chlorine, the process used for most commercial pads, nor is the absorbent material bleached with chlorine gas. Some very sensitive women have been able to tolerate them.

Under no circumstances should chemically sensitive women use tampons. In fact, it isn't wise for any woman to use them because of the danger of toxic shock syndrome. Incidentally, it is suspected that victims of toxic shock syndrome are chemically sensitive people who are unaware of their condition.

10

LESS-TOXIC PEST CONTROL

Every year the news media is filled with information about a new insect infestation which threatens agricultural crops. Scientists proclaim that pesticides are the only protection for our crops and talk about the need to make stronger pesticides to combat new infestations.

Survival of the Fittest. When are they going to connect Darwin's thesis of the survival of the fittest with pest control? Strong pesticides kill weak insects; the strong surviving insects mate and produce a stronger insect. A stronger pesticide is then needed to kill these insects and the weaker insects perish while the strong which survive mate and produce a more resistant strain of pests. This vicious cycle will continue as long as the chemical companies are financially strong and the American people so gullible to advertising.

🐚 🐚 🐚

I was gullible too. When I was studying at Columbia, I persuaded the exterminator to spray in my apartment whenever he sprayed in the building because I did not want bugs from other apartments escaping into my apartment.

While the spraying did kill many bugs it made those which survived stronger. Unfortunately, it had the opposite effect on me and I ended up paralyzed on the left side of my body. I learned the hard way. Hopefully, you will take a warning from my own experience and at least control the insects in your building with less-toxic procedures.

The Mystery of My Paralysis. For four weeks in a row, every Wednesday, I had a partial paralysis in my left arm and leg. But by the end of the week, having used my cellibration therapy techniques, I had regained use of my left arm and leg and was able to ride my bicycle again. The strangest part of this was that it took me longer to recover every fifth week.

Months went by and we could think of nothing unusual that would cause this problem. Since I am a delayed reactor, my doctor finally suggested that I ask the superintendent of this brand new, 25 story luxury apartment building what happened on Tuesday. I discovered that every Tuesday for prevention purposes an exterminator sprayed the compactor shoots down which we threw the garbage. They sprayed five floors at a time; the week that it took me longer to recover was the week in which they sprayed my floor.

I learned this only by the good detective work of my doctor and gained a certain relief knowing the cause. I moved as soon as I was able but even afterward I had a recurrence every time I was exposed to certain insecticides.

During those periods when I was confined to my bed and couldn't even watch television or have a radio in my room I began to write my first book. Even though I had extreme pains in my right side and the numbness of paralysis on my left side I had the use of my brain and my right arm. I decided that with the right mental attitude there can always be a way for me to be productive. But I must say how grateful I am that I found Dr. Randolph and Dr. Kailin before pesticides totally destroyed my immune system.

ᘐ ᘐ ᘐ

My co-author and I would like to share with you some easy, less-toxic pest control methods. We—and the entire field of environmental medicine (EM)—are deeply indebted to Francis Silver, P.E., the real pesticide expert who taught us so much about safer methods.

Salvaging a Pesticide-Treated Home. (See *Do-It-Yourself Housecall.*)

Insect Repellent. One which is especially effective for spider mites, silverfish, ants, and roaches is *Rugged Red*. It works best when used in combination with the recommendations which follow under specific insects. Clean the affected area as directed in Chapter, *Keeping It Clean,* and then apply *Rugged Red* full strength. You will note immediate improvement but will need to repeat this several times over a period of weeks to completely eliminate the problem. Rugged Red can also be used to spray and paralyze an individual insect, such as a bee, hornet, or roach; it is then easy to finish it off with a flyswatter.

Steam Cleaning. If there is an infestation of insects you may steam the area. This has worked to dislodge fleas from carpets and upholstery. Bill Rea's patients have also used steaming to eliminate termites and mites, and you may find that it works with other insects. Companies which do steaming can be located in the yellow pages under "Steam Cleaning."

Avoid Shell No-Pest Strip. This type of strip is very toxic and should be avoided.

Insect Pests

Ants. Ants are attracted by food. While some like sweet foods others choose grease. Cleanliness—leaving no crumbs around and keeping the sink spotless—is the most effective control. Red pepper, borax, or boric acid left in the areas where ants are discovered can also help in controlling ants. Planting mint by both front and back doors has served as a deterrent in keeping ants from entering some houses.

Beetles. The beetle which presents most problems is the sawtoothed grain beetle which is found in cereals, cracker meal, cookies, flour, and macaroni. A bay leaf placed in each container or freezing these items effectively control this beetle.

Cereal Moth. This insect infests grain and cereal products. The most effective control is to clean the kitchen thoroughly to locate the source of these moths. All contaminated cereal products should be discarded and any crack in the kitchen which has a food build-up should be cleaned. Keeping flours and grains frozen is effective. If freezer space is at a premium, freeze flours and grains for 48 to 72 hours and then store in tightly sealed glass jars in the coolest place in the house.

Clothes Moth. This common moth likes dark, quiet, stationary locations. Many of its forms are soft-bodied and cannot stand activity. To control moths keep clothes in light places and move them occasionally. Eggs, larvae, and other forms will be killed by a vigorous brushing. Placing a dried tobacco plant in a closet or chest, or peppercorns in a chest can also repel these moths. Rugs may be vacuumed or hung on a line outside and beaten with a broom or rug beater. Salt sprinkled on rugs and furniture also wards off moths.

Flies, house flies, cluster flies. These insects lay their eggs in decaying flesh, vegetables, garbage, or manure. They first hatch as maggots before turning into flies. The vacuum cleaner can be effective by suctioning up cluster flies in the attic. Fly ribbons or paper placed on a decorative fixture near the ceiling also help in control. Window and door screens are essential and the common fly swatter can be used against individual flies. Electrocutors work in some outdoor and indoor areas. A fly trap can be made of screen wire with a funnel and the bait at the bottom. Cooling food should be covered; garbage should be disposed of promptly or ground immediately in the disposal unit.

German or small kitchen roach. This insect loves damp places, mildew, mustiness, and water. It stays in cracks and appears when the room is dark. Again the most effective control is painstaking cleanliness leaving nothing such as garbage, food, or dirty dishes around for them to eat.

When you bring your groceries into the house immediately inspect the bags and boxes for bugs; as soon as they are emptied discard them. Sprinkle boric acid liberally in crevices, corners, nesting places, and around the molding. In about six weeks they will disappear and you can then keep the worst areas covered with a small amount of boric acid. (See *Keeping It Clean*)

Mosquitoes and Gnats. There are electric zappers that are sometimes effective against these pests. *(See Appendix E)*

For personal protection some very sensitive people have been able to ward off mosquitoes by generously applying full strength *Organic Green* on all exposed areas of the body except the eyes. *(See Appendix E).*

11

COSMETICS AND TOILETRIES

Because cosmetics frequently contain such contaminents as hidden coloring dyes, preservatives, coal tar petroleum products, alcohol, witch hazel, formaldehyde, and because it is less expensive to use homemade procedures on a regular basis, prepare your own makeup whenever possible.

Facial Mask

For example, think how inexpensive it is to use two eggs, the whites for your skin and the yoke for your hair. On your "egg day," liberally spread the whites of two eggs over your face and neck. Let it dry, then put on a second application and let that dry. If there is enough egg left over, make a third application so there is a liberal mask. Leave it on for at least a half hour (longer if possible) and then wash it off with cool water. Those two eggs will act as a tightener, moisturizer, conditioner, and cleanser.

Hair Care

Use the two yolks that are left over from the skin care for your hair. Whip them to a froth with two teaspoons of almond oil.

Massage into scalp and spread through hair. Leave on until it stiffens, at least one hour—the longer, the better. Then rinse thoroughly with water only. This is a very satisfactory treatment for your hair; after trying this method for a period of time, some people use it exclusively. If you cannot tolerate almond oil, substitute another oil. If you are allergic to eggs, avoid this treatment.

In some cases, allergic patients who must use organic products internally can tolerate mixtures containing nonorganic products externally. However, they must avoid external use of foods to which they are allergic.

Dandruff Treatments. Mix one-half cup apple cider vinegar with one-half cup water and apply to your scalp several times a week before shampooing.

Rinse with a solution of Zephiran 1:750 (one-half teaspoon to one cup water). Zephiran also works well as a general disinfectant.

Dry Hair Treatment. Gently massage two tablespoons mayonnaise into your hair, rinse, and shampoo.

Nonchemical Hair Spray. Combine one-eighth teaspoon powdered gelatin and one-sixth cup cool water. Heat in top of double boiler, stirring to dissolve. Pour into a spray atomizer and store in refrigerator. Heat before using.

As a quick fix for flyaway hair, pat fresh lemon juice on the problem area, or make your own lemon hair spray. Chop one whole lemon and cover with water. Boil until only half of the water remains. Cool. Squeeze lemon and liquid through a thin cloth or cheesecloth. If necessary, add water to thin and mix well. Refrigerate in a pump valve dispenser (such as those used for window cleaners).

Setting Lotions. Dissolve six teaspoons superfine sugar (beet or cane if tolerated) in one-half cup warm water and apply to hair while warm.

Many sensitive patients can tolerate Organicure (distributed by *La Maur, Inc.*), a product useful as a setting lotion, hand cream, or body cream. While not perfumed, it does have a natural scent. It works well as a bodifier even for fine hair.

Skin Care

The juices of fruits and vegetables are the least expensive and healthiest form of skin care. You can use them for astringents, cleansers, conditioners, moisturizers, face rinses, tighteners, or softeners.

Astringents. Use the juice of two lemons, cucumbers, or lettuce; the enzymes will remove the oil from your face.

Bath Water. If you are chlorine-sensitive, add a few crystals of sodium thiosulfate to your bath water to change the chlorine to chloride. As an alternative, consider buying a shower water filter. *(See Appendix E.)*

Dusting Powder. Use any tolerated starch such as arrowroot or tapioca.

Deodorants. Dark green plants (especially parsley and comfrey) are the best deodorants. Buy in quantity when available, juice them, and store as ice cubes. Drinking the juice (either alone or mixed with another juice to make it more palatable) will deodorize the body.

For another effective deodorant or body powder, blend in a blender one-half cup baking soda and one-half cup arrowroot starch. If sensitive to arrowroot starch, substitute another type of starch.

You can also use plain baking soda or alkali salts (two parts soda bicarbonate to one part potassium bicarbonate).

As an antiperspirant, Dr. Randolph suggests asking a druggist to combine: aluminum chloride 4 gm. and water to make 100cc., or (especially if you cannot tolerate aluminum) oxyquinoline sulfate 1 gm. and rose water to make 500cc. Test both on a small area for individual tolerance.

Lipstick and Blush. Unfortunately, to our knowledge, no one has found a really pure substitute for lipstick. However, some sensitive people can tolerate Clinique lipstick and Clinique blush although not their rouge or any other products. Try them and use them for special occasions but give your lips and cheeks a rest when you're at home.

Rough Skin. The tannic acid of a tomato softens rough skin on elbows and heels. Or use avocado as an alternative.

Skin Cream. Preservative-free Duane's Special Formula Cream is excellent for chapped hands and rough skin. Dinet and Delfosse, Inc., a Chicago-based prescription druggist, make it for Dr. Randolph's patients. *(See Appendix E.)* Store the jar in the refrigerator to prevent molding.

Tonic for Oily Skin. Use the juice of a tomato, cucumber, or orange. If you're feeling lazy, simply rub your face with a slice of the fresh tomato, cucumber, or orange.

For complete cosmetics and toiletries recipes, see *Coping With Your Allergies (Appendix F).*

12

REBUILDING TOLERANCE

The Body's Adaptive Ability. Through physiologic adaptation the body is able to adjust to new conditions and maintain its homeostasis (the body's balance). A good example of homeostasis is the way the body responds to external temperature changes. During an ice cold shower the body heats itself and on a hot day the body cools itself. The body also adjusts to other factors in the environment which present strange conditions. Environmentally-triggered illness results when the body loses it ability to adapt and loses tolerance.

After you have stabilized your diet and improved your environment and your body has had a chance to recover, it is important for you to rebuild your tolerance. Three factors should determine the extent to which you become involved in an adaptive program: the extent of your illness, the total number of foods and chemicals that produce reactions, and your own schedule. You are usually the best judge of the timetable to follow but consult with your doctor or counselor if you have any doubts about proceeding.

Stabilize Your Diet First. An appropriate time to begin this process is six months after you have stabilized your diet with food injection therapy or avoidance of untolerated foods. Before retesting a food or testing a food you have not previously eaten, relax using the shortcut in Cellibration Therapy. Then eat the food using the testing procedure (See "Testing").

Dr. James Cox, who supervised a pilot project of ten very sensitive patients, first suggested this process. Most of these patients were able to add many new foods and return some previously troublesome foods to their diet. However, some patients who had been doing well for a year or two would suddenly find their major complaints returning and would also experience new symptoms. When questioning revealed that they had become careless in the rotation, the logical conclusion was that continuing to rotate indefinitely would prevent symptoms from returning. Patients who continued the rotation reported that it maintained their health and helped them regain a tolerance for many foods.

Methods Used. To make it possible for patients to adapt to the eating patterns of social functions—dinner parties or restaurant meals—several methods were devised. Some patients reported success from taking two tablespoons of an oil permitted that day before eating an "unsafe" meal. One possible explanation, advanced by Dr. Randolph, was that the oil slowed down the absorption rate. The rate of absorption is a major factor in food allergy.

Some patients took additional measures when they first broke their diets. One preventative measure was to take their alkaline salts or milk of magnesia right after the meal, even before they had a reaction. If there was any sign of a reaction they took a spring water enema as soon as possible. Another anti-allergy measure was the use of large quantities of pure vitamin C. This may cause loose stools or diarrhea for some persons and a doctor should be consulted if this method is used.

A deliberate and controlled exposure, rather than a haphazard one, was found to be most successful in rebuilding tolerance. Following each exposure with a time of cleansing helped to reduce the stress on the individual. This consisted of returning to eating only one food per meal for several days. Gradually patients were able to increase the quantity of food and the number of meals they could tolerate in one exposure.

Follow Your Own Schedule. Each person had to discover his own time frame in rebuilding tolerance. However, the process was so successful that some were able to indulge all day on Thanksgiving and be able to do so again by Christmas. Some extremely sensitive patients were even able to travel and eat in restaurants for a week or two. These patients were advised to rotate when possible and avoid stews, fried foods, and fast foods.

To reduce their total stress they were also cautioned not to become agitated about matters beyond their control. Other suggestions to reduce stress included: exercise, breathing exercises, drinking large amounts of tolerated water, and the relaxation techniques which Dr. Cox had taught and are now incorporated into cellibration therapy. Occasionally these persons found that they either had to eat some foods daily or were tempted to do so and they again became addicted to those foods.

ಜಾ ಜಾ ಜಾ

This happened to me after I had my diet under control. In the beginning, before we knew about food injection therapy, I had lived for two years on exotic foods—elephant, moose, hippopotamus, nami, yucca, malanga, etc.) After using the process described above, I was able to regain all of my foods except foods with yeast and beets—as long as I rotated and ate organic foods.

I then took a two week trip during which I ate eggs and potatoes every day. When I returned home I avoided eggs and potatoes. After three months I could again tolerate them on rotation. I believe my case illustrates how successfully your capacity for tolerance can be rebuilt. With every subsequent trip I was less troubled by the food and I was able to decrease my period of avoidance. Finally I was able to reintroduce the foods into my rotation after a twelve-day avoidance.

Two major barriers discouraged me from a lifetime or indefinite commitment to rotation. Making changes in the rotation seemed too difficult since mistakes could be made in minor foods such as oils, herbs, teas, etc., and there could be greater exposure to a food family. It was also difficult to enjoy favorite recipes using the rotations. Because of these complaints I developed a formula which allows me to change my rotation frequently (See "The Formula"). Dr Sidney Baker of the Bio-Brain Center told me that his patients could use it with ease after they had practiced it a few times. You can do it too—without breaking the rotation, you can cook or bake any recipe from scratch.

ಜಾ ಜಾ ಜಾ

The Chemical Environment

Patients in the pilot project were also able to regain a degree of tolerance to toxic chemicals but this required great caution. Not only is testing more complicated but control of the environment is costly and requires a lot of time. Controlling the amount of the exposure is extremely important because overexposure to one toxic chemical can trigger a decrease in tolerance to all chemicals and the patient can lose tolerance for all chemicals. There is also an interaction between chemical sensitivities and food allergies. A chemically free environment helps to increase food tolerance but an overexposure to chemicals usually retriggers food allergies.

The procedures outlined in "Home Testing" were easy for individuals to use in their own chemical testing. Francis Silver's method "That Crawly Feeling" was one important testing method used. Other individuals with a keen sense of smell were trained in the Randolph method as "noses" to help detect hidden contaminants in houses.

The Project Lesson. From this pilot project we have learned, however, that individuals who tried to implement all the changes immediately ran into problems such as financial difficulties, lack of family cooperation, and lack of strength. Discouragement from these problems caused one person to drop the project altogether so we learned to teach people to plan priorities. Persons with financial problems were able to build a "haven"—even just one small bedroom—where they could spend some time in a relatively pure environment.

Procedure. After members of the project had a "haven" it was possible to begin rebuilding tolerance. Before beginning to rebuild tolerance one had to reach a level where he could function in reasonable comfort—call it "Plateau A." Then he deliberately had a small exposure to a chemical, proceeding in the method described above for rebuilding food tolerance.

Insight Gained. While people discovered that their first few attempts to rebuild tolerance to the chemical was successful, they reported that they would then encounter a setback for an extended period of time. At first we thought that they had been imprudent in their exposure to the chemical but we soon learned that this was part of a pattern: two steps forward, one step back, two steps forward. When the people improved after the setback they would reach a level of health better than that they experienced in Plateau A; we called this sustained level Plateau B. This has become accepted as a part of the process of rebuilding tolerance.

ஐ ஐ ஐ

Now about my own recovery of tolerance to toxic chemicals. When I resumed exposure to newsprint I had a reaction after five minutes. It would last for two or three days. Gradually I could increase exposure to an hour or two. Now I can spend hours working with print as long as I use my cleansing techniques which I described.

My sister doesn't smoke but she worked in a smoke-filled environment. Before she came to visit me she would bathe and change her clothes. However, the smoke had also permeated her hair and I would have to ask her to leave within 15 minutes. Now after a full day in a smoke-filled room, I have only minor problems if, as soon as I reach home, I bathe and wash my clothes and hair.

Now I can also be away from my haven for two or three weeks at a time, exposed to all types of toxins including nonorganic food. I begin to "crash" if I stay away too long and have withdrawal symptoms, a short period of setback, and then I reach a higher plateau. As long as I do not do this too frequently I find the withdrawal periods are less reactive and of shorter duration.

≈ ≈ ≈

Making Choices for Exposure

During the pilot project an important part of the training was learning to make choices for exposures — learning what to avoid and which one to learn to tolerate without too much trouble. Helping patients set their priorities required extensive education and reading in this field. Each person had to find his own way but certain principles could be applied to the process. The procedure could be approached in two ways: exposure to one toxin at a time or exposure to a combination of unavoidable toxins.

Paint is one toxin with which many persons have difficulties. Only if the patient were an artist and could not be convinced to begin creative endeavors not requiring turpentine and paints, would the procedure be tried with paint. Then the artist was advised to begin the procedure slowly by using a toxin not as strong as paint. When the artist was aware that the procedure was succeeding, painting could be tried for a short time working outdoors with a brisk wind and using all other procedures. The amount of exposure to paint would be increased only very gradually.

Some toxins, such as smoke, gas, and perfume, are so pervasive in our society that everyone had to learn to deal with them. The best way to begin to tolerate these toxins was by visiting the home of a friend or relative who understood the situation and would not be upset if the patient suddenly had to leave abruptly, go outside for a brisk walk, or take oxygen. Patients were advised to be selective in choosing outings, selecting only those they really enjoyed and wanted to adapt to. Another consideration was the degree of exposure — an outing to a home filled with cigarette, cigar, pipe, and fireplace smoke and people wearing heavy perfumes would be counterproductive.

Patients have learned that to be successful in the process they must carefully plan the buildup of exposures. "Cheating"—an indiscriminate, spur-of-the-moment and uncontrolled exposure—is counterproductive in this slow process.

Summary

While testing, avoidance, and/or treatment are very important for chemically sensitive people, these alone are not the answer. For patients to return to society they need to be educated and guided in a planned program by a physician. Patients also need help and support from each other through local chapters of a support group. The pilot project indicated that local support groups are important in augmenting the help given by the physician and helping people return to mainstream life faster and safer than if they only receive treatment by a doctor. Had this project been conducted today it would have been greatly improved. With no local environmental medicine (EM) specialist to guide us, treatment was restricted to education of the patient and avoidance of excitants such as offending foods and chemicals. With the innovations and progress in the field of EM that have since taken place the process today would have been speeded up.

Family Cooperation

Family cooperation is essential in providing optimal conditions for patient recovery. Indeed, the success of the treatment may be directly related to the support, especially the moral support, given by the family. At the same time the patient must not take advantage of any special status because of the illness. Family members should work to educate themselves either by taking part in the patient-education classes or through reading. They should also be an active part of the support group.

Your Responsibility. There are many ways for the extremely chemically sensitive person and your family to work at solving problems which occur in everyday relationships. You can assume some responsibility in this cooperative effort. For example:

- Set an example by avoiding cheating with foods that cause behavioral changes that may affect your family.
- Keep a positive attitude and join a support group with whom you can talk about your problems. Encourage family members to join also so they can talk with other families having the same experience.

- Help family members locate products that do not aggravate your health.
- Learn to tell others in a polite way what bothers you and to suggest alternative products or procedures.
- Learn to be as independent as possible and to forget your aches and pains. Doing chores, for example, gives you something to think about and exercise helps to improve circulation and clear some of the reactions.
- Suggest family activities in which you can participate with a minimum of exposure and a maximum of enjoyment. Learn to enjoy yourself during the function without worrying about after-effects and spoiling everybody's fun.
- After an intentional exposure remember that you made this choice knowing you would have to pay the price.

Your Family's Support. There are suggestions you can make to your family to give you support.
- Educate themselves so they understand the nature of the illness and how to cope with it.
- Remember that you need understanding, support and positive help from your family.
- Learn to recognize your symptoms so they can help you avoid things which contribute to illness.
- Remember that you often have cerebral reactions which may interfere in making necessary decisions to take relief measures when needed.
- Remind you to take prescribed treatments, drink water, exercise, and other measures that help alleviate reactions.
- Learn to proceed with gentle insistence and with great understanding.

Take a Firm Stand

In the case of some toxins, if you are extremely sensitive persons you must learn to take a firm stand and refuse to make any compromise. Tradespeople and family visitors alike must be told that these restrictions are essential for your health.

Aerosal Cans. Avoid aerosal cans, especially the perfumed hair sprays.

Perfumes. Perfumes are toxic and you should restrict the use of perfume and any perfumed products.

Smoke on Clothes. When family members smoke or come from a smoke-filled environment, ask them to change clothes, placing the smoke-filled clothes where they will not make you ill, and shower and wash their hair to remove the smoke which clings to the hair and body.

Smoking. Set restrictions that others can follow: no smoking in your presence, your house, or your car.

PART V

ALLERGY FREE COOKING

13

FOOD ROTATION

Food and Environmentally-triggered Illness

What unmitigated gall! But I was desperate! At 2:30 a.m. from my hospital bed, I called my brother Ellery (collect!) and blurted out, "Please make me laugh so I won't cry." Of course at that time I didn't know that laughter is a stress reduction mechanism. I just needed a diversion from the excruciating pain in my legs and back. By painful experience, I was learning that withdrawal from chemicals and addictive foods can be as agonizing as withdrawal from addictive drugs. It was my first day on a water fast in 1966 in the hospital under the care of Dr. Theron Randolph.

ᴥ ᴥ ᴥ

Fasting

Among his many contributions in environmental medicine, Dr. Randolph will be most honored and remembered for the development of comprehensive environmental control. In a hospital ecology unit, patients are diagnosed and treated for food and chemical sensitivity through this method. All possible toxic substances have been cleared from the unit as described under recommendations for nontoxic living in the chapter titled "Make Your Own House Call." After four to seven days of fasting, drinking only pure water until allergic symptoms disappear, patients are once again exposed to foods and toxic substances one at a time, to learn which ones are the cause of the allergic reaction.

Although environmental medicine is more than 50 years old, many hospitals do not yet have ecology units, and some patients must go through the fasting period at home. This is less effective, even though it is done under a doctor's supervision, because the patient may be reacting to things in the environment rather than to the foods and the allergy pattern may emerge less clearly.

WARNING: Never try a do-it-yourself fast. Fasting should always be done under medical supervision; otherwise, complications could develop. If you want to try a self-test, you can use the rotary diversified diet or the simple food tests described in the chapter on "Home Testing." In this chapter you will learn how to keep a record of foods eaten and symptoms experienced.

🐾 🐾 🐾

But first, back to my hospital room in Chicago, or rather, how I was fortunate to get there. When I developed diarrhea, could hold no food or water, and kept losing weight, I went to a doctor who was chief of medical staff in a leading hospital in the local area. (I won't mention his name or tell you what I think of him.)

He put me though a series of tests, then referred me to a surgeon because all he could find was a tiny gall stone. The next word I heard was "operation." Operation? But I'd never had a gall bladder attack; never any pain.

Three days after the operation, I developed a hoarse throat. "Don't worry," said my surgeon, "it sounds sexy! I'll see that you get inhalation therapy." The same day my diarrhea returned. "Don't worry," said my internist, "it's probably a grain allergy. In six weeks, after you've recovered, I'll send you to an allergist." !*#*#! Why didn't he do that before the operation???

No, it was not the anesthesia or the inhalation medication I received through toxic tubing that caused my illness. They were just the "straw that broke the camel's back," causing my body to overload and the symptoms to show up. Or to use Dr. Rea's analogy discussed earlier, they were the drops of water that caused the barrel to spill over.

My health went steadily downhill during the intervening weeks. Fortunately, Dr. Kailin, the allergist to whom I was referred, recognized my problem as grain allergy and also a sensitivity to plastic; she sent me to Dr. Theron Randolph's hospital in Chicago. That is where I learned about food addiction, masking, and the rotary diversified diet.

ƷÀ ƷÀ ƷÀ

Food Addiction

It usually takes about 96 hours for food to clear the gastrointestinal tract and other parts of the body's food absorption system. If you eat a particular food often enough that the system never becomes free of it, you can become addicted to that food in the same way people become addicted to drugs. What makes things worse is that you can become a food addict without knowing it. The reason for this is masking.

Masking

Suppose you are allergic to corn. If you avoid eating corn or anything made with corn for a period of ten days, then reintroduce it into your diet, you are likely to have a definite reaction very quickly or at least within 18 hours of eating the offending food.

By eating corn every day, the reactions may become weaker, and eventually you may not notice a reaction. This does not mean that corn no longer aggravates you, but simply that the symptoms are hidden, or masked, so that they are no longer associated with the food that caused them. New symptoms and chronic disorders may develop. You may find that eventually you feel relief from certain ailments only after eating corn, and so you eat corn more and more frequently. Once the problem becomes severe, you begin to crave corn.

Food Addiction Cycle

The *food addiction cycle* is very similar to drug addiction, with two additional problems that cause even more difficulty in diagnosing the underlying cause. First, corn oil or syrup is found in many prepared foods, so it is not always possible to know when corn is being introduced into your system. Also, there is the possibility that you may be addicted to several foods at once and in varying degrees. This confuses the issue so that only an experienced clinician may be able to decipher the puzzle.

Rotary Diversified Diet (RDD)

The *rotary diversified diet,* devised by the late Dr. Herbert J. Rinkel in 1934, is the key to identifying the proper treatment approach for food addiction. Because food addiction is frequently linked to such problems as schizophrenia, alcoholism, and obesity, it seems logical that the rotary diversified diet could be used routinely as a first step in the treatment process for these disorders.

The rotary diversified diet is for people who have multiple food sensitivities and can be used as a short-term eating method or for a lifetime. You can use it either to prevent food allergies and addictions or to diagnose and treat food allergies and addictions.

The diet is based on the premise that the most frequently eaten foods are the most common allergens. The plan allows you to eat foods no more than once in a four-day period. So, if you eat rice on Monday, you would not eat it or any other form of rice again until Friday. Usually four days is the maximum bowel transit time; in some cases (such as chronic constipation), transit time is longer and so a longer rotation is necessary.

Not only are individual foods rotated, but food families are as well. Foods from the same family tend to share common characteristics and so often react similarly. Foods from the same family are rotated two days apart, so that if you eat wheat on Monday, you would not eat corn until Wednesday.

Appendix A contains an alphabetical List #1 which you can use to familiarize yourself with foods and their botanical families (based on biological origin). To use the alphabetical list, look up the food and note the number shown to the left of that food. Then use that number to refer to the food family guides (Appendix B) and locate the appropriate family. Listed under the family name are all closely related foods (botanically or biologically).

Ideally, according to Dr. Joseph Morgan, a pediatrician in Coos Bay, Oregon, infancy is the best time to begin rotating foods. A great majority of food allergies could be prevented by feeding infants in this way, and the child would learn good eating habits. In fact, there is now clinical evidence to suggest that allergic parents on a rotation diet before conception can, in some cases, prevent food allergies in their unborn child.

Don't be discouraged by the number of foods you find you cannot tolerate on your rotary diversified diet. The good news is that eventually you may be able to tolerate many more foods than in the initial stages of the diet. When you suddenly shift to a rotary diet or have just finished a fast, your system is unusually sensitive, and mildly allergic foods may cause a stronger reaction than normally would be the case. However, foods that caused only minor reactions can be returned to the diet with little or no problem *after avoiding* them a few weeks or a month.

Cyclic Allergies

Also, many food allergies, called cyclic or nonfixed allergies, come and go depending on frequency of exposure. At times they cause mild reactions; at other times severe. Although nonfixed allergies may compose up to 70 to 80 percent of a patient's allergies, with proper management on the rotary diet, some foods that create severe symptoms can later be eaten safely. This happens because the body has had a rest period during which it regains tolerance. Waiting time varies—some foods can be eaten after a rest period of three to four weeks; for others, it may be necessary to wait two to six months before they can be eaten safely. A few foods may remain permanent allergens.

Types of Diets

Two basic types of rotation diets are the mono-rotary diversified diet (RDD) which is limited to one food item per meal, and the liberalized rotation diet which allows multiple food items per meal. How many foods you eat per meal and how many meals per day is an individual decision based on your food tolerances, other sensitivities, and physical needs.

Principles in the Diet

- Eat each food item no oftener than once every four days. (See "Understanding the Formula.")
- Choose foods with fewer chemical contaminates. Whenever possible, select foods labelled "certified organic." Fresh or frozen foods are better than canned foods.
- Use sea salt for seasoning rather than regular salt which may contain dextrose, aluminum, and other harmful ingredients.

- When dining out, ask questions about food preparation. Choose simple a la carte items, the salad bar, plain meats or fish, steamed vegetables without sauces, and fresh fruit.
- Drink and cook with spring water in glass containers.
- Space meals a minimum of three to four hours apart.
- Eat the desired amount at each meal within one hour. Do not repeat a food in the same day unless directed otherwise.
- For remedies to a food reaction, see "First Aid" chapter.

Nutritional Considerations

The nutritional advantages of the rotary diversified diet are many. Because you eat a wide variety of foods, it is easier to achieve a nutritionally balanced diet. Eat whole, unrefined, high fiber foods which are high in complex carbohydrates and low in salt. Because these foods have not been processed, they still contain important nutrients.

The rotary diversified diet helps ensure that the individual with multiple food omissions still maintains a nutritionally balanced diet. However, if you have numerous food sensitivities, one or more important nutrients may be missing from your diet. Calcium is the nutrient that is most difficult to obtain in adequate amounts. As a common allergen, cow's milk is often omitted from the diet, and a calcium deficiency results. To prevent long-term vitamin or mineral deficiencies, it is extremely important for such individuals to have the guidance of a physician or dietitian knowledgeable about the nutritive content of foods.

Calcium. Calcium combines with phosphorus and vitamin D to form bones and teeth, and works with vitamin K to ensure blood clotting. It also helps maintain healthy nerve function and muscle tone in the tissues.

Although most calcium comes from dairy products, foods from other food groups may also contain calcium.

Calcium	Sardines, goat's milk, salmon, mustard greens (cooked), amaranth leaves, raw, almonds, amaranth seeds and flour, kale (cooked), Brazil nuts, quinoa, soybean milk, beet greens, sesame seeds, orange,sea vegetables, rhubarb (raw), carob flour, broccoli (cooked), spinach (cooked), egg, green beans, whole wheat bread.

Sources of Other Nutrients:

Vitamin A	Fish liver oils, milk, butter, whole-milk cheese, liver, egg yolk, spinach, turnip tops, chard, beet

greens, asparagus, broccoli, carrots, sweet potatoes, winter squash, pumpkin, apricots, peaches, cantaloupe.

Thiamin (B1) Brewer's yeast, wheat germ, brown rice, pork, liver, dried beans, peas, soybeans, peanuts, egg yolks.

Riboflavin(B2) Excellent sources are liver, milk, and milk products. Moderate sources are oysters, meat, dark green leafy vegetables, eggs, mushrooms, asparagus, broccoli, avocado, Brussels sprouts, tuna, salmon.

Niacin (B3) Poultry, meats, fish, organ meats, peanuts, brewer's yeast, potatoes, legumes, green leafy vegetables.

Pyridoxine(B6) Meats and organ meats, poultry, fish, egg yolk, soybeans and dried beans, peanuts, walnuts, bananas, avocados, cabbage, cauliflower, potatoes, whole grain cereals and breads, prunes.

Vitamin B12 Excellent sources are organ meats (liver, kidney, heart), clams, and oysters. Good sources are nonfat dry milk, crab, salmon, sardines, egg yolk. Moderate sources are meat, lobster, scallops, flounder, swordfish, tuna, fermented cheese.

Pantothenic Acid Liver and organ meats, fish, chicken, eggs, cheese, whole grain cereals and breads, avocados, cauliflower, green peas, dried beans, nuts, dates, sweet potatoes.

Folic Acid Organ meats, kidney beans, asparagus, broccoli, beets, cabbage, yeast, cauliflower, orange juice, cantaloupe, green peas, sweet potatoes, wheat germ, whole grain cereals and breads, lima beans.

Biotin Organ meats (liver and kidney), egg yolk, milk, yeast, legumes, nuts, chocolate, some vegetables.

Choline Snap beans, soybeans, egg yolk, beef liver, peas, spinach, wheat germ.

Inositol	Lima beans (dried), liver, cantaloupe, grapefruit, peaches, peanuts, oranges, peas, raisins, wheat germ, cabbage.
Vitamin C	Citrus fruits (oranges, grapefruit, lemon, lime), tomatoes, green peppers, parsley, fresh dark leafy vegetables, broccoli, cantaloupe, strawberries, cabbage, potatoes, fresh peas, lettuce, asparagus.
Vitamin D	Milk, eggs, butter, cod liver oil, exposure to sunlight, fortified foods, commercial vitamin D preparations.
Vitamin E	Vegetable oils (corn, soy, cottonseed, safflower), whole grains, dark green leafy vegetables, broccoli.
Phosphorus	Milk and milk products, meats, fish, poultry, eggs.
Magnesium	Nuts, legumes, whole grain cereals, breads, soybeans, seafood.
Manganese	Liver, kidney, lettuce, spinach, muscle meats, whole cereals and breads, dried peas and beans, nuts. Moderate sources are leafy green vegetables, dried fruits, and the stalk, root, and tuber part of vegetables.
Iron	Excellent sources are liver and other organ meats, beef, dried fruits, lima beans, ham, legumes, dark green leafy vegetables, sardines, prune juice, oysters. Good sources are whole grain cereals and breads, tuna, green peas, chicken, strawberries, egg, tomato juice, enriched grains, Brussels sprouts, winter squash, blackberries, pumpkin, nuts, canned salmon, broccoli
Chromium	Whole grains, brewer's yeast, pork, kidney, meats, cheeses
Copper	Good dietary sources are whole grain cereals and breads, shellfish, nuts, organ meats, eggs, poultry, dried beans and peas, dark green leafy vegetables

Iodine	Iodized salt and water. Food content varies depending on the soil and water supply.
Molybdenum	Dietary intake depends on soil status on which grains and vegetables are raised. Hard water can provide up to 41% of daily intake. Other good sources are meats, whole grains, legumes, leafy vegetables, and organ meats.
Potassium	Meat, milk, fruits (especially bananas, orange juice, and apricots), vegetables (especially potatoes)
Selenium	Excellent sources are liver, kidney, meats, seafood
Zinc	Excellent sources are oysters, herring, milk, meat, egg yolks. Good sources are whole grains.
Bioflavanoids	Grapes, rosehips, prunes, citrus (especially the white parts), cherries, plums, parsley
Sodium	Most commercially prepared foods have a high sodium content; this is one of many reasons to cook from scratch.

Mold and Yeast Sensitivities

Many people are allergic to foods in the fungi family such as brewer's and baker's yeast, mold, and mushrooms; this is especially true for those who live in humid or moldy environments. If you have yeast or mold sensitivities, avoid the following foods or use them with caution:

Brewer's yeast is found in fermented foods, including all alcoholic beverages, aged cheeses, soy sauce, cider, sauerkraut, and root beer. Vinegar, which is an ingredient in salad dressings, ketchup, prepared mustard, mayonnaise, pickles, olives, steak sauce, and barbecue sauce, contains brewer's yeast, as does malt, an ingredient in many cereals and candies.

In addition, brewer's yeast is often used to fortify foods with B vitamins such as flour, breads, and cereals. Many nutritional supplements contain brewer's yeast, unless the label states "yeast free." If you are sensitive to brewer's yeast, avoid these items.

Depending on your degree of sensitivity, you may be able to tolerate some lower mold cheeses such as cottage cheese, cream cheese, ricotta, mozzarella, monterey jack, and farmers (pot) cheese.

Baker's yeast is found in yeast leavened breads, rolls, and buns, as well as donuts, pastries, pizza dough, pretzels, and sourdough products. Some canned refrigerator biscuits and some crackers, cookies, canned soups, and flour tortillas also contain baker's yeast. Avoid these foods if you have a baker's yeast sensitivity.

Mold is found in many foods such as nuts and seeds, root vegetables, and dried fruits. It is also airborne. Take certain precautions with foods that contain mold. Roast all nuts and seeds and store them in the freezer.

You can also destroy most of the excess mold by baking at 325° for 10-15 minutes. In most cases, nut butters prepared from roasted nuts are safe.

Peel and steam root vegetables that grow under the soil such as potatoes, carrots, beets, onions, turnips, and sweet potatoes. You may bake a potato in its skin, but remove the skin before eating. If your sensitivity is not too high, you may be able to eat raw carrots if they are well peeled.

Fresh fruit juice is acceptable for some people; immediately freeze any leftover juice to avoid fermentation.

14

COOKING HINTS AND SUBSTITUTIONS

Allergy free cooking can be a chore or a challenge. With a positive attitude, you can make it a fun filled experience, a new adventure. I wish I had had that attitude back in 1966 when I first returned from Dr. Randolph's hospital unit.

ë€ ë€ ë€

In the hospital I learned that I was allergic to all the foods I loved. I had trouble locating organic foods; and because there was no provocative neutralization (P/N) treatment for foods, I had to import the exotic foods I could eat (hippopotamus, moose, elephant, name, malanga, etc.)

Picture This Scenario. Before I was hospitalized, I did not know how to cook; well, that's not quite true—I could broil liver or a steak and bake a potato. But most of the time I'd stop at a deli on the way home and buy some chocolate bars, a quart of chocolate ice cream, and for nourishment, a luncheon meat sandwich and a Pepsi. Yes, I was a real candidate for food sensitivities!

To this day, Dr. Randolph teases me for calling Dr.
Kailin's office to request directions for cooking
something that required boiling water. I asked the
nurse, "How do I know when the water is boiling?" (In
my own defense, I must protest that the question was
not so stupid as it sounds. As a novice, I did not
know how to phrase my question to learn whether the
recipe called for "rapid boil" or "simmer.")

At any rate, my question made the rounds and
everyone had a good laugh. I made up my mind that I'd
show them. The chore became a challenge. I was like a
sponge, learning recipes from other patients and
later inventing my own. I learned all there was to
know about the rotary diversified diet, nutrition,
and substituting foods.

🐚 🐚 🐚

Things have changed since then. We hope that the cooking hints and
substitutions in this chapter will help you become inventive on your own.

One of the ways you can begin is to learn to cook without sugar. So
many warnings have been issued about the dangers of sugar that none of
our recipes use it. Most doctors and nutritionists have also recommended
avoiding honey; however, if you must use a sweetener, try tupelo or sage
honey.

Sugar Substitute

- One-half cup of honey equals one cup sugar.
- When using honey in place of sugar, deduct one-quarter cup
  liquid from recipe.

Substitutes for the Grain/Potato-Sensitive Patient
(See also recipe sections under "Grain Substitutes.")

Amaranth. This is a non-grain plant family, available in seeds and
flour. (See recipe section of Day 2.)

Arrowroot Flour *(Starch).* Use to make cookies, to thicken fruit juice
to pudding consistency, or to thicken meat sauce or gravy.

Artichoke. Available as a flour.

Avocado. High in calories.

Banana. Slice into citrus or pineapple juice. Bake in oven and use
with chicken. Broil thin slices of plantain brushed with oil, mash when

soft, and broil again to make a "banana chip." Steam green bananas and serve like steamed potatoes; they are starchy rather than sweet.

Buckwheat. Use buckwheat flour in pancakes, groats as hot cereal. If allergic to wheat, use buckwheat no more than once every two weeks, or you may develop an allergy to it.

Ground Nuts and Seeds. Use for fruit cake. Pumpkin or sunflower seeds make good snacks.

Lima or Navy Beans, Green Peas. Use in lentil soup, pork and beans, split pea soup. Lima bean flour can be purchased for use in making bread.

Ñame, Malanga, Yuca. These starchy tubers are similar to white potatoes (available in stores catering to Spanish-speaking people). Another root you can cook and eat is the tropical potato.

Pancakes. (See recipes.)

Quinoa. Although quinoa looks like a grain, it is a member of the goosefoot family, related to spinach, beets, and chard. It is one of the best grain substitutes because it contains high values of oils and carbohydrates and is an excellent source of plant protein.

Snack Foods. Nuts, dates, figs, raisins, dried fruits such as apple, peach, apricot. (Go easy—they tend to generate intestinal gas.)

Soybean. You can use flour in pancakes, muffins, cookies, waffles. Note: Processed soy flour contains wheat. Health food stores sell wheat-free soy flour.

Sweet Potato. Boil, mash, bake, or steam.

Tapioca. To thicken fruit juice, soak pearl tapioca overnight, then cook it with juice. Use tapioca starch for puddings, cookies, cake.

Winter Squash. Hubbard, butternut, acorn squash; use pumpkin similarly.

Yuca. Yuca, from which tapioca is made, grows as a fleshy protuberance on the roots of a small tree. Its proper name is cassava. With a knife remove the coarse, stringy outer layer to get to the yellow layer between the bark and the white tuber. Then quarter the tuber and steam like a potato.

Other Substitutions

Baking Powder.
- One teaspoon baking powder is equal to one-third teaspoon baking soda and one-half teaspoon cream of tartar.
- Combine one part potassium bicarbonate, two parts cream of tartar, and two parts arrowroot powder.
- Combine one-quarter teaspoon baking soda and one-half teaspoon of any acid—lemon or lime juice, cream of tartar, powdered vitamin C (ascorbic acid).

- For every cup of flour, use one-half teaspoon baking soda plus one of the following: one tablespoon lemon juice or vinegar, two tablespoons pineapple juice, or one-quarter teaspoon vitamin C crystals. Add baking soda and vitamin C crystals to dry ingredients and sift to blend *or* add the lemon juice, vinegar, or pineapple juice to the liquid ingredients.

Bread Crumbs for Meat Loaf and Patties. Replace with cooked oatmeal, grated nuts, grated potato or other starchy vegetable, or, for dieters, grated cauliflower.

Butter. When using oil as a substitute, combine seven-eighths cup oil with one-half teaspoon salt. (Not recommended for cookies). Oil pie crust is easier to press into pan with fingers than to roll or spoon it.

Cane Sugar. One cup cane sugar is equal to any of the following:

- Seven-eighths cup honey (Reduce liquid in recipe by three tablespoons per seven-eighths cup honey substituted. Unless recipe calls for sour milk or sour cream, add pinch of baking soda to reduce acidity.)
- Three-quarters cup pure maple syrup (Reduce liquid by three tablespoons for every cup of syrup substituted.)
- One-half cup fructose
- One cup maple sugar
- Seven-eighths cup fig syrup (Reduce liquid in recipe by three tablespoons per seven-eighths cup fig syrup substituted.)
- For baking, corn syrup is not an effective substitute for cane sugar.

Chocolate or Cocoa. For one ounce of chocolate, heat three tablespoons carob in one and one-half teaspoons oil, or for one tablespoon of chocolate, use one tablespoon carob flour.

Coffee or Tea. Rotate herb teas.

Cornmeal. Use millet, potato meal, or soy flour.

Cow's Milk. Substitute an equal amount of any of the following:

- Artichoke milk. Mix one-half cup artichoke flour and two cups water with electric beater, bring to a boil, and simmer for 20 minutes. Drink plain or sweeten to taste.
- Coconut milk. In blender, puree one-half cup coconut or coconut meal with one cup water. Or whip one cup fresh coconut chunks plus its own milk in blender until pulp is fine. Store in covered jar in refrigerator.
- Fruit juice.
- Fruit milk. Puree chunks of pineapple or banana in blender. Use in breads, puddings, or other desserts.
- Goat's milk.

- Nut or seed milk. Soak one-half cup of nuts or seeds in one cup liquid (water or juice) overnight. With blender or food processor, blend to taste. Add enough liquid to paste for desired consistency.
- Soy milk. Gradually add one quart soy flour to four cups water in blender. Strain. In double boiler, heat drippings 15 minutes, stirring frequently. Refrigerate until needed. (See also "Recipes for Day 4, 8, 12, Etc."
- Soybean milk. Soak one and one-half pounds dried soybeans in spring water for 12 hours. Drain. While grinding beans in grinder, slowly and steadily pour in one gallon of water. Heat to 131° F. Put into clean cloth bag and allow to drip. Put drippings in double boiler and heat for 45 minutes, stirring often. Sweeten to taste. Add enough water to make 5 quarts and refrigerate.
- Vegetable milk. In blender, puree peeled zucchini or cucumber and use for baking. You may need to use a bit more liquid or less flour than the recipe calls for.

Egg. Substitute two tablespoons water, one tablespoon oil, and two teaspoons baking powder for one egg.

Flour. For baking, one cup of white or wheat flour is equal to any of the following:

- 1 1/4 c rye flour
- 5/8 c potato flour
- 1/2 c barley flour
- 3/4 c soy flour—reduce baking temperature 25° F.
- 3/4 c corn meal
- 1 1/2 c ground rolled oats
- 7/8 c rice flour

As a thickening agent, one tablespoon flour is equal to any of the following:

- 1 1/2 t cornstarch
- 1 1/2 t potato flour
- 1 1/2 t tapioca flour
- 1 1/2 t arrowroot flour

Salad Dressing. Use sea salt, oil, lemon juice, or vinegar, either singly or combined. (E.g., for French dressing, blend one-quarter cup lemon juice or vinegar, three-quarters cup oil, one-half teaspoon salt, pinch of herbs.)

Vanilla Extract. Substitute one-quarter teaspoon dried ground vanilla bean for one teaspoon vanilla extract. Or place a vanilla bean in quart jar filled with flour and leave for at least a week (the longer the better). Use in recipes calling for both vanilla and flour.

Food Preparation

As a food sensitive person, what you may miss most is the convenience of prepared foods. Without commercially packaged foods, it is difficult to throw together a quick meal. Although it may not be so simple as buying frozen dinners at the supermarket, you can speed up your food preparation time by organizing your shopping and your kitchen. To save time, you can cook in large quantities and freeze meal-sized packages.

The first step toward making the diet easier is to go through your kitchen cupboards and refrigerator, discarding the prepared and processed foods you no longer need. You may find it helpful to separate your cupboards, pantry, refrigerator, and freezer into four areas, one for each day of the rotation diet.

Plan ahead by deciding what staples you need to begin the diet. You will probably want to buy some foods in bulk depending on how long they can be stored. Following are some staples you will need to begin the rotation diet (depending on your sensitivities):

- A variety of dried beans;
- A variety of grains and flours such as wheat (whole grain and flour), corn (cornmeal, corn grits, and popping corn), rye (flour), millet, barley, amaranth (flour and puffed), quinoa (whole grain and flour), rice (brown, white, wild, or rice flour), buckwheat (groats), oats (rolled and flour), teff, and spelt;
- Four or more different starches;
- Four or more different oils;
- Four or more different nuts and seeds;
- Vitamin C crystals (*non*-buffered);
- A variety of dried fruits (if permitted).

Plan meals in advance. Set aside time each week to prepare several meals at one time. To reduce daily preparation time, freeze in individual portions. Whenever possible, use the open-freeze method. On a cookie sheet or in a large pyrex baking dish, place your food in a single layer and quick-freeze before packaging, preferably in glass or cellophane. If you are not extremely sensitive, try aluminum foil.

Open Freezing

Combining Foods. When cooking in quantity, cook each food individually and freeze separately. Combine foods only after they are defrosted and ready to eat for maximum flexibility, as you may wish to change rotation. Also, there is a possibility you could become allergic to a food once considered safe.

Flours and Starch. Buy in bulk quantities, then freeze for 48 hours and defrost. Stored in tightly capped glass containers, they will keep for months.

Fruits. The healthiest and most enjoyable way to eat fruits is when they are fresh. But because of the increasing cost of fruits (particularly organic fruits), it is wise to buy in quantity when they are in season and freeze them. Unless you have a shortage of freezer space, do not can fruits because the heating process destroys much of their nutritional value.

You must acquire a taste for some frozen fruits such as bananas. Many people say they enjoy them while still partially frozen. You can make a delicious fruit shake by placing frozen fruit and a juice in a blender.

Some fruits you can wash and freeze whole: apples, apricots, blueberries, cherries, grapes, peaches, pears, persimmons, and plums. To prevent discoloration in apples, peaches, or pears that have been cut, dip in a brine solution of sea salt and well water.

To freeze pineapple or melons, peel and core or remove seeds. Divide oranges into sections.

To freeze bananas, buy them in quantity when green. When they are very ripe and will no longer keep, peel, slice, and put in blender, first at low speed, then at high. Spoon into pint jars and freeze. Defrost just enough to be edible for best taste and combine with chopped nuts.

You can open-freeze very ripe, peeled, whole bananas. Defrost only enough to slice, as taste is best when still frozen. Nuts on cold bananas are a great substitute for an ice cream sundae.

Herbs. If you are sensitive to molds, use only fresh herbs. Growing your own is easy, or buy them in large quantities at the height of the season. Herbs that freeze well are dill, tarragon, oregano, and mint. Others may also work well.

Wash them and pat them dry on a cotton or linen towel. Cut into one-half inch pieces, keeping the leaves and finer stems and discarding the rest. Open-freeze so you can take out small quantities as needed.

Leftover Vegetables. Arrange leftovers in individual portions, wrap, and freeze. Use as soon as possible in salads or for the next rotated meal. Marinate if you wish. Freeze vegetable juice in small cubes and place in a cellophane bag or in wide-mouth jars for later use in stews and soups.

Liquids. Always cool liquids before pouring them into freezer containers. Fill glass jars half full to allow for expansion. As an alternative juice container, use two cellophane bags, one inside the other and close with a rubber band or twist tie. Freeze immediately. The bags can tear easily, so handle with care. Place in a bowl to thaw, as the cellophane occasionally weakens and may leak.

You can also freeze fruit juices, meat and vegetable juices, or stock in ice cube trays. Then store in cellophane bags or glass jars. (See Appendix E.)

Meat slices. Place slices of meat one layer deep on a cookie sheet and quick-freeze before packaging. This prevents them from sticking together after freezing, allowing you to store all slices in one bag and later to remove one serving at a time.

Nuts. Freeze nuts in their shells or shelled to save space. They will keep as long as two years in the freezer. Place them in restaurant carry-out cartons or glass jars.

Nuts are an excellent source of protein, calcium, and energy for those who can tolerate them. Mold-sensitive patients may have a problem, although freezing does help retard the growth of mold. One possible solution is to heat nuts before eating them. Steaming works best.

To grind quantities of nuts, seeds, or coconut for freezing, a Vita-Mix 3600 food processor is a worthwhile investment. The money you save by making your own nut, seed, and peanut butters will pay for it.

Vegetables. The following vegetables can be sliced or cubed for cooking, arranged in a single layer on a cookie sheet, and frozen quickly. Blanching is not necessary. As soon as they are frozen, place in an appropriate container and use as needed.

carrots	nutmeats
celery	onions
celery leaves (chopped)	parsley
chives	parsnips
corn (remove from cob)	peas
green beans	rhubarb
green pepper	shell beans
herbs (fresh, chopped)	squash

COOKING METHODS

Meat

Organically grown meats are the best choice. If you must compromise because of expense or availability, be selective in buying meats at your regular market. Buy lean meat or meat from grass-fed animals, not prepackaged meat, thus decreasing your intake of additives.

Avoid meats from animals injected with hormones and antibiotics. Before cooking remove all fat because that is where most of the pesticides are located. It is more difficult to avoid antibiotics, as they are distributed throughout the meat.

Moist heat works better for less tender meats. Cook all meats at a low temperature for optimum tenderness, flavor, and nourishment; less shrinkage; and no burned pan drippings.

Boiling. Never boil meat; "simmer" it with the temperature of the liquid never going above 185° F. With higher temperatures the meat will be stringy, dry, and tough. Add salt only when the meat is ready to serve. To receive the full nutritional value, use leftover liquid for gravy, stock, or as a drink mixed with vegetable juice.

Liquid Cooking or Stewing. Cut meat into small pieces of one inch or smaller. Cover with liquid and simmer until done. Do not boil. Simmering temperature is below 185° F.

If you are rotating foods, do not cook meat and vegetables together if you plan to freeze either of them for future use. You may wish to change the rotation next time you eat them.

Pot Roast. Add three to four cups of boiling liquid (water, milk, tomato juice, vegetable juice, or cube-frozen gravy) to pot roast, enough to cover bottom of pan.

Chemically sensitive persons often react to fats subjected to high temperatures because fats separate into glycerol and the glycerol into the toxin acrolein. To pot roast meat means braising or searing at a high heat; thus, it is better to make pot roasts in a crock pot for better taste and healthfulness.

Roasting. After meat has defrosted in the refrigerator for at least 24 hours, place it with the (formerly) fat side up, uncovered, on a rack in a low-sided pan, in a preheated oven at 325° F. Add no water. Insert a meat thermometer in the thickest part of the meat (do not touch a bone). Cook until the temperature is right for the degree of doneness you prefer. Turn at least once during cooking if meat is boneless or very large.

It is better to cook exotic roasts such as venison or moose in a covered roaster with water for a longer period of time. Place meat on a rack above the water if possible.

To test meat for doneness without a thermometer, pierce with a skewer. If the juice runs red, it is rare; if pink, medium rare. If the juice is not red, but brown, the meat is well done, except for pork or poultry.

Steaming. Steaming is a much healthier cooking method than frying or broiling. To steam meat, place a stainless steel baking rack in a covered roasting pan with water up to but not touching the meat. You can bake or steam a large roast or fowl in the oven at 250° F. overnight and have it ready for breakfast.

Fish and Seafood

Frying and broiling are not healthy cooking methods; steaming is much better. Use the same process as for steaming meat. The ten-inch Corning Ware baking dish with cover is ideal for steaming (poaching) fish. Test after five to eight minutes (depending on the thickness of the fish); do not overcook. The fish is ready to eat when it flakes off easily with the gentle touch of a fork.

Hint: Use boiling water in the bottom of the pan and place in a preheated oven. This will both save time and decrease the amount of time the fish is exposed to heat.

Vegetables

Eat raw vegetables as frequently as possible unless your doctor advises against it. If you do cook vegetables, observe the following suggestions to assure that they are not overdone, waterlogged, colorless, and tasteless.

Water. Add as little water as possible to vegetables and save all leftover liquid. Freeze in small cubes to use in soup, stews, gelatin for salad, or beverage.

Cook Very Briefly. When just tender, as soon as you can pierce with a fork, remove from heat and serve immediately.

Peel Only If Necessary. Leave skin on unless it is tough, bitter, or too rough to clean well. Vitamins, minerals, and flavor are concentrated just under the skins of fruits and vegetables. However, if you don't like the skin, you can remove it more easily after cooking with less waste of both vegetables and nutrition. With raw vegetables such as cucumbers, begin by leaving some of the skin on and gradually increasing the amount until your taste buds learn to enjoy the most wholesome part of the vegetable.

Root vegetables accumulate mold very quickly, so if you are extremely sensitive to mold, avoid preparing them yourself. Unfortunately, mold sensitive people cannot eat the skins of root vegetables. If someone else peels them, you may be able to eat the inside of the vegetable.

Always Refrigerate Vegetables Until Use. Keep vegetables covered and use them as soon as possible before food value is lost.

Cover while cooking. To cut down contact with oxygen cover during cooking, as well as for storage.

Seasoning. Season just before serving, after cooking is finished.

Avoid Reheating. Use cold, cooked vegetables in salads.

The basic cooking methods for vegetables are as follows:

Pressure Cooking. Follow manufacturer's directions for pressure cooker. Cooking time must be very precise to avoid overcooking. Use very little water and bring to a boil before adding vegetables.

Raw Fruits and Vegetables. As mentioned earlier, unless your doctor recommends otherwise, eat foods raw whenever possible. Heat destroys many nutrients, especially high heat. Use our recipes for such foods as baked apples only occasionally, and gradually develop a taste for raw fruits and vegetables. Many traditionally cooked vegetables actually taste better raw.

Steam (Waterless Cooking). Steaming is the best way to cook vegetables. Place a small amount of water in a heavy saucepan and preheat using low heat and keeping it tightly covered. Place the vegetables on a rack above the water level or in a stainless steel steam basket inside the pan. This keeps the nutrients and flavor in the food instead of being lost in the water. Leave vegetables whole and unpeeled whenever possible and cook only until fork tender. Shred or grate chilled vegetables and steam quickly for a tasty dish.

Sprouts

Seeds That May Be Sprouted. (See Appendix for sources of sprouting seeds.) Alfalfa (41), beans (41), cereal grain (6), red clover (41), cress (36), fenugreek (41), lentils (41), mung beans (41), Oats (6), parsley (65), dried peas (41), radishes (41), and rye (6). Most other seeds that will grow may be sprouted, too.

Why Sprout Seeds? Seeds are more easily digested when sprouted and nutritional value increases. Sometimes patients who are allergic to certain seeds can tolerate them when sprouted.

How To Grow Sprouts. Be sure to select good quality seeds that have not been sprayed or treated with chemicals. Use a one- or two-quart wide-mouth jar. Put one level tablespoon of alfalfa seeds or two level tablespoons of mung beans or other large seeds in jar with a tight lid and cover with several inches of lukewarm water. Place a piece of cheesecloth or a fine stainless steel screen over the mouth of the jar and secure with a rubber band or a canning ring.

Place seeds in a dark cupboard and allow to soak for about five hours or overnight. Drain and rinse well. Then lay jar on its side in a rather dark place for a couple of days. But be sure to rinse with lukewarm water (flood) and drain well two or three times daily. *Rinsing is an important key to good sprouts. As the seeds produce heat and waste during germination. they need to be cooled and washed at least twice a day.*

It is very important to keep sprouts warm and moist all the time, but not wet. Too much heat may result in molding, while cold retards growth. About the fourth day, leaves will begin to show. At this point place the jar near a window for more vitamin A and chlorophyll. Sprouts are ready to use when two green leaves have opened out fully.

One-fourth cup mung beans will give you about two cups of bean sprouts.

When to Eat Sprouts. Alfalfa sprouts are best when one to two inches long; this takes about five days. Mung beans taste best at one and one-half to three inches long, which takes about four to five days. Lentil sprouts are ready to eat in 36 hours when they are about one inch long. Sunflower seed sprouts are best when no longer than the seed. Pea and soybean sprouts taste good whether short or long. When sprouts reach the desired stage, put into a glass jar and keep in refrigerator. If properly covered, they will keep for several days, but one week is the maximum storage time.

Alfalfa Sprouts. Always eat them raw. Mix a handful with a favorite spread such as tahini (sesame butter), mayonnaise, or tofu for a snack. Or add to salads, soup, or stew just before serving.

Lentils Sprouts. Add to soups just before serving. You may eat them plain, with herbs, diced onions, or any seasoning of the day.

Mung Bean Sprouts. These taste like raw fresh pod peas and are one of the highest vegetable proteins. Add to omelets or soups of the day.

Peanut Butter. Buy pure peanut butter with peanut oil, if oil is added. Better yet, make your own. It is usually cheaper and much safer. (See recipe for nut butter.)

Warning: Mold and Chemicals

Diagnosing food allergies can be complicated by mold on food skins. You may test negative to your doctor's provocative testing but react to the food at home. Read about provocative testing in "Sex in the Clean Bedroom," or for an in-depth explanation, see the books, *Chemical Sensitivities* by William Rea, M.D.; *Is This Your Child?* by Doris Rapp, M.D.; or *Relief at Last* by Joseph Miller, M.D.

How to deal with sensitivity to mold depends on the degree of sensitivity. Some patients must wear a mask and wash the vegetables thoroughly, while others must have someone else do the washing. Those with high sensitivity need to have someone else wash, peel, and dispose of the peelings from this type of vegetable. The biggest danger of mold comes from root vegetables that mature underground, such as carrots, potatoes, and yams. Other threats come from dried foods such as fruits or herbs. Use only fresh or frozen foods if you are sensitive to molds.

Chemical Sensitivity. *There could be another reason for reacting to a food to which you are not allergic. You could be allergic to chemicals* in the food or chemicals that were used to grow the foods.

Time and Money Savers

Fast Food. Cooking with a crock pot is a great way to save time. Wash and season your meat the night before. When you wake up, put it into your crock pot on high for about an hour. Be sure to turn it to low before you leave the house.

When you return, it is ready to eat. You can even place the vegetables in the crock pot with your meat if you wish. Crock pot cooking is not only convenient, but cooking at a low speed is thought to be healthier.

You will discover other ways of saving time and money as you gain more experience with the program. One good way is to buy when prices are low, and cook and freeze in large quantities.

15

CHANGING YOUR EATING HABITS

Modifying Your Diet

Diet modification is an important step for all health-oriented individuals. It can help prevent sensitivities or, for those who have mild allergies, it can help prevent additional trouble. If you or a family member have food sensitivities, diet modification gives the option of easing into dietary changes.

DON'T TRY TO BE A ONE HUNDRED PERCENTER who must do it all or nothing. You can be as flexible as you wish when you start to change your diet, making it easier for you to incorporate changes acceptable to you and your family. Begin to modify your eating habits by cutting back.

Sugars. Nutritional experts usually recommend cutting back on any form of sugar, especially crystallized sugars. When you cook, substitute honey, maple syrup, or a grain syrup such as corn, rice, sorghum, or molasses for sugar. Gradually begin to cut back on these, too. Dates, figs, raisins, and coconuts are the best substitutes for sugar, however, persons who have a yeast problem should avoid these completely. As you reduce your intake of sweeteners your need for them will also decrease and you will be able to enjoy instead the natural sweetness of fresh fruit instead of dried for snacks and desserts.

Cooking. Cutting back on cooking, unless there is a medical reason for cooking your foods, will help preserve the taste and nutrients in the vegetables and fruits. See "Food Rotation" for ideas for a nutritious approach to cooking. As you learn to enjoy eating raw broccoli, cauliflower, and spinach, you will want to use the salad suggestions in the recipe sections.

Junk Food. Cut back on junk food. Substitute nuts, sunflower seeds, roasted soy beans, and dried fruits for candies. Buy pure popping corn to make your own wholesome popcorn. If you buy corn chips or potato chips buy brands which use pure safflower or canola oil, contain no additives or preservatives, and are packaged instead of canned. Instead of buying soft drinks and fruit drink buy pure fruit juice or low salt, natural sparkling waters.

Refined grains. Most of the nutrients have been removed from refined grains; although some nutrients are added to enriched grains, these manufactured nutrients can be harmful. Learn instead to use whole wheat, whole rice, and other whole grains.

Salt. Because salt places unnecessary stress on your system, we recommend that you become less dependent on it by gradually reducing your consumption. Herbs make a tasty seasoning alternative.

You will note that we have recommended cutting out the worst diet offenders—refined sugars and grains, preservatives (especially nitrates, BHA and BHT), and artificial flavors and colors. This book places more emphasis on how to change than on the reasons to change. You can find a detailed explanation in the book *Chemical Sensitivities* by co-author William Rea, M.D. or *Is This Your Child* by Doris Rapp, M.D. (See Appendix F.) Learning more about food allergies will help in your commitment to diet modification.

Eating out. This presents some problems in changing your dietary habits, but even here you do have choices. For example, instead of French fries, which may have been treated with preservatives, are highly salted, and are usually fried in unsafe fats, you can order a baked potato.

Prepackaged foods. This is another area where you can cut back. If you do use them read the labels carefully to omit those with chemicals, additives, or preservatives. You should know, however, that even when the food is pure, packaging may not be. For example, the insides of cans are often treated with the preservative phenol.

Misleading Labels

Nickel in Food. The Food and Drug Administration (FDA) does not regulate the term "natural" in foods, so it is possible for some manufacturers to label a food "natural" even though the food contains hydrogenated oil or margarine or most companies process it with the use of nickel.

Monosodium Glutamate (MSG). The FDA does regulate labeling MSG on packaging, however, it is possible to find on labels the words "natural flavoring" without any further explanation. That natural flavoring could contain MSG. Fortunately, since Ed Bradley on the CBS program "60 Minutes" started the expose on MSG problems, the FDA is now investigating this. Be very cautious until the problem is solved.

Sulfites. Although FDA regulates the amount of sulfites in food and requires labelling for them, food can contain hidden sulfites. For example, in a processed food the label can list among the ingredients wine vinegar. However, it does not list the ingredients of the wine vinegar and this can contain sulfites.

Easing Into Rotation

Rotating the food families that you eat clears your system of food to which you are mildly allergic while preserving your tolerance for foods to which you are not allergic. It also prevents any new allergies developing from overexposure to any one food. If it is difficult for you to change a lifelong eating pattern, you may wish to ease into rotation instead of making a dramatic change.

Because foods come in families an allergy to one food may likely carry over to the rest of the family. An allergy to zucchini, for example, may mean that you also react to cantaloupe, a member of the same food family. (See Appendix C, *"Daily Food Charts."*)

To begin make note of the first categories: Animal Protein, Vegetables, and Fruits. Start with animal protein; you can rotate vegetables and fruits later when you are ready. Choosing from the more familiar proteins in the chart you could select from the following:

Day 1 — Monday: Cheese, milk, cod fish, haddock, or beef.
Day 2 — Tuesday: Tuna, carp, or turkey.
Day 3 — Wednesday: Trout, perch, salmon, ham, or pork (uncured).
Day 4 — Thursday: Sole, flounder, halibut, eggs, or chicken.

Unless fish is the only animal protein you can eat, eat fish every other day selecting from the choices given for each day. In "Cooking Hints and Substitutions" you will find some suggestions on preparing these foods.

Food Rotation Made Easy. Acceptance of rotating food by family members can be difficult. One way around this is to educate the family about good eating habits. It is also wise to involve the whole family in the rotation and not just the individual who is "sick."

The order of the rotation can be changed as long as you take into consideration the facts we used in preparing the rotation. Good nutrition was our primary objective, and we designed the rotation so that the daily diet was balanced and the four-day rotation provided the required nutrition.

Every day contains a green leafy vegetable, a yellow vegetable, fruit, and protein. The two families highest in vitamin C — the potato family and citrus fruits — are on different days. Likewise, the two foods highest in vitamin A — carrots and apricots — are separated. Each day also contains seeds and nuts, fats and oils, herbs and spices, beverages, and a starch for making sauces and puddings. A sweetener has been included each day although we recommend that the amount be reduced each time so you can gradually lose your taste for sweets.

Eliminating Name Confusion. We have placed some foods together to make the system easier to understand. Although technically silver perch belongs to one family and white perch to another we have treated them as one family. The same situation exists with arrowroot; although it may come from eight different sources we have treated it as one family and put all of them on one day.

Taste Appeal. Another consideration in this rotation was taste appeal; traditional combinations such as cranberries and turkey are on the same day. Another factor we considered was including cheese and yeast—mold products—on the same day; that same day also includes beef and goat since cheese is a milk product. This facilitates recipes for wholesome spaghetti and pizza. This gives you an idea of the complexity of factors we considered in drawing up this rotation.

Simplifying Rotation : Inventing Your Own Recipes. One approach to rotating multiple food meals is building the recipe around the foods available on a particular day. Example # 1, vegetable salads, illustrates this approach.

Example #1 — Vegetable Salads

These can be simple or varied but they should always contain a leafy green vegetable and/or sprouts. To limit the food families used per meal you may use vegetables from one family.

One-Food Family. On day 3 combine endive, lettuce, sunflower seeds (also sprouted), Jerusalem artichoke, the herb tarragon, and sunflower or safflower oils.

Two-Food Families: Cabbage, cauliflower, and radishes, from Day 4, make a good combination. Add another family, sesame seeds and oil, to give you extra protein.

Four-Food Families: Substitute canola oil, omitting sesame oil and seeds. Now you can add two new families by making mayonnaise with the canola oil, mustard (both from the cabbage family), and adding lemon and egg. Chopped egg and diced cold chicken can be added; without increasing the number of families you have a satisfying and filling main dish. Staying within these four families you can serve grapefruit as an appetizer and oranges for dessert.

Change your pattern. Adding one more family, the Lily Family, allows you to use asparagus as the vegetable, the salad above as a side dish, and add baked chicken and garlic- or onion-flavored chicken soup. One substitution for the recipe already given shows how you can work within the rotation and change food families. If you substitute peanut oil (peanuts are from the legume family) you open up a wide number of possibilities. You can add alfalfa sprouts and/or cold cooked beans to the salad and noodles made with peanut starch to the chicken soup. Carob cookies (see recipes Day 4, 8, 12, etc.) can be served with the oranges for dessert.

Using the foods of the day, you can follow this example on any day of the rotation.

Example #2 — Fish of the Day

Unless you are sensitive to all other animal protein and must eat fish every day, eat fish every other day. If you eat fish every other day combine Day 1 and Day 3; also combine Day 2 and 4. Check any given recipe to be sure you are not breaking rotation. Certain days contain specific recipes but the ingredients of the day can be used to change or spice up the fish.

Baked Fish

*3 lbs fillet of fish of
  the day
4-6 c mixed vegetables of
  the day*

*1/2 to 1 c water
2 T herb of the day
salt to taste before serving*

Preheat oven to 350 F. In baking dish add vegetables to one cup boiling water. Put the fish on top, sprinkling it with herbs. Fish is done when it flakes easily with a fork. If additional water is needed make sure it is boiling.

For instructions on steaming fish or seafood see "Cooking Hints and Substitutions." Steamed fish may be served plain, with an oil/herb dressing, a garnish, or a dressing from the recipes of the day.

Good combinations:

Day 1 — cod, haddock, shrimp, or lobster with avocado dressing or rice oil or corn oil seasoned with bay leaf, basil, sage, savory, or a combination of these.

Day 2 — tuna, chub, or carp with apricot oil, almond oil, or olive oil seasoned with allspice or with olive oil dressing.

Day 3 — bass, perch, trout, croaker, or walleye with saffloweroil seasoned with kelp, dill, or tarragon.

Day 4 — flounder, halibut, sole, or turbot with peanut oil or sesame oil seasoned with chives.

Example #3 — Dried Fruits of the Day

Dried fruits have a very high sugar content and should be avoided in a yeast free diet. If you intend to try them, first bake, steam, or stew them. To stew them, use only enough water to cover them, and simmer for 10 or 15 minutes. To steam use a steamer basket, cover tightly, and steam until tender. For additional variety stuff fruit with other fruit or nuts of the day.

Example #4 — Fruit Butter

Peel, remove seeds, and cut into quarters any fruit of the day. Berries and other small fruit may be used whole. Use an oil of the same family as the fruit or an oil of the day to lightly grease a crock pot and place the fruit in pot leaving at least an inch clear on top. You may add about 1 teaspoon of an herb or spice of the day if you wish. Simmer on low until it is the texture of apple butter (usually 24 hours or more). If you wish, sweeten just before using with the sweetener of the day. Some delicious choices are:

Day 1:   Apple or pear with cinnamon.

Day 2:   Blueberry with maple syrup or ginger, peach with banana, cherry with banana and/or ginger.

Day 3:   Strawberry, raspberry or blackberry with coconut, nutmeg and/or date sugar.

Fruit butter can be canned by filling sterilized Mason jars, closing top tightly, and placing them on a rack in a pan of boiling water. Be sure water is about an inch above the jars, cover, and boil for 10 minutes.

Example #5 — Nuts of the Day

Hardshell nuts (butternuts, Brazil nuts, filberts, walnuts, pecans) can be shelled more easily when you pour boiling water over the nuts and leave them for 15 minutes. When shelled a pound of nuts yields about a half pound of nut meats.

Example #6 — Nut or Seed Butter

1 c nuts or seeds of the day

1 T oil of the day
herb of the day (optional)

In a grinder, blender, or food processor, process until it has a smooth consistency, and refrigerate or freeze. Naturally, use almond oil with almonds, sesame oil with sesame seeds, sunflower oil with sunflower seeds. Otherwise, choose a mild oil for the seeds or nuts. For example, your choices of oils on Day 2 to use with pumpkin seeds are apricot, almond, or olive. The best selections are apricot or almond oils rather than the stronger-tasting olive oil.

Example #7 — Nut or Seed Fruit Cheese

1 lb dried, seeded fruit of the day

1/2 lb nuts or seeds of the day

Process the fruit and nuts or seeds in a grinder, blender, or food processor until very fine. Mix well and press mixture firmly in a glass baking dish between 1/4 to 1 inch thick. Cover and allow to dry for 2 or 3 days and then cut into small strips. Additional ground nuts or seeds may be rolled in.

Example #8 — Nut or Seed Fruit Pie

The crust can be made with any nut or seed of the day that has been blended or processed into a meal. Soft nuts like cashews should be processed on chop speed and hard nuts on grind speed. (For this procedure a food processor works faster than a blender.) The nuts nearest the blade lump together and contain more oil; use these for the bottom crust adding additional oil if needed. Use the drier nuts for the top crust.

Press oily nuts or seeds into sides and bottom of a greased pie plate. The best thickness is 1/4 inch although some people favor a thinner crust. (Eight full teaspoons will provide a generous crust for a small deep dish pie while about two cups are required for a nine-inch pie.) Press the oily nuts firmly into plate with a spoon and thumbs until you have the thickness you prefer. If too much oil has been added use additional nut meal.

Filling:

2 c liquid of the day
  optional:

2 T starch of the day
fresh or frozen fruit of the day
1 T sweetener of the day
(avoid on a low yeast diet)

Liquid used may be any juice of the day (for citrus a different recipe is needed), a stewed fruit, and/or defrosted frozen fruit which is soaking in its own juice. The best four thickeners for fillings are arrowroot, tapioca, cornstarch, and potato starch. Other starches that may be used are rice flour, rye flour, and artichoke flour.

Mix liquid and starch thoroughly and heat at medium temperature stirring constantly to prevent burning. Remove from heat when thick. Tapioca is a starch that thickens after removal from heat. (The best way to thicken filling is to use a double boiler.) When filling is cool pour it over the bottom crust; you may wish to leave space for fresh fruit. Crushed dry nuts, seeds, coconut, or meringue (on your egg day) may be placed on top. Cover the pie to keep the topping from browning before the pie is baked.

Preheat oven to 400° F. and bake for 20 to 40 minutes or until bottom crust has browned lightly.

Some suggested tasty combinations:

	Day 1	Day2	Day3
Crust:	Pecans	Almonds	Filberts
Liquid:	Apple Juice	Cherry, apricot or peach juice	Strawberry juice
Oil:	Walnut	Almond	Sunflower
Starch:	Potato or corn	Arrowroot	Agar-Agar
Sweetener:	Partially cooked sweet apples, or grain syrup (cinnamon optional	Cherries or peaches, maple syrup	Strawberries, date sugar, or coconut

For Day 3 follow directions on agar-agar (sometimes called agar) package.

Example #9 — Nut or Seed Fruit Pudding

To make an easy variation of the pie in Example #8, make the pie filling recipe for the day and add chopped nuts or fruit of the day just before serving.

Example #10 — Nut or Seed Milk

1 part nuts or seeds of the day   1 part water or juice of the day

Mix and soak 24 to 48 hours. Pour liquid off, reserving it, and blend nuts on low as for nut or seed butter using reserved liquid instead of oil. Add the remaining liquid when smooth; add additional liquid if it is still too thick.

Optional: Sweeten to taste or season with an herb of the day.

NOTE: Some people like to strain the milk or use the leftovers on recipes that call for nuts or seeds.

Example #11 — Nut or Seed/Starch Pancake (Blender)

1 c starch of the day   Liquid as needed (water or
1 c seeds or nuts of the day   nut milk of the day)

Begin blending mixture at low speed and gradually increase the speed as liquid is added. Note: Because this recipe has no leavening the pancake will be flatter than normal and the batter should be thicker than normal. You will need to experiment for the right consistency but remember that adding liquid is easier than adding dry mixture. When possible, use the oil of the seed or nut in the pancake to grease the griddle. For example, use almond oil with almonds, sunflower oil with sunflower seeds. Otherwise any oil of the day may be used.

Example #12 — Popsicle of the Day

1 pint of any juice or combination of juices of the day

Place ice cube tray filled with juice in freezer. After juice begins to solidify place wooden uncolored, unflavored toothpick into each cube. After about 24 hours when they are quite solid, remove from the tray and put in a glass jar. Both children and adults can enjoy an unlimited number of wholesome popsicles.

Example #13 — Soup of the Day

Using your imagination, select a mammal or fowl of the day and combine the meat and bones (for stock) with a few teaspoons of some herbs of the day to prepare a hot soup that will warm up any cold day. For variation, add several vegetables of the day for a filling soup that can be a meal in itself.

Example #14 — E-Z Tortillas of the Day

These quick and easy tortillas are satisfying to eat, work well for "brown-bag" lunches (packing topping separately), and freeze well. A variety of grains can be used to suit your preferences and tolerances.

1 1/4 c of any flour of the day:
 corn, millet, oat, rye, wheat, amaranth, milo, buckwheat, quinoa
1/4 t salt
1/2 c water at room temperature
1/2 t to 1 t oil of the day
 (Optional with this exception: required with quinoa and millet)

In a bowl whisk 1 cup of flour and salt together. Pour the oil and water into a "well" in the center of flour mixture and stir several times until the dough clumps together in a ball.

Preheat a large griddle or two skillets. Sprinkle the rest of the flour on a bread board. Break off golf-ball-sized portions of dough, roll them in flour, and flatten with your hand, turning frequently to keep them floured. The texture becomes more workable as the dough soaks up flour. Further thin tortillas with a rolling pin; when they are quite thin and six to seven inches across, check to see that they are well floured on both sides. Using no oil, bake them on the hot griddle one or more at a time.

Bake about three minutes on each side and place baked tortillas on wire racks or cotton towels to cool. Once you are used to making and baking tortillas, you can do this quickly and easily. (Reprinted by permission from *Mastering Food Allergies.* See Appendix F.)

Example #15 — Substitute Slushies and Slurpies of the Day

These two commercial drinks that teenagers enjoy are usually partially frozen (like crushed ice), flavored, colored, and sugared drinks. To make a wholesome replacement, fill an ice cube tray (with dividers removed) or a flat dish with any fruit juice of the day and partially freeze. Stir frequently and serve when it reaches the consistency of crushed ice.

For variation add any tolerated carbonated water and an herb, spice, and/or sweetener of the day.

Example #16 — Trail Mix of the Day

Combine equal parts of two or more nuts of the day with equal parts of chopped dried fruit of the day. Note: Not recommended for people on a yeast free diet.

16 .

UNDERSTANDING THE FORMULA

In planning a rotation diet, the ideal would be to devise a universal system that could meet everyone's needs. However, because there are so many variables to consider, this was virtually impossible to achieve. So it was necessary to design an extremely flexible system. You may better understand the scope and versatility of the rotary diet by becoming aware of the complications in developing a formula.

Factors considered:

The individual's health: Are you a healthy person who is allergy prone; a mildly sensitive individual; a patient with food allergies; a patient with multiple sensitivities to food, inhalants, and chemicals; or a patient on the road to recovery?

The purpose of the diet: Is it for allergy prevention, diagnosis (allergy testing), treatment, or maintenance? The plan must allow for necessary dietary changes to accommodate the individual's changing food allergy tolerances.

Rotation Changes

Under certain circumstances you may want to make permanent dietary changes. Suppose you are allergic to one or more foods of every vegetable family listed for a particular day. Unless you made a permanent change, that would leave you with no vegetable on that day.

If all your favorite vegetables are listed for one day and all the ones you dislike on another day, you would want to adjust the diet. An exciting reason to make a temporary change is to provide maximum variety so that you can use any "from scratch" recipe without breaking your rotation.

How to Make Changes

To make changes you need to understand the numbering system we have given to the food families and how we use it.

Turn to Appendix A (List #1) and note that each food is accompanied by a number. There is no botanical reason for these numbers; you will not find them in a botany book. They have been assigned to families for your convenience in planning the rotation diet. Each food is listed in two ways, alphabetically with its corresponding food family number, and numerically with all the other foods in the same family listed under the family name.

Look under C in Appendix A and you will see the word "cabbage" preceded by the number "36." Then turn to Appendix B (List #2), the numerical list of food families, where you will find that "36" is the Mustard Family; you will then see all the foods that are in the same family as cabbage.

Whenever a member of the family appears on the diet chart, the numbers are repeated, simplifying food switches from one day to another.

Now turn to Appendix C. At the beginning of each day's food chart is a list of numbers of all the food families included that day, as well as corresponding numbers listed before each family in the day's listings.

Notice that all members of the same family are listed on the same day. See Day 1, Family #6. However, as previously noted, different foods within the same family (known as related foods) may be rotated every other day (i.e., wheat on Day 1, corn on Day 3).

By listing the entire family on the same day, you have the opportunity to choose which related foods you wish to separate—we don't make the decision for you. However, with our recipes we have frequently separated members of the same family, so, for example, you could have a wheat recipe on day 1 and a corn recipe on Day 3. Whenever we separate related foods, we refer you back to the formula.

Recommendations

To make simple alterations to the diet:
- Eat the same food item no oftener than once every four days. For example, if you eat rice on Monday, do not eat rice again until Friday.
- You may eat different foods from the same food family every other day. For example, if you eat wheat on Monday (Grass Family, #6), you may eat corn on Wednesday. Use this guideline for the Grass Family (grains): If you eat gluten-containing foods on Monday, select one of the three nongluten grains (rice, corn, or millet) on Wednesday.

Temporary Changes

Foods may be moved to other days if you also move the entire food family. For example:
- To move wheat (Grass Family) from Day 1 to Day 2, be sure to move the entire Grass Family to Days 2 and 4.
- You may interchange foods from Days 1 and 3 or Days 2 and 4. For example, if you move wheat (Grass Family) from Day 1 to Day 3, it is not necessary to move the food family since you are staying within the Grass Family. However, be sure not to repeat the same food two days later.

Do not repeat foods or food families twice in the same day unless at the same meal.

Permanent Changes

When you make a permanent change you must record an additional change in your chart. Look again at Appendix C. At the top of the food chart for Day 1, locate "Food Families Used." If you decide to move grains, "Family #6," to Day 2, be sure to remove the number "6" from the top of the page where all the food numbers for that day are listed, and add "6" to the list of numbers for the new day. This will ensure that your own charts are up to date.

When you first begin to make changes, it may seem very complex. But after working with it a few times, it will become as easy as any other meal planning system.

Keep in mind that the recipes refer to the numbering as we presented it, and that the same number system is used throughout the book.

ટ&ા ટ&ટ&

Before you begin working with the charts, a little
background. Because I had no prior knowledge of
botany, I struggled with the food families for 11
years, trying to make changes in my diet while
remaining on rotation. Without a knowledge of botany
and food families, I found it difficult to follow the
excellent chart of food families prepared by my
botanist, Jane Roller. Finally, for us lay people,
Jane agreed to my request to number the families
(List #2) and prepare the alphabetical listing using
the corresponding numbers as found in List #1.

Now imagine using List #2 without the numbers,
having to look through every family until you stumble
onto the correct food. That's what I (and the readers
of my 1969 book) had to do each time we added a new
food to our diets or made a change in our diets. Now,
thanks to Jane's help and my formula, all you have to
do is spend a little time practicing the formula.
Before long you'll be able to do it automatically.

ટ& ટ& ટ&

Easy Temporary Changes

You already know but it is worth repeating that you may interchange
foods from Days 1 and 3, or Days 2 and 4, so long as you do not repeat
the same food two days later.

The formula also allows you to change foods on days adjacent to each
other, i.e. Days 1 and 2, 2 and 3, 3 and 4, or 4 and 5, with Day 5 being a
repetition of Day 1. Whenever you wish to make temporary changes it is
best to plan ahead, checking your charts on the first day of any rotation
cycle.

For example, you might decide to eat maple syrup with your
buckwheat pancakes on Day 3. A check of the charts shows you that
maple syrup must be moved from Day 2 to Day 3. So you follow the
usual rotation except for omitting the Maple family (50) on Day 2. In
your next cycle return to the original rotation, eating maple syrup on Day
2 if you wish.

Or, in the event you want to add onions to the Day 1 spaghetti sauce
recipe (see "Recipe Day 1, 5, 9, Etc."), a check of the food chart tells you
that onions belong to the Lily family (11) and are included on Day 4. So
follow the rotation as outlined on Days 1, 2, and 3, but omit the Lily

family on Day 4 because you are switching onions from Day 4 to Day 1 of the next cycle.

CAUTION: If you are highly allergic to certain foods, or if you are moving foods for more than one day, omit the switched food family for two full cycles, one before and one following the switch.

By now it will be obvious that this approach to recipes and menus is very different from the average cookbook. Because foods cannot be repeated daily, conventional recipes are not available every day. The recipe section is divided into four chapters, with each chapter devoted to one day of the four-day cycle.

To help you through the transition period until you become accustomed to one-course meals, we have included suggestions to help you conform more closely to conventional meals. Later on you may become accustomed to eating one course meals such as a half pound of fish for breakfast, three papayas for lunch, or a pound of broccoli for dinner.

Remember, these menus are only suggestions to get you started. You can mix or match them to suit your own needs. You might wish to eat breakfast from one menu and lunch from another. Or you may want to omit those that take too much time and repeat the favorites or the easiest and least expensive ones.

Salt and Sweeteners

Manufactured foods have so much salt and sweeteners in them that the average consumer has difficulty giving them up. For this reason we reluctantly include these unhealthy ingredients in our recipes with the suggestion that you begin decreasing the amount you use. This will help you decrease your dependence on them and develop an appreciation for nature's flavors.

Organic Foods

We can never understand the public's reaction to pesticides. Many people protest the use of pesticides on lawns but still eat pesticide-filled commercial food instead of organic food. Isn't injesting worse than inhaling these poisons?

It's a well known disgrace that the government has been lax in warning us about cancer-causing toxic chemicals in our food. If you still have doubts about the hazards of non-organic foods, other than cancer, write to the U.S. General Accounting Office (GAO) for the "Report to the Chairman on Governmental Affairs, U.S. Senate: Reproductive and Developmental Toxins — Regulatory Action Provides Uncertain

Protection"; October 1991. It includes a list of 30 toxic chemicals not properly regulated in foods.

In addition to cancer, reproductive and developmental health problems, environmental medicine (EM) specialists have clinically identified many other problems stemming from toxic chemicals in foods—diabetes, arthritis, etc.

Begin your changeover to less-contaminated food AS SOON AS POSSIBLE. *(See B. Gordon's Market, Appendix E.)*

Unused Food Families

Not all of the 137 food families listed in Appendix A have been used in the food charts in Appendix B. These foods fall into several classes:

a) Non-edible plants: 15-orris, 38-yellow dye, 67-chicle.

b) Food or food factions that are not recommended: 5-gin, 12-tequila, 21-black and white pepper, 57-tea, 76-coffee, etc. If you use these occasionally, be sure to rotate your use.

c) Vegetables that add to a salad (mostly green leafy vegetables). This includes vegetables which grow wild or are available only in certain areas. If you want to use them, fit them into your charts on a day you can use an extra vegetable: 29-New Zealand spinach, 37-caper, 42-oxalis, 43-nasturtium, 78-fetticus, commonly known as corn salad.

d) Animal protein which is not widely available. Check Appendix A if you wish to add any of these to your charts: 84, 85, 86, 89, 90, 92, 93, 94, 95, 97, 99, 101, 104, 105, 108, 110, 116, 118, 119, and 128.

PART VI

ALLERGY FREE
COOKBOOK

17

MENUS AND RECIPES FOR DAYS 1, 5, 9, ETC.

Food Chart for Days 1, 5, 9, ETC.

Suggested Menus for Days 1, 5, 9, ETC.

Recipes for Days 1, 5, 9, ETC.

Beverages
Dairy and Dairy Substitutes
Dressings, Garnishes, Sauces, and Spreads
Fish, Fowl, and Meat
Grain and Grain Substitutes
Salads and Side Dishes
Snacks, Sweets and Desserts
Soups

See also recipe section in "Changing Your Eating Habits" and "Understanding the Formula."

FOOD CHART FOR DAYS 1, 5, 9, ETC.

Food Families: 2, 6, 22, 34, 35, 40a, 42, 46, 52, 61, 62, 73, 74, 82, 87, 88, 105, 112, 137.

Animal Protein: 82-Crab, crayfish, lobster, prawn, shrimp. 87-Cod, haddock. 88-Ocean catfish. 105-Herring, sardine. 112-Catfish species. 137-Beef (butter, cheese, kefir, milk, veal, yogurt), buffalo, goat, sheep (lamb, mutton).

Vegetables: 2-Mushroom, truffle. 6-Corn, bamboo shoots. 74-Eggplant, sweet pepper, potato, tomato.

Fruit: 34-Avocado. 40a-Apple, crabapple, loquat, pear, quince. 42-Carambola. 46-Acerola. 52-Dried currants, grape, raisin. 61-Pomegranate.

Seeds & Nuts: 22-Hickory nut, pecan, walnut. 62-Brazil nut.

Fats and Oils: 6-Corn oil, rice oil. 22-Walnut oil. 34-Avocado oil. 137-Butter and any fat from above.

Other: 2-Yeast. 6-Barley, bulgur, cornmeal, corn starch, millet, oats, oat flour, rice, rice flour, rye, rye flour, spelt, teff, wheat, wheat flour. 52-Cream of tartar. 74-Potato meal, potato starch.

Sweeteners: 6-Grain syrups: barley, corn, malt, molasses and sorghum. 52-Raisin.

Herbs and Spices: 6-Lemon grass. 34-Bay leaf, cassia, cinnamon. 35-Poppyseed. 73-Applemint, basil, mint, lemon balm, marjoram, oregano, peppermint, rosemary, sage, spearmint, summer savory, thyme, winter savory.

Beverages: Juice, soup, and tea from any of the above. 73-Tea from catnip, chia seed, dittany, horehound, hyssop, pennyroyal. 137-Milk.

SUGGESTED MENUS FOR DAYS 1, 5, 9, ETC.

Breakfast

Grape juice or grapes
Oatmeal with nut milk
Walnuts and/or raisins

Grape juice
Granola with milk or
Oatmeal with butter and
milk

Apple juice
Potato pancakes
Applesauce

Pears and/or pear juice
Rice pancakes with pear
sauce

Lunch

Sardines
Apples and apple juice
Avocado

Rice wafers or bread
Sardines
Pecans and/or raisins

Baking powder biscuits
Whole wheat, sprouted wheat
or batter bread
Cheese with wheat sprouts
Walnuts and dried currants
or raisins

Fruit salad with cottage
cheese
Applesauce cookies with milk

Dinner

Tomato juice
Raw tomatoes
Raw green peppers
Beef stew

Tomato juice
Stuffed peppers
Avocado, wheat sprouts
Popcorn for snack

Spanish rice, spaghetti
or pizza
Vegetable salad
Grape pie or applesauce
cake with milk

Hamburgers
Vegetable salad
Wheat balls
Milk shake

WARNING: Only the first suggestion follows the proper rotation plan. The three additional suggestions are for those people who are easing into rotation.

RECIPES FOR DAYS 1, 5, 9, ETC.

Beverages

BUTTERMILK

Powdered dry skim milk
Commercial buttermilk (unpasteurized)

Follow instructions for 1 quart skim milk using 1 cup less water than called for. Add 1 cup of commercial buttermilk, stirring well. This gives a source of preferred bacteria; from now on a cup of your own buttermilk will work as a starter. Add a dash of salt, stirring well, and let it set at room temperature for 24 hours. Stir before using.

MARJORAM MILK

For a late night soothing drink place a sprig of sweet marjoram in a cup of warm milk. May be sweetened to taste.

Dairy and Dairy Substitutes

BUTTERMILK

Powdered dry skim milk
Commercial buttermilk (unpasteurized)

Follow instructions for 1 quart skim milk using 1 cup less water than called for. Add 1 cup of commercial buttermilk, stirring well. This gives a source of preferred bacteria; from now on a cup of your own buttermilk will work as a starter. Add a dash of salt, stirring well, and let it set at room temperature for 24 hours. Stir before using.

COTTAGE CHEESE, HOMEMADE

Place sour milk over heat until the whey (clear liquid) comes to the top. Do not boil! Pour off the whey, place the curd into a cheese cloth bag and let it drip for six hours without squeezing the bag. Place it in a bowl and chop it to desired coarseness, adding salt to taste. If you wish add some cream or work mixture to the texture of soft putty or paste adding some cream and butter as needed. Shape into pats or balls and keep in a cool place. Best when fresh.

Variation: Fried Cheese (India-CHANNA): Instead of chopping curd, divide it into small cubes or slices and fry lightly at moderate heat until golden. Salt and serve. Eat plain or as a garnish over vegetables.

COTTAGE CHEESE, LOW FAT

Use buttermilk made with previous recipe and let it stand for 48 hours or
when the bottom third of liquid is clear (curds and whey). Without stirring
pour gently into cloth-lined colander and large strainer and let it drain. Use
this as cottage cheese.

MARJORAM MILK

For a late night soothing drink place a sprig of sweet marjoram in a cup of
warm milk. May be sweetened to taste.

YOGURT, HOMEMADE

2 c fresh cow's milk   *2 heaping T sour cream*

Heat milk over low heat until lukewarm. Take off heat, put into widemouth
jar, and add sour cream while stirring briskly. Cover and place in warm spot.
After mixture is thickened, chill for several hours or overnight and serve with
fruit or vegetables.

Dressings, Garnishes, Sauces, and Spreads

AVOCADO SALAD DRESSING

1 ripe avocado
4 T juice (sour grape or tomato)

Place cubed avocado into blender with juice and blend on medium. Add
more juice if needed to give consistency of mayonnaise. This can be used as
a mayonnaise substitute and is especially good with fish and seafood.

MINCED BASIL and MARJORAM

Minced basil and marjoram are excellent seasoning for hamburg croquettes.

MINT GARNISH

1/4 c shopped fresh mint   *1/2 c apple cider vinegar*
1 T grain syrup   *pinch of sea salt*

Mix together and let stand for several hours before use. Serve with roasts
(especially lamb).

MOLASSES BUTTER

2 c cooked apples   *1 c molasses*

Stir constantly over heat until it is thick and buttery. Good with pancakes.

SPAGHETTI MEAT SAUCE

3 T walnut oil
1/2 c chopped green peppers
1 lb fresh sliced mushrooms
salt and cayenne pepper to taste

2 1/2 c pressed, drained tomatoes
1 - 2 T basil, rosemary, and/or thyme
1 1/2 lbs ground beef
1 bay leaf (optional)

Saute green peppers and mushrooms in walnut oil. Add meat and saute until nearly cooked. Add tomatoes and seasoning and simmer uncovered 20 or 30 minutes. If more liquid is needed add 1/2 c hot beef stock or tomato juice. If thicker sauce is desired add 1/2 c homemade tomato paste.

Serve over spaghetti, noodles, rice, or wheat or rye sprouts.

Variations: Serve over steamed potatoes.
               Add seasoned meatballs and simmer for 30 minutes.

TOMATO PASTE

6 large ripe tomatoes
2 T melted butter or oil (corn
* or rice)*
1/4 t paprika

3/4 t sea salt
Optional: 1/2 t grain syrup (rice
* or malt, etc.)*

Cook all ingredients over low heat or double boiler, stirring constantly. When it is the consistency of thick paste, strain paste or blend at low speed.

TOMATO PASTE (Juicer)

When tomatoes and green peppers are juiced, save the pulp from the seeds and skins. Freeze in small portions and use as a paste for flavoring and thickening of tomato sauces.
  Also see Fish, Fowl, and Meat.

TOMATO PASTE or SAUCE (Blender)

2 parts tomatoes (fresh, frozen
* or home canned)*
1 part green pepper
* (fresh or frozen)*

Sea salt and cayenne pepper to taste
Optional: herb of the day

To use as a paste: Pour off excess juice and save to use for sauces. Blend on slow or puree. Core, skin, and seeds add flavor to paste or sauce.

To use as a sauce: Keep excess juice and process as above.

Fish, Fowl, and Meat

BEEF STEW, #1

Combine: Cubes of beef with potatoes and green peppers
Optional: Flavor with bay leaf or herbs from mint family.
Optional: Add mushrooms and/or tomatoes.

Simmer on low in crock pot for 6 to 8 hours.

BEEF STEW, #2

2 lbs beef stew meat   1 T potato starch
2 potatoes, cut into chunks   2 t sea salt
2 fresh sliced tomatoes   dash cayenne pepper
1/2 chopped green pepper   1/2 c cold water

Remove excess fat, cut meat into bite-sized pieces and brown. Place meat and water in covered pot and simmer for 30 minutes. Add potatoes and tomatoes and simmer for 30 more minutes. To prevent lumping, dissolve starch in 1/2 cup cold water and add slowly to stew stirring well. Season, stir, and serve.

COUNTRY PIE

1 - 1 1/2 lbs ground beef   2 T finely chopped green pepper
1 T finely chopped mint   4 or more c Spanish rice (see
1 t sea salt   below)

Preheat oven to 350°F. Mix beef, mint, green pepper, and salt; press into pie dish for a pie crust. Fill crust with Spanish rice. Cover with large ovenproof lid and bake for 25 minutes. Uncover and bake for 10 to 15 minutes longer. Serve with grated cheese (optional).

GAME MEAT SAUCE (SPECIAL FEATURE RECIPE)

2 quarts tomato juice or 1 quart   Oregano (1/2 t per lb of meat up
  whole tomatoes to 1 lb   to 1 1/2 t)
  ground meat   Green pepper to taste
(In large quantities use more   Basil (1/4 t per pound of meal)
meat in proportion to juice.)

Flake meat and mix ingredients together, cooking over medium heat until mixture comes to a boil. Simmer about 3 1/2 to 4 hours. May be frozen.

GNOCCHI

1/2 c melted suet, beef, or goat   1 t sea salt
   animal fat or butter   1/2 t paprika
2 c potato (riced or mashed)   1/2 c potato meal
1/2 t baking powder

Preheat oven to 400°F. Mix ingredients together well and roll into cylinders 1 1/2" in diameter. Chill and cut into 1/4" slices indenting with finger. Grease baking dish with oil of the day, put cylinders in baking dish with edges overlapping, and cover with meat or tomato sauce.

   Variation: Add herbs from mint family; rosemary and marjoram are a good combination.

LAMB CHOPS PARMIGIANA

2 lamb chops   2 slices goat's cheese
1/2 thinly sliced onion (Day 4*)

Broil chops for about seven minutes on each side. Put sliced onion on each chop and cover with cheese, broiling about two more minutes or until cheese melts. (*Use formula.)

LAMB PATTY

8 oz ground lamb   1/4 c chopped pecans or filberts
1 mashed potato   1/2 t sea salt

Mix ingredients together and shape into patties. Saute in skillet until meat loses pink color.

MEAT BALLS

1 lb ground meat   1 1/2 t sea salt
1/2 c raw rice   2 T fine chopped mint, if desired
2 - 4 t finely chopped green   3 1/2 c tomatoes
 pepper

Combine ingredients shaping into 8 to 12 balls. Brown in skillet, add tomatoes, and simmer 30 to 45 minutes until done or cook in pressure cooker for 20 minutes.

MEAT BALLS, SAVORY

1 1/2 lbs ground beef
3/4 c crumbled starch (walnuts
  or steamed potato)
1/4 c chopped green pepper
2 t salt

2 T butter
dash cayenne pepper
1 T basil
1 c tomato juice

Blend ground beef, starch, pepper, and spices. Shape into 2" balls and brown
in butter. On low heat cook approximately 25 to 30 minutes. Add tomato
juice and simmer 20 to 25 more minutes.

MEAT LOAF

1 1/2 lbs ground meat
1/4 - 1/2 c starch

1 1/2 t salt
1/2 - 1 c liquid

Preheat oven to 325^{oF}. Combine ingredients, shape into loaf, and bake 1 1/2
hours. Use beef, buffalo, or goat for ground meat. For starch use either
potato meal, raw grated potato, or rye or wheat flour. Use either meat juice,
tomato juice, or cow's milk for liquid.

MEAT LOAF, BASIC

1 1/2 lbs ground meat
1/4 - 1/2 c starch

1 1/2 t sea salt
1/2 - 1 c liquid

Preheat oven to 325^{oF}. Combine ingredients, form into loaf, and bake 1 to 1
1/2 hours.

For ground meat use:	ground beef, buffalo, goat, or lamb.
For starch use:	potato meal, riced cooked potato or raw, grated potato or corn meal.
For liquid use:	meat juice/or gravy, tomato juice, milk, or milk substitute.
Season with:	1/8 teaspoon marjoram and 1/8 teaspoon thyme or 1/4 teaspoon rosemary and 1/4 teaspoon savory. Chopped cooked liver may be mixed into meat.

MEAT LOAF, EASY

1/2 c mashed potatoes
1 lb ground beef

1 t salt
dash of cayenne pepper

Prepare potatoes by boiling and mashing with desired amount of water. Mix
ingredients well, shape into 9" x 5" loaf pan, and bake at 350^{oF} for 45
minutes.

PIZZA

Crust: Use a recipe in Pies and Crust section or toast slices of breads or biscuits on both sides.

Base: Use thickened spaghetti meat sauce or tomato paste covering with cheese layer and sprinkling with oregano.

Variation: Add chopped or sliced mushrooms and/or chopped sauteed green peppers and chopped meat seasoned with cayenne pepper.

SPANISH RICE

Brown 1 to 1 1/2 pounds ground meat. Add:

3 1/2 c raw or cooked tomatoes   *2 t sea salt*
2 c raw brown rice   *1 chopped green pepper*
2 c water

Place all ingredients in saucepan with tight fitting lid, bring to a boil, and cook on low heat about an hour or until rice is done.

Variations: Italian flavor - 1/2 t oregano and 1/4 t thyme.
Spicy flavor - 1/2 t basil and dash cayenne pepper.

Use as filling for baked, stuffed green peppers, tomatoes, etc.

Meat roll - using 1 to 1 1/2 lbs ground meat and 1 t sea salt, roll meat into a rectangle 12" x 15". Spread rice about 1/2" thick over this and roll as for a jelly roll. Bake as for a Country Pie or slice, place cut side up in dish and bake.

Using seasoned ground beef - make thin patties 4" across. Place large spoon Spanish Rice in patty center and turn edges up as for a tart. Put in covered frying pan and cook at 300^{oF} until crust is firm and browned.

STUFFED AVOCADO WITH CRABMEAT

1 avocado   *10 pecans*
1 c crabmeat, flaked

Cut avocado in half and pit. Combine pecans and crabmeat and spoon into avocado.

STUFFED PEPPERS

1 quart tomato juice   *3 - 4 green peppers*
1 lb chopped meat   *dash of sea salt*
Optional: 1/4 t Basil

Preheat over to 350°F. Shape meat into 1" balls, place in saucepan with tomato juice, cover, and simmer at very low heat for two hours or until juice turns to sauce. Salt to taste. Core and blanch green peppers by parboiling for two minutes. Put thickened sauce and meat in green peppers and bake in covered pan for 15 minutes.

TAMALE PIE

4 ounces meat (goat, lamb, beef,   *pinch thyme*
* buffalo, veal)*   *dash of chili or cayenne pepper*
1 t sea salt   *1 pint tomatoes*
pinch basil   *1/2 c corn*
pinch oregano

Add seasonings to meat and cook, adding tomatoes and corn to mixture. Simmer until done.

VEAL LOAF, JELLIED

1 veal knuckle bone; either saw   *1 bay leaf or 1/4 - 1/2 t other*
* in half or use 2 T gelatin*   * herb (mint family, #73)*
1 lb diced veal   *bits of red (chopped tomato and/or*
                                      * red sweet pepper)*

Combine, cover with water, and simmer two hours. Take veal and bone out; chop meat into fine pieces. Strain broth and cook down to one cup. If geletin is used, add to broth at this point and stir until dissolved. Using oil of the day, oil sides and bottom of loaf pan and add meat and broth. When chilled, slice with sharp knife.

Note: A broth that jells can be made with veal bones; other meats will need gelatin. The flavor of veal is so mild that herbs and vegetable juices (instead of water) should be added.

Grain and Grain Substitutes

BAKING POWDER BISCUITS

2 c flour
1 T baking powder
1 t sea salt

1/3 c walnut oil
2/3 c milk or water

Preheat oven to 475°F. Sift all dry ingredients together three times. Combine liquids without stirring and add liquid all at once to flour mixture. Avoid lumps by mixing thoroughly.
Variations:

Drop Biscuit:	Drop onto ungreased cookie sheet and bake 10 to 12 minutes.
Roll Biscuit:	Roll or pat dough to 1/4" or higher and cut with unfloured biscuit cutter. Bake 10 to 12 minutes.
Sweet Roll:	Roll out and add raisins, apples, or pecans; shape and bake.
Pot Pies:	Use 1/4" thickness. Dish must be very hot and filling as close to boiling as possible. Bake 12 to 15 minutes.

BARLEY BAKING POWDER BREAD

1 c plus 1 T whole barley flour
2 t melted butter or walnut oil
3 t baking powder*

1 t grain syrup
1/4 t sea salt
1 c water

Preheat oven to 350°F. Sift flour before measuring. Mix dry ingredients. Mix water, oil, and syrup and add to dry ingredients, using long strokes. Place in 4" x 7" x 2" pan and bake for 25 minutes. (*See food substitutions.)

CORN BREAD

1 c cornmeal
1/4 c corn oil
1/2 c water

1 t sea salt
1 t baking powder*

Preheat oven to 450°F. Combine all ingredients pouring into 9" x 9" pan greased with oil of the day. Bake 10 to 15 minutes. (*See food substitutions.)

CRUNCHY RYE CRACKERS

1 3/4 c rye flour   *1/4 t salt*
2 T corn or walnut oil   *4 T water*

Preheat oven to 325^{oF}. Mix flour, oil, and salt by hand adding water as necessary; knead. Roll out dough, cut into round circles, and bake on oiled cookie sheet for 10 to 12 minutes.

GRANOLA

3 qts oats   *1/3 c walnut oil*
1 c oat flour   *2 c walnuts*
1 c water

Combine oats, flour, and nuts. Combine oil and water and add to oats, stirring until everything is thoroughly coated. Use more water if needed and more oil if desired so that mixture is a little moist. Spread evenly on cookie sheets and bake for 30 to 40 minutes at 250^{oF}. Allow to cool on cookie sheets, place in jars and store preferrably in freezer.

   Variations: Use corn oil and pecans.
                   Sweeten with raisins and/or dried apples and pears.
                   Serve with milk, cream, pecan nut milk, and/or sprouted
                   rye seed.

OAT WAFFLES

2 1/4 c water   *1 T walnut oil*
1/2 t sea salt   *Optional: 1/2 c walnuts or*
1 1/2 c rolled oats   *pecans*

Combine ingredients and blend until light and foamy. Let batter stand for 10 minutes until it thickens, blend quickly again just before pouring on waffle iron. Bake 10 to 15 minutes.

Note: These need more baking time than regular waffles. Do not try to peek for at least 8 minutes because they may stick. If they do stick, wait for awhile. Do not try to open or top and bottom will separate. Ingredients may be combined and allowed to soak for 30 minutes or overnight in refrigerator before beating. Chilling will aid in forming steam to promote rising action. Vigorous beating is required.

OATMEAL SHEET BREAD WITH NUTS

1 c oat flour   *2 t baking powder**
1 T potato starch   *2 T walnut oil*
1 t sea salt   *1/3 c nuts (pecans or walnuts)*
2/3 c water

Preheat oven to 475^{oF}. Mix ingredients and pat batter onto an oiled 9" x 9" pan greased with oil of the day. Bake 10 to 20 minutes. (*See food substitutions.)

POTATO BISCUITS

5/8 c potato starch flour   *3 T butter*
3 t baking powder*   *1/4 c cow's milk*
1/4 t salt

Sift dry ingredients together and cut in shortening until it is pea-sized. Gently stir milk to mixture to form a soft dough and knead lightly on board dusted with potato starch. Roll to 1/2" thickness, cut with 1 1/2" cutter, and place on ungreased baking sheet. Bake 425^{oF} for 10 to 12 minutes until lightly browned. (*See food substitutions.)

RAISIN BREAD

1 c chopped raisins   *1 t sea salt*
2 t baking soda   *1 1/2 c warm water*
2 t baking powder*   *1 c butter or corn oil*
1 c potato flour   *1/3 c grain syrup*

Preheat oven to 350^{oF}. Let raisins soak in warm water until it cools then add baking soda, butter or oil, syrup, baking powder, potato flour, and salt. Bake 45 minutes in loaf pan greased with corn or rice oil. (*See food substitutions.)

RICE, BASIC

1 c brown rice   *2 1/4 c cold water*

Rinse rice well and drain. Add cold water, bring to a boil over high heat, and boil 2 to 3 minutes. Cover pan tightly, reduce heat, and steam for 50 minutes. Remove covered pan from heat, allow to set for 10 minutes, and fluff.

RICE, FLUFFY

1/4 c walnut oil   *2 1/4 c water*
1 c brown rice

Add rice to heated oil stirring constantly until rice is brown. Add water, cover, and simmer for 50 minutes. (In tropical countries, rice is usually browned in oil to separate grains before being steamed.)

RICE, FRIED

3 T walnut oil   *1 c cooked rice*

Heat oil in skillet, add rice, and stir often as rice browns.

RICE PUDDING, OLD FASHIONED

2 c cooked rice   *1 1/2 c cows or coconut milk*
1/4 c chopped dates   *Day 3*)*

Mix above ingredients, place in 2 quart casserole dish, and bake at 325^{oF} for 20 minutes. Serve hot with additional nut milk. (*Use formula.)

RICE WAFERS

1/2 c rice (gritty)   *1 T potato starch*
1/2 c rice polish   *1/2 c ground pecans*
1/2 t baking powder*   *1/2 c grain syrup*
1/2 t sea salt   *3/8 c oil of the day*

Preheat oven to 425^{oF}. Mix ingredients and pat batter onto 9" x 9" oiled pan. Bake for 10 to 20 minutes. (*See food substitutions.)

ROLLED OAT MUFFINS

1 c ground rolled oats   *1 t cinnamon*
3/4 c rice flour   *1/8 c grain syrup (2 T)*
2 T baking powder*   *1 1/8 c water*
1 t sea salt   *1/2 c raisins*
1/4 c melted butter or beef fat

Preheat oven to 425^{oF}. Using fine cutting blade, grind rolled oats in food chopper. Using oil of the day grease muffin tins. Thoroughly mix dry ingredients adding raisins, water, and fat. Add syrup mixing well. Fill muffin pans about 2/3 full and bake until lightly browned — about 20 minutes. Makes 12 medium-sized muffins. (*See food substitutions.)

RYE BREAD

1 1/2 c plus 2 T sifted whole   *1/4 t salt*
 rye flour   *5 t baking powder**
3 1/2 t oil   *1/2 c water*

Preheat oven to 375°F. Mix dry ingredients, add oil and water, and beat with long strokes. Bake in 4" x 9" x 2" pan for about 20 minutes. (*See food substitutions.)

RYE CRACKERS

1 3/4 c rye flour   *1 t baking soda*
1 c rice flour   *1/2 c butter or beef fat*
1 1/2 t sea salt   *1 c buttermilk*

Preheat oven to 375°F. Mix dry ingredients well and add fat mixing only until mixture is crumbly. Add buttermilk, mix well, and place dough on well-floured surface. Roll very thin and cut into strips 3" x 1 1/2". Place with sides touching on baking sheet and bake until lightly browned, about 18 minutes. Makes 75 crackers. Note: Coarse salt may be sprinkled on top of crackers before baking, if desired.

RYE FLAKE CEREAL

6 c water   *2 c rye flakes*
2 T corn or walnut oil

Saute flakes in heated oil for about 5 minutes. Add boiling water, cover well, and simmer for 20 minutes, stirring occasionally.

RYE MUFFINS

1 1/4 c rye flour   *3/4 t sea salt*
1/2 c rice flour   *1/8 c grain syrup*
4 t baking powder*   *1 scant c water*
1/4 c melter butter or beef fat

Preheat oven to 375°F. Thoroughly mix dry ingredients and add grain syrup, water, and fat and mix well. Grease muffin tins with oil of the day and fill about half full. Bake until lightly browned, about 25 minutes. Makes 12 small muffins. (*See food substitutions.)

SPELT HOT BISCUITS

1 c minus 2 T tepid water   *1/2 t salt*
1/2 t vitamin C crystals   *2 t baking soda*
2 c spelt flour   *3 T walnut oil*

Preheat oven to 425°F. Mix water and vitamin C crystals; set aside to dissolve. Whisk flour, salt, and soda together in mixing bowl. Whisk oil in with dissolved crystals and add all at once to flour; beat 10 strokes. Drop in mounds on baking sheet and bake 12 minutes until firm to touch and brown on the bottom.

SPELT HOT CEREAL

1 c fine or coarsely ground   *2 c water*
  spelt   *1/4 t salt*

Mix ingredients in saucepan, bring to boil, and simmer for 10 to 12 minutes, stirring occasionally. Serve with small amount of sweetener and nut milk (optional).

SPELT TORTILLAS

1 c spelt flour   *1/2 - 1 t walnut oil*
1/4 c flour for board   *1/3 c water*
1/4 t salt

Blend salt, oil, water, 1 cup flour, placing 1/4 cup on bread board. Roll ball of dough in flour, flattening, and folding dough; it will become more workable. Divide dough into 4 to 6 small balls. Working on the floured board, roll or pat each ball until it is thin and about 5" to 7" in diameter. Heat griddle until a drop of water "dances" on it and bake the tortillas about 2 minutes on each side; if you want crisper bread bake longer. Cool on wire racks.

Salads and Side Dishes

AVOCADO WHEAT OR RYE SPROUT

1 cubed avocado   *3 c vegetables (green peppers and*
wheat or rye sprouts   *tomatoes cut in chunks)*

Toss avocado and vegetable together. Dressing is not needed.

> Variations: Cut a ripe tomato almost through to bottom leaving leaves attached.
> Place on mound of wheat or rye sprouts and spread lightly.
> Fill center with scoop of mashed avocado which had a few drops of vinegar or sour apple juice added. Sea salt to taste.
>
> Instead of tomato, substitute green pepper.

BANNOCK, NEW HAMPSHIRE

1 c whole white corn meal   1/2 t sea salt
2 T soft butter   boiling water

Preheat over to 350°F. Combine corn meal and salt and pour enough boiling water over it to make a batter the consistency of thick cream. Add butter. Pour into large well-greased pan, spreading mixture thin. Bake for about 45 minutes or until crispy brown. Serve with melted butter, cream, milk, or nut milk.

Variation: Serve with soup.
               Sweeten to taste with a grain syrup.

FRENCH FRIES, BAKED

4 medium potatoes   1/4 c walnut oil
1 t salt

Preheat oven to 400°F. Pour oil into 9" by 13" pan. Peel and slice potatoes, coat slices with oil, and arrange in pan. Bake for 30 to 40 minutes and sprinkle with salt.

FRUIT SALAD

Combine: Chopped apples, pears, and grapes.
Add: Pecans or walnuts.
Optional: Apple juice, yogurt, or avocado dressing (See Salad Dressings).

POTATO PANCAKES

4 large potatoes   3 T potato meal

Peel and grate potatoes and combine with potato meal. Oil pan with oil of the day, heat over very low heat, and spoon mixture into pan. Brown and turn over. Serve alone or with apple or pear sauce.

Variation: Place in oiled cake dish and bake in oven at very low heat until brown and cooked through.

POTATO SOUFFLE, HOT

6 eggs   1/4 t cayenne pepper
1/2 c heavy cream   11 oz cream cheese
1 t salt   1 c cooked, cubed potato
1/4 t celery seed (Day 3*)   1/4 c chopped green pepper

Blend eggs, cream, and seasonings until smooth. Add cream cheese in chunks, potato, and green pepper and process until smooth. Butter a 6 cup souffle dish or 5 to 6 individual dishes. Pour into prepared dish and bake

350° for 45 minutes (soft center) or 50 minutes (firm center). Serve immediately. Yields 6 servings. (*Use formula.)

VEGETABLE SALAD

Combine: Sprouted wheat or rye, raw sweet green or red peppers, and tomatoes.
Dressing: Corn or rice oil with mint or other herb of the day for flavoring.
Optional: Flavor with poppy seed.
Add avocado, raw mushrooms, and/or bamboo shoots.
Add diced steamed potatoes, cheese, diced lobster, or shrimp.
Variation: Use avocado dressing (see recipe later).

WALDORF SALAD

Toss lightly together:

2 c diced apples   *1/2 c seedless raisins*
1/2 c chopped walnuts

Serve with avocado dressing.

Variation: Add 1 cup seedless grapes.

Snacks, Sweets and Desserts

APPLE BUTTER

2 c cooked apples   *1 c maple syrup (Day 2*)*

Mix ingredients and cook over medium heat, stirring constantly, until thick. Use as a spread. (*Use formula.)

APPLE SAUCE

Fresh apples   *Dash cinnamon*

Quarter apples, removing core and seeds, and steam in covered pot until tender. Puree in blender and sprinkle cinnamon on top. Serve hot or cold.

APPLE SAUCE CAKE

1/2 c grain syrup
1 c unsweetened applesauce
1/2 c butter
1 t baking soda

1 3/4 c unbleached flour
1 c raisins
1 c walnuts or pecans
optional: 1 t ground cassia

Preheat oven to 375°F. Combine butter and syrup. Add sifted flour, soda, spices, and applesauce and mix well. Bake in sheet pan 35 to 40 minutes until done.

APPLE SAUCE COOKIES

1/4 c butter
1 1/4 c grain syrup
1/3 cup thick applesauce
1 c potato starch

1/4 t sea salt
2 t baking powder*
1/2 c nuts (pecans or walnuts)

Preheat oven to 350°F. Cream butter and grain syrup together well and add applesauce. Sift dry ingredients together and stir into mixture. Add nuts. Drop onto cookie sheet and bake for about 12 minutes. (* See food substitutions.)

APPLES, BAKED

Cut tops out of apples, funnel-shaped, and dig out most of core with teaspoon being careful not to get to the bottom. Place apples in baking dish, fill with walnuts, and place pinch of mint or cinnamon on top. Add cup of water and bake at 350°F until tender. Eat hot or cold.

APPLES, GLAZED

Pare and core small tart apples. Place in greased baking pan or casserole, sprinkle with 1 part grain syrup mixed with 3 parts boiling water, and bake uncovered in moderate (350°F) oven until tender (about 1/2 hour). Basting syrup over apples several times while cooking makes an attractive glaze. Fill centers with raisins and/or pecans.

BARLEY FLOUR PIE CRUST

1 1/2 c whole barley flour
1/2 t sea salt

3 or 4 T ice cold water
4 T butter

Preheat oven to 400°F. Sift flour before measuring. Add salt, stir in butter, and gradually add water. All pie crusts made from flour other than wheat are hard to handle so this will not roll out as nicely as ordinary pie crust. Roll out, lift into pie dish, and pat into shape. Bake for 15 minutes.

GARNISHED BREAD SNACKS

Thinly slice home-made bread, butter slices, and sprinkle with spearmint, mint, marjoram, and/or cinnamon. Toast lightly under broiler until golden brown and serve hot.

GELATIN DESSERT

Soften one package plain gelatin in 1 cup apple or grape juice and dissolve over low heat. Add 1 cup of same liquid, mold, and chill.

    Variation: Add apples and/or pecans.

GRAPE PIE FILLING

If you are not allergic to yeast or mold use bottled grape juice; if you are allergic, cook seedless grapes in small amount of water and juice grapes to make juice. Bring 1 cup grape juice to a boil and thicken with 2 tablespoons potato starch and 2 tablespoons water. Sweeten to taste with grain syrup.

GRAPE PUDDING

1/3 c rice flour   *3 c concord grape juice*
1/4 c butter

Combine rice flour and grape juice in saucepan and cook over medium heat approximately 10 minutes until thickened. Remove from pan and puree in blender adding butter.

GROUND OATS PIE CRUST

2 c ground organic oat flakes   *6 T walnut oil*
 (use blender, not too fine)   *2 T water*
1/4 t sea salt

Preheat oven to 425^{oF}. Toss ingredients together and press into 9" glass pie pan which has been greased with oil used in crust. Bake until lightly browned, cool completely, and fill with pie filling of choice.

MOLASSES CRISPS

1 1/4 c flour   *1/4 c butter*
3/4 t baking soda   *1/2 c molasses or other grain syrup*

Preheat oven to 375^{oF}. Bring syrup and butter to boil and cool slightly before adding sifted dry ingredients. Chill, roll, and cut. Bake on buttered sheets for 8 to 10 minutes. Makes 2 dozen.

MOLASSES MOUNDS

4 1/2 c unbleached wheat flour   *1 1/2 c molasses*
1 c bran   *1 c + 2 T walnut oil*
1 t baking soda   *1/3 c water*
2 t baking powder*

Preheat oven to 350°F. Blend dry ingredients in bowl. In another bowl mix liquid ingredients, putting oil in first. Combine ingredients. If batter does not look shiny add more oil. Roll in balls, place on ungreased pan, and bake exactly 7 minutes. (*See Food Substitutions.)

    Variation: Add 1 to 2 t cinnamon.

NUT PASTRY PIE CRUST

1/2 c ground walnuts or pecans   *3/4 t sea salt*
1/2 c water   *1 t potato starch*
1 c oat flour

Preheat over to 475°F. Combine ingredients, mixing well, and press into pan. Bake 3 to 5 minutes. Fill with pie filling and bake as needed for filling.

OAT AND BARLEY PIE CRUST

1 c barley flour   *1/2 c oat flour*
1/2 t salt   *1/3 c safflower oil*
4 T ice water

Preheat oven to 400°F. Brush 9" pie pan lightly with oil. Sift dry ingredients together. Mix oil and ice water and add to dry ingredients using fork to stir until mixture forms a ball. Press into pie pan with fingers making crust as thin as possible and leaving a high edge around the outside. Prick with fork and bake for 10 to 12 minutes or fill with fruit filling and bake for 35 minutes.

OIL PIE CRUST

2 c sifted, unbleached blour   *1 1/2 t sea salt*
1/2 c walnut oil   *1/4 c cold water or milk*

Preheat oven to 475°F. Do not mix ingredients but add all at once to flour and stir lightly until blended. Roll. It is easier to press bottom into pie pan and to pat top flat on cutting board. With fork prick both top and bottom well. If desired, fill with fruit filling and bake at 425°F for 40 minutes. If making tart shells, bake for 10 minutes.

RAISIN PUDDING

1 c raisins   *1 c hot water*
1/3 c walnuts

Soak raisins in hot water until softened and blend raisin and nuts until pureed. Because this recipe is very sweet use it as an alternative to sweetener in recipes.

RICE PANCAKES

2 c rice polish   *1/2 c dried skim milk (water may be*
2 T syrup of the day   *substituted)*
3 T rice bran oil   *1/2 t baking soda*
                                                1/2 t sea salt

Add spring water for proper consistency. Mix ingredients and bake on griddle greased with corn or rice bran oil. Serve with applesauce.

RICE PIE CRUST

1/4 c walnut oil   *about 1/3 c water*
3/4 c rice flour

Preheat oven to 425^{oF}. Work the oil into flour and add enough water to make soft dough. Press dough as thinly as possible into oiled pan and bake for 10 to 12 minutes or until brown.

SHOO-FLY PIE

1 c flour   *1/4 c boiling water*
1/4 c walnut oil   *1/2 t baking soda*
1/2 c unsulphured molasses   *1/2 t apple cider vinegar*

Mix flour with oil for crumbs. In blender mix unsulphured molasses and boiling water. Dissolve baking soda in apple cider vinegar and add to liquid, stirring until foamy. Put about 1/3 of crumbs in 8" pie pan, add liquid, and add remainder of crumbs on top. Bake in 450^{oF} oven for 10 minutes or 350^{oF} for 30 minutes.

SPELT PIE CRUST

3 T walnut oil   *1/4 t salt*
2 T cool water   *1 c plus 2 T spelt flour*

Whisk oil, water, and salt together and stir in flour mixing only until evenly moistened. Press into 9" pie plate. Fill and bake as needed for the filling. If baking empty crust, prick bottom with fork and bake for 12 minutes at 375^{oF}. Fill when cool.

WHEAT BALLS

1 c sprouted wheat   2 c seedlss raisins
1 c brazil nuts or pecans   pinch of sea salt

Grind ingredients through food mill, add salt, and mix well. Roll into one-inch balls. Use as a dessert.

   Variation: You may use two raw apples, grated fine, or dried apples or
                  pears.

WHEAT FLOUR PIE CRUST

1 1/2 c wheat flour   4 T water
1/2 t sea salt   1/3 c walnut oil

Preheat oven to 400^{oF}. Brush 9" pie pan lightly with oil. Sift dry ingredients together. Mix oil and water and add to dry ingredients, stirring until a ball is formed. Press with fingers into pie pan, making crust as thin as possible and a high edge around outside. Prick with fork and bake for 10 to 12 minutes or fill with prepared fruit and bake at 425^{oF} for 30 to 35 minutes or until crust is golden.

Soups

BEEF BROTH

1 1/2 lbs chuck, chopped   1/2 lb split beef bones
4 c cold water

Place beef and bones in stock pot, add water, place over medium heat, and bring to boil allowing to boil for five minutes. Simmer for two to three hours over reduced heat checking occasionally to make sure beef is not sticking. The broth is done when beef has no flavor. Taste after two hours and if beef still has flavor simmer an additional hour. After cooking strain broth through cheese cloth. Cool, cover, and refrigerate overnight. Remove solidified fat from top. Broth may be kept in refrigerator for five days, frozen for two months. Yield: 2 cups.

CREAM OF POTATO SOUP

4 T butter
1/4 c diced celery (Day 3*)
1/4 c diced green pepper
1/3 c buckwheat flour (Day 3*)
4 c diced potatoes

2 c beef broth
1 c cream
1 c milk
generous pinches salt and pepper

Cook potatoes and set aside. Melt butter in 2 quart saucepan and saute green pepper and celery until tender. Blend in the flour and then the beef broth. Stir vigorously with a wire which and cook over medium heat, stirring until thickened. Add the cream, milk, and potatoes; season to taste with salt and pepper. Yields about 5 servings. (*Use formula.)

18

MENUS AND RECIPES FOR DAYS 2, 6, 10, ETC.

Food Chart for Days 2, 6, 10, ETC.

Suggested Menus for Days 2, 6, 10, ETC.

Recipes for Days 2, 6, 10, ETC.

Beverages
Dressings, Garnishes, Sauces, and Spreads
Fish, Fowl, and Meat
Grain and Grain Substitutes
Salads and Side Dishes
Snacks, Sweets and Desserts
Soups

See also recipe section in "Changing Your Eating Habits" and "Understanding the Formula."

FOOD CHART FOR DAYS 2, 6, 10, ETC.

Food Families: 4, 9, 13, 14, 16, 17, 18, 19, 24, 26, 28, 30, 31, 32, 40b, 40d, 47, 50, 63, 64, 66, 69, 71, 72, 79, 98, 107, 109, 111, 117, 120, 122, 126.

Animal Protein: 98-Tuna, mackerel. 107-Whitefish. 109-Pike. 111-Carp, chub. 117-Frogs legs. 120-Turtle. 122-Dove, pigeon (squab). 126-Turkey, turkey eggs.

Vegetables: 9-Malanga, poi, taro. 14-Ñame, yam. 28-Beet, chard, spinach. 47-Yuca. 69-Olive. 71-Comfrey, 79-Cucumber, pumpkin, squash, zucchini.

Fruit: 16-Banana, plantain. 32-Cherimoya, custard apple, pawpaw. 40b-Apricot, cherry, peach, plum. 63-Guava. 66-Bearberry, blueberry, cranberry, huckleberry. 79-Cantaloupe, melon, watermelon.

Seeds and Nuts: 24-Chestnut. 26-Macadamia. 40b-Almond. 79-Pumpkin seed.

Oils: Fats from any of the above. 40b-Apricot oil, almond oil. 69-Olive oil.

Other: 4, 9, 13, 16, 17, 18, 19, 28-Quinoa. 30- Amaranth. 47-Arrowroot starch, poi, tapioca starch.

Sweeteners: 50-Maple syrup.

Herbs and Spices: 17-Ginger, turmeric. 40d-Burnet. 63-Allspice, clove. 71-Comfrey. 72-Lemon verbena.

Beverages: Juices, soups, and teas from any of the above. 31-Golden seal. 64-American ginseng, Chinese ginseng. 71-Comfrey.

SUGGESTED MENUS FOR DAYS 2, 6, 10, ETC.

Breakfast	Lunch	Dinner
Apricot juice Cherries and almonds	Tuna fish with olives (and oil Cucumber, steamed squash, cantaloupe	Turkey Spinach and beets Macadamia nuts and/or bananas
Dried stewed fruit (cherries, apricots, peaches, and/or prunes) with almonds Bananas	Tuna salad Pumpkin seed crackers Pumpkin seed butter or almond butter Melon	Roast turkey (with chestnut stuffing) Vegetable salad Squash (baked) Banana nut sundae
Pancakes (arrowroot and pumpkin seed) served with dried fruit jam or blue- berry butter	Salad (Vegetable, Turkey) Bananas	Steamed whitefish Zucchini (stuffed) Vegetable salad Cherry almond pie or pudding
Cherry arrowroot pudding with bananas Ginseng tea	Fruit salad Pumpkin seed crackers Almond nut butter	Carp or chub almondine Squash pudding Vegetable salad Cucumbers Banana ice cream with almond cookies

WARNING; Only the first suggestion follows the proper rotation plan. The three additional suggestions are for those people who are easing into rotation.

RECIPES FOR DAYS 2, 6, 10, ETC.

Beverages

COMFREY DRINK

15 almonds (soaked overnight in water)
5 t pumpkin seeds (soaked overnight in water)

16 oz unsweetened cherry juice
1 banana
green leaves - spinach, beet greens, comfrey leaves

Place approximately 8 ounces of juice in blender, add softened nuts and seeds, and banana and liquefy. Pour into pitcher. Add four large handfuls of green leaves and rest of juice and liquefy. Combine mixtures. It should not be too thick; you may want to strain combined mixture.

Variation: If possible, juice green leaves in juicer and then mixture will not be too thick. Prepare the rest as above.

Dressings, Garnishes, Sauces, and Spreads

BANANA DRESSING

2 bananas
4 T maple syrup
2 T apricot juice

8 t water
dash of sea salt

Bake or steam bananas. Cool, mash, add other ingredients, and beat well with rotary or electric beater.

BLUEBERRY PUREE

4 c blueberries

liquid as needed
(water or blueberry juice)

Puree blueberries in blender using liquid sparingly. Serve with chopped nuts, pancakes or crackers.

Optional: Sweeten to taste with maple syrup.

DRIED FRUIT JAM

Drain stewed fruit. Puree in blender.

Optional: Sweeten to taste with maple syrup.

OLIVE OIL DRESSING

3 parts olive oil   *1 part cucumber juice*
                                             (more if desired)

Add juice slowly to olive oil.

    Optional: Add finely minced olives or season with ginger, turmeric, or
                         lemon verbena.

SEED OR NUT BUTTER

1 c pumpkin seeds   *1 T almond oil (more if needed)*

Grind or blend until smooth; store in refrigerator.

    Variation: For pumpkin seeds substitute almonds.

Fish, Fowl, and Meat

FISH ALMONDINE

1 fish fillet (whitefish, pike,   *1/4 c shredded blanched almonds*
  or carp)   *4 T almond oil*

Steam fish 5 to 8 minutes or until it flakes. Saute almonds in oil and pour
over fish.

ROAST TURKEY

Preheat oven to 350^{oF}. Rub turkey, including cavity, with ginger and
liberally brush turkey with garnish of ground allspice and almond oil.

Put 1/4 inch of water in roaster and place turkey on rack above the water.
Roast uncovered for an hour, basting with garnish (adding more liquid if
needed) at 30 minute intervals. Lower oven to 250^{oF}, cover roaster, and bake
about 6 more hours or until meat thermometer registers 190^{oF}.

To bring out natural juices, for the last half hour pour 3/4 cup of juice
(blueberry, cranberry, or cherry) over turkey and baste every 10 minutes.

    Variation: After rubbing cavity with ginger, stuff turkey 3/4 full.
                         (See "Chestnut Stuffing" under Salads and Side Dishes.)

TUNA FISH

See Salads and Side Dishes.

TURKEY LEFTOVERS
See Salads and Side Dishes.

Grain and Grain Substitutes

ALMOND ARROWROOT PANCAKES

1 c arrowroot starch   *liquid as needed (water or almond*
1 c almonds   *nut milk)*

On low speed blend dry mixture and add liquid increasing speed. Add only enough liquid to reach the right consistency.

Note: Because there is no leavening, the pancake will be flatter than usual and the batter should be thicker than usual. As you experiment for the right consistency, remember that it is easier to add liquid than dry mixture. Use almond or apricot oil to grease griddle.

> Variation: Substitute pumpkin seeds for almonds.
> Serve with dried fruit jam, maple syrup or pureed blueberries.

AMARANTH WAFFLES

2 1/4 c amaranth flour   *1 2/3 c cool water or almond milk*
1/3 c arrowroot   *1/4 c almond oil*
1/2 t salt   *1/3 c boiling water*
3/4 t unbuffered vitamin C   *2 t baking soda*
  crystals

Preheat waffle iron to medium. In mixing bowl combine flour, salt, arrowroot, and vitamin C crystals. Whisk to blend ingredients and whisk in oil and water. When waffle iron is ready, combine soda and boiling water in small bowl (it will foam), stir to dissolve, and whisk into batter. Pour 1 cup batter onto waffle iron, wait 10 minutes to check; loosen waffle with fork and remove when done. Repeat until batter is used. Yields four 9" x 9" square waffles.

BUCKWHEAT AND QUINOA

4 c water   *1 c unroasted buckwheat (Day 3*)*
1/8 - 1/4 t sea salt   *1 c quinoa*

In 1 1/2 quart saucepan bring water and salt to boil. As water heats place buckwheat in a wok or skillet and toast over high heat, stirring continuously, until it turns a shade darker in color (about 10 minutes)and then set aside. When water boils add quinoa first and slowly add buckwheat. Change heat to low, cover, and simmer about 15 to 20 minutes until all water is absorbed.

Remove from heat and let stand 5 to 10 minutes. Gently mix the grain from top to bottom in the pot with a damp wooden spoon. Cover again and allow to set for 5 to 10 minutes. Makes 6 cups. Serve in a wooden bowl. (*Use formula.)

QUINOA, BASIC

1 c quinoa	2 c water
1 pinch sea salt	

Rinse quinoa several times to remove bitter saponins by running fresh water over it in a pot and pouring through strainer. Place water and salt in saucepan and bring to a rapid boil. Add quinoa, reduce heat, cover, and simmer until water is absorbed (15-25 minutes). Makes 4 cups. For rich, nutty flavor toast quinoa (with or without oil) in skillet, stirring constantly, before adding to water.

QUINOA WAFFLES

2 c quinoa flour	3/4 t vitamin C crystals
1/2 t salt	1/4 c oil
1 1/2 c cool water or almond	1/4 c boiling water
milk	2 t baking soda

Blend the flour and salt and add the cool liquid, vitamin C crystals, and oil. Beat or whisk hard for 2 minutes and set aside for 10 minutes. Preheat waffle iron to "medium." In small container dissolve the baking soda in boiling water and whisk the soda water into mixture. Pour one cup of batter onto hot waffle iron and let it set for 10 to 14 minutes. Remove with a fork and place on a plate. Yield: 4 9" x 9" waffles.

Salads and Side Dishes

BAKED SQUASH

1 butternut or acorn squash	1/4 t ground ginger (optional)
2 T almond oil	2 t maple syrup (optional)

Preheat oven to 350°F. Cut squash in half and remove seeds. Combine other ingredients and brush on squash. Bake until tender, about 20 minutes.

Variation: Serve with finely chopped chestnuts.
              Stick a whole clove in the end of each half of squash.

BUTTERNUT SQUASH PUDDING

Steam and puree equal amounts of butternut squash and pumpkin. For flavor add ground cloves and/or ginger.

Variation: Substitute mashed steamed plantain or raw bananas for the pumpkin.

CHESTNUT STUFFING

2 1/2 c cooked chestnuts   *3 T almond oil*
2 c cooked ñame   *sea salt to taste (optional)*

Combine riced chestnuts, mashed cooked ñame, and almond oil. Use for stuffing with turkey or as a side dish.

Variation: Season with 1/2 teaspoon ground ginger.

FRESH FRUIT SALAD

watermelon chunks   *whole blueberries*
casaba melon chunks

Combine above ingredients. May serve on bed of spinach, if desired.

FRUIT COMBINATIONS

1. Apricot, cherry, peach, and almonds.
2. Cantaloupe, honey dew, watermelon, and pumpkin seeds.
3. Banana, blueberry, guava, and macadamia nuts.

Variation: Serve any of the above with banana dressing. (See Dressings, Garnishes, Sauces, and Spreads.)

NUTTY SPINACH SALAD

1 c fresh spinach   *1 c crushed almonds*
1 T almond oil   *1 clove garlic, crushed (Day 4*)*

Rinse spinach well in cold water, pat dry, and tear into bite-sized pieces. Toss lightly with oil. Add garlic and nuts, toss, and serve. (*Use formula.)

STUFFED ZUCCHINI

6 - 8 inch large zucchini   *1/4 c finely chopped chestnuts or*
1 c chopped spinach   *pumpkin seeds*
2 T almond oil

Steam zucchini about 7 to 8 minutes until tender. Drain and cut lengthwise, scooping out and discarding seed. Drain again and sprinkle remaining shell with salt; stuff with spinach and chestnuts. Place stuffed zucchini in shallow baking pan or oven-to-table dish greased with almond oil. Sprinkle each portion with almond oil. Reheat for about 20 minutes in 350°. oven before serving.

TUNA FISH SALAD

Combine tuna fish with raw spinach and cucumbers.

Dressing: Olive or almond oil flavored with allspice, ground clove, or
             ground ginger.

Optional: Add olives.
             Add diced steamed beets or flame.

VEGETABLE COMBINATIONS

1. Beet greens, chard, steamed winter squash, and pumpkin seeds (see
olive oil dressing).
2. Raw spinach, cucumbers, and chestnuts with almond oil and allspice.

Variation: Add diced turkey.

Snacks, Sweets, and Desserts

ALMOND COOKIES

3 c almond meal (or finely   *1 T cherry juice (optional)*
  ground almonds)   *1 1/4 t ginger (optional)*
3 T maple syrup   *Boiling water as needed*
1 1/2 T almond oil

Preheat oven to 250^{oF}. Mix all ingredients and add just enough water to hold
ingredients together. With wet rolling pin, flatten dough on cookie sheet
greased with almond oil. Bake until firm enough to cut into squares.

AMARANTH PIE CRUST

3/4 c amaranth flour   *1/4 t salt*
1/2 c arrowroot   *3 T almond oil*
1/4 c almonds, finely ground   *3 - 4 T water*

Mix the flour, arrowroot, and nuts in large bowl. Mix the oil and water in a
cup and blend into the flour mixture with a fork until a ball can be formed. If
dough is dry and crumbly, add more water, 1 teaspoon at a time, until dough
sticks together. Oil a 9" plate and either pat the dough directly onto the plate.
Handle carefully, dough is fragile. Prick all over with a fork. For an unfilled
crust, bake empty shell at 400^{oF} for 3 minutes. Add desired filling and finish
baking as recipe directs.

ARROWROOT PUDDING

2 T arrowroot starch   *1 c juice (apricot, cherry, peach,*
                                          or blueberry)

Add liquid gradually to prevent starch from becoming lumpy. Heat at medium temperature, stirring constantly until it thickens. Cool and add any fruit and/or nuts of the day. Excellent for pie filling with an almond crust.

Optional: Sweeten with banana.
               Sweeten to taste with maple syrup.

BANANA BERRY CRUSH

2 bananas   *1 c cherries*
2 c blueberry juice

Freeze fruits and puree with juice. Serve as is or top with almonds or macadamia nuts.

BANANA ICE CREAM

2 bananas   *Cherry juice to taste*
1 1/2 c nut milk (macadamia   *1/2 c maple syrup*
or almond)   *2 T apricot oil*

Mix in blender or mash bananas and mix ingredients with electric beater. Freeze, whip again, and re-freeze.

BANANA NUT SUNDAE

2 large or 3 small bananas   *chopped almonds*

Peel and slice bananas and freeze. Partially defrost and serve with chopped almonds.

PLANTAIN, SAUTEED

1 plantain   *1 c oil of the day*

Using either green or ripe plantain, cut in rounds and saute in oil of the day. Green plantain makes a good biscuit substitute while ripe plantain is sweet. Serve with meal or as a dessert.

Variation: Sweeten to taste with maple syrup.

PUMPKIN SEED CRACKERS

3 c pumpkin seed

Grind the pumpkin seed and add:

1/3 c ground almonds   *3 T oil (almond)*
3/4 t sea salt

Preheat oven to 250^{oF}. Add enough boiling water to make stiff dough. Roll as thin as possible on oiled cookie sheet with roller kept wet with water. Bake for 10 minutes and increase heat to 350^{oF} for 15 minutes.

SIMPLEST DESSERT OF ALL

1 ripe banana

Peel banana and freeze. Serve frozen and whole with napkin wrapped around bottom, or sliced in serving dish. Yield: 1 serving. Note: Frozen bananas taste delicious and have the consistency of ice cream.

STEWED DRIED FRUIT

3 c dried fruit (apricot, cherry, peach, prune)

Cover fruit with boiling water and soak overnight or until tender.

   Variation: Serve with chopped almonds or macadamia nuts.

Soups

TURKEY BROTH

1 1/2 lb chopped turkey   *4 c cold water*

Place turkey in stock pot, add water, and bring to boil over medium heat. Boil for 5 minutes then reduce heat and simmer 2 to 3 hours. You should check the pot occasionally to make sure turkey does not stick. The broth is done if turkey has no flavor so taste the turkey after 2 hours. If it still has flavor, simmer an additional hour. Strain fully cooked broth through cheese cloth; cool, cover, and refrigerate overnight. Remove hardened fat from top of broth. It may be refrigerated for 5 days or frozen for 2 months. Yield: 2 cups.

   Variation: Debone roast turkey, place turkey bones and gravey in crock pot, cover bones with boiling spring water, and cook on low heat for 8 - 10 hours.

19

MENUS AND RECIPES FOR DAYS 3, 7, 11, ETC.

Food Chart for Days 3, 7, 11, ETC.

Suggested Menus for Days 3, 7, 11, ETC.

Recipes for Days 3, 7, 11, ETC.

> Beverages
> Dressings, Garnishes, Sauces, and Spreads
> Fish, Fowl, and Meat
> Grain and Grain Substitutes
> Salads and Side Dishes
> Snacks, Sweets and Desserts

See also recipe section in Changing Your Eating Habits" and "Understanding the Formula."

FOOD CHART FOR DAYS 3, 7, 11, ETC.

Food Families: 1, 7, 8, 10, 23, 27, 33, 39, 40c, 51, 65, 68, 70, 80, 81, 91, 96, 102, 106, 113, 114, 115, 129, 134, 135.

Animal Protein: 81-Abalone, clam, cockle, mussel, oyster, scallop, snail, squid. 91, 96, 102, 106, 113, 114, 115-All bass, all perch, all trout, croaker, grouper, salmon, sauger, walleye. 129-Rabbit. 134-Swine (bacon, ham, pork). 135-Caribou, deer (venison), elk, moose, reindeer.

Vegetables: 7-Chinese water chestnut. 65-Carrot, celeriac (celery root), celery, parsley, parsnip. 70-Sweet potato, camote. 80-Artichoke, dandelion, endive, Jerusalem artichoke, lettuce.

Fruits: 8-Date, coconut. 10-Pineapple. 27-Rhubarb. 39-Currant, gooseberry. 40c-Blackberry, raspberry, strawberry. 51-Litchi. 60-Prickly pear. 68-Persimmon.

Seeds and Nuts: 8-Coconut. 23-Filbert (hazelnut). 80-Sunflower seeds.

Fats and Oils: Fats from any of the above. 80-Safflower oil, sunflower oil.

Other: 1-Agar-agar. 8-Sago starch or pearls. 27-Buckwheat. 80-Artichoke flour, sunflower seed meal.

Sweeteners: Date sugar.

Herbs and Spices: 1-Kelp (seaweed). 33-Nutmeg. 65-Anise, caraway, celery seed, chervil, coriander, cumin, dill, fennel. 80-Santolina, tansy, tarragon.

Beverages: Juices, soups, and teas from any of the above. 80-Tea from boneset, burdock root, chamomile, chicory, goldenrod, yarrow.

SUGGESTED MENUS FOR DAYS 3, 7, 11, ETC.

Breakfast	Lunch	Dinner
Buckwheat cereal Coconut milk and dates	Salmon Vegetable salad (lettuce, Jerusalem artichokes, endive, sunflower seeds, and oil Sweet potatoes	Pork stew or rabbit stew Raw carrots, celery Filberts and pineapple
Filberts and straw-berry pudding made with agar-agar	Sunflower seed wafers Fruit salad	Steamed salmon or baked trout #1 Buckwheat stuffing Date nut balls with pineapple
Buckwheat pancakes #1 with date nut dressing	Salmon Vegetable salad #1 Baked rhubarb	Roast pork Sweet potato with pineapple Filbert berry pie or pudding
Buckwheat/seed pan-cakes #2 with pureed pineapple	Vegetable salad #2 Steamed scallops Barbecued spareribs or Filbert berry date pie	Baked fish #2 Baked rhubarb with sweet potato Vegetable salad Date cookies

WARNING: Only the first suggestion follows the proper rotation plan. The three additional suggestions are for those people who are easing into rotation.

RECIPES FOR DAYS 3, 7, 11, ETC.

Beverages

COCONUT CREAM, MILK, AND SKIM MILK

1 coconut (fresh or frozen)   *water as needed (about 3-4 c)*
coconut milk from 1 coconut

Puncture holes in three eyes of the coconut with ice pick. Drain coconut milk, strain, and refrigerate.

Place coconut shell in oven 15 to 20 minutes at 250° F. to make it easier to crack.

After cracking shell, cut coconut into cubes, cover with about 3 cups of water, and soak overnight in covered jar.

Pour into blender and blend first on low speed, then on high. Strain liquid, separating it from shredded coconut. Combine liquid with coconut milk to make coconut cream.

Return shredded coconut to blender and add more water, just enough to let blender work. Strain again for coconut skim milk.

Variations: Use coconut cream as you would regular milk to drink by itself or season it with nutmeg, sunflower seeds, or date cookies. Try it on buckwheat cereal with strawberries. Or serve it with fresh strawberries as a special treat.
Use coconut skim milk instead of water to give a coconut flavor to any recipe.

Note: Your produce manager can tell you when is the peak season for coconuts when they will be least expensive. Buy them in quantity. Prepare the extra coconuts into cubes and freeze, placing one in each package. Freeze coconut milk in ice cube trays. When frozen solid, remove from tray and store with the coconut, a few cubes in each package.

COCONUT MILK #2

3 c hot water
1 shredded fresh coconut

Blend and coconut together in blender. Strain is desired. Cool before using.

PINA COLADA

1 part cocconut cream
1 part pineapple chunks or pineapple juice

Combine in blender.

STRAWBERRY FRAPPE

1 c strawberries (rinsed and hulled)
1 chopped mint sprigs
6 ice cubes, crushed

Whip all ingredients in blender until smooth. Use formula.

Dressings, Garnishes, Sauces, and Spreads

DATE NUT SALAD DRESSING

1/2 c boiling water   *1/4 c filbert nut butter*
1/4 c date butter   *1/8 t sea salt*

Pour boiling water over salted butters and beat with rotary beater.

BAKED RHUBARB

2 c sliced rhubarb   *boiling water as needed*
1/2 c date sugar

Preheat oven to 300° F. Dissolve date sugar in boiling water. Alternate layers of rhubarb and date sugar syrup in a baking dish greased with oil of the day. Bake until rhubarb is red.

   Variation: Eat with sweet potatoes or buckwheat pancakes.

SEED/NUT BUTTER

1 c sunflower seeds   *1 T safflower oil*

Grind or blend until fine and smooth. Store in refrigerator.

   Variation: Substitute filberts for sunflower seeds.

Fish, Fowl, and Meat

BAKED BATTER FISH

Bass, perch, trout, or other fish of the day.

Preheat oven to 400° F. Pour a little water or pineapple juice over fish. Dip in ground filberts, sunflower seed meal, or artichoke flour. Bake until fish is flaky (about 10 to 15 minutes).

> Variation: Saute three to four minutes in safflower oil seasoned with dill and/or fennel.

BAKED FISH

Bass, perch, trout, or other fish of the day.

3 lbs fish, dressed   *1 c water*
2-3 c sliced carrots   *1 T minced parsley*
2-3 c chopped celery   *1 1/2 t sea salt*

Preheat oven to 350° F. Place vegetables and one cup of water in the bottom of a pyrex cake dish. Place fish on top of vegetables. Bake 25 to 30 minutes or until fish flakes easily with a fork.

BARBECUED PORK SPARERIBS

12-14 spareribs   *1 c tarragon*

Partially cook ribs in crock pot for one hour on high and three hours on low. Pour small amount of juice from ribs into pyrex dish. Coat ribs with minced or dried tarragon, and place in dish. Bake in oven for two hours (longer if you like very crisp ribs).

FRIED RABBIT

2 cleaned young rabbits (dress   *4 tablespoons tarragon*
as you would a chicken)   *sunflower oil*
1 c artichoke flour or crushed   *salt to taste*
* sunflower seeds*

Preheat oven to 325° F. Cut meat into serving pieces. Place in cellophane bag with seasoned artichoke flour or sunflower seeds, close, and shake vigorously. Pour oil of the day into stainless steel skillet or electric frying pan to 1/2" depth. Heat oil until sizzling. Cook rabbit in oil, browning on all sides. Finish by roasting until crisp, about 20 minutes or until fork tender.

Variation: For a healthier alternative, place the floured and seasoned
               meat in a liberally oiled baking dish and bake at 300° F. for
               two hours or until fork tender.

FRIED VENISON

1 lb venison (Day 1*)   *1 c sunflower oil*

Dip venison in water, shake, and roll in flour. Fry in hot oil, turning once.
(*Use formula.)

GRAINLESS BREADED PORK CHOPS

1 c sunflower seeds   *2 pork chops*

Preheat oven to 350° F. Blend seeds in blender. Dip chops in water, shake,
and roll in seeds. Bake about 45 minutes or until internal temperature
reaches 170° F.

PORK ROAST

1 pork roast   *1 c pineapple juice*

Preheat oven to 325° F. Pour juice into pan with meat. Bake until tender,
about one hour.

Variation: Cook in crock pot for eight to 10 hours.

PORK STEW

Cut pork into bite-size pieces and season pork with tarragon. Add celery,
carrots, and parsley.

Optional: Add parsnips and/or celery root.

Place in crock pot for one hour on high. Turn to low for six to eight hours.

Variation: Instead of using vegetables from the Carrot Family, add
               Jerusalem artichoke and sweet potato.

RABBIT STEW

Combine pieces of rabbit meat with carrots, celery, and parsley. Cook in crock pot eight to 10 hours on low, the last 30 minutes on high.

Optional: Add Chinese water chestnut, celery root, and/or parsnip.

SALMON OR OTHER FISH STEAK

For a delicate fish steak such as salmon, place on a cake rack over a broiler pan with one-quarter inch of water in the bottom. For an unique flavor, add a little pineapple juice, safflower oil, or kelp.

STIR FRY PORK

2 c pork cut into 1" bite-size pieces
3/4 c sliced celery
5 sliced Jerusalem artichokes
3/4 c sliced carrots
1/3 c sunflower oil

Heat oil in a wok or skillet until very hot. Add pork and stir fry until meat turns white (eight to 10 minutes). Add vegetables and stir fry until done.

Grain and Grain Substitutes

BUCKWHEAT CEREAL

1/2 c buckwheat   *1 c water*

Combine buckwheat and water and simmer 30 minutes until tender.

BUCKWHEAT PANCAKES #1

3/4 c water   *1/2 t sea salt (optional)*
1/2 c buckwheat flour

Mix ingredients until full of bubbles. Spoon on hot griddle greased with safflower or sunflower oil.

BUCKWHEAT SEED CAKES #2

1 c buckwheat or   *1 c filbert or sunflower seed*
* artichoke flour*   *liquid as needed*

Follow recipe instructions for Example #11 in Chapter 15. Grease grill with safflower or sunflower oil. Serve with pureed strawberries, pineapple, or baked rhubarb.

BUCKWHEAT PANCAKES #3

1 c organic buckwheat flour   *1 T date sugar (optional)*
1 t sea salt   *1 1/4 c water*

Combine ingredients and stir well, then beat with electric or hand beater until bubbly. Spoon on griddle greased well with sunflower oil. Serve with date, coconut, strawberry puree, or date/nut salad dressing.

BUCKWHEAT STUFFING

Saute four minutes in three tablespoons safflower oil:

1 stalk celery   *2 T parsley*

Add to two cups cooked buckwheat. Season with kelp and/or nutmeg.

CORN PONE

1/4 c corn meal (Day 1*)   *1/3 t salt*
1/2 c boiling water

Preheat oven to 400° F. Sift corn meal and salt together. Add boiling water and mix. Shape into cakes and place on cookie sheet greased with corn oil. Bake for 15 to 20 minutes. Yields four small cakes. (*Use formula.)

TEFF NO-EGG PANCAKES

1 c teff flour (Day 1*)   *1 c water*
1 t baking soda   *1/4 t (rounded) vitamin C crystals*
pinch of salt   *1 1/2 T safflower oil*

Preheat griddle. Combine dry ingredients and whisk together well. Dissolve vitamin C crystals in water before adding the oil. Whip liquids together, then quickly pour over dry ingredients and mix. Spoon onto hot griddle, turn when tops are bubbly and edges are brown. (*Use formula.)

TEFF HOT CEREAL

1/2 c teff (whole seed or flour) (Day 1*)
1 c water
pinch salt

> Method A: Combine ingredients and simmer 20 minutes. Stir occasionally. For better digestibility, cover and set aside for another 10 to 15 minutes.
>
> Method B: Combine ingredients in a small slow cooker/crockpot. Cook on low overnight. Stir briskly, but avoid pulling much of the crusty ring around the top of the cereal. Oil the side of the cooker beforehand if desired. (*Use formula.)

TEFF PIE CRUST

1/4 c water   *1/8 t salt*
1/4 c safflower oil   *1 c teff flour (*Day 1)*

In a small bowl, whisk together the water, oil, and salt. Stir in the flour.
Press into a nine-inch pie plate. Fill and bake at 350° F about 45 minutes or
until filling is done. To bake empty shell, prick and bake for 12 to 15
minutes. (*Use formula.)

Salads and Side Dishes

FRUIT SALAD COMBINATIONS

#1: Blackberries, strawberries, dates, and coconut.
#2: Pineapple, persimmons, gooseberries, and filberts.

HAWAIIAN SALAD

1 ripe pineapple, cut into chunks   *1 c roasted and chopped*
(may substitute stewed dried   *filberts*
pineapple—about 1 1/2 c)   *1 t ground ginger (Day 2*)*
1 1/2 c strawberries, rinsed
and sliced

Mix all ingredients together. (*Use formula.)

JERUSALEM ARTICHOKES

Prepare artichokes by scrubbing and then scraping or peeling thinly.
Immediately cover with cold water to which one tablespoon pineapple juice
or one-quarter teaspoon vitamin C crystals had been added to each quart to
keep good color. (This step may be omitted if they are sliced one-third inch
thick and steamed. Steam appoximately five to six minutes.) Place in
boiling salted water, cover, and simmer until tender, about 20 to 30 minutes.
Overcooking may cause sogginesss.

Variation: Steam in jackets and peel afterwards.
Variation: Coat with oil of the day and bake whole at 400° F for 30
               minutes.
Variation: Saute.
Variation: Slice raw for salads.

SWEET POTATO WITH PINEAPPLE

4 large sweet potatoes   *1 pineapple*

Chop and combine steamed sweet potato with pineapple.

VEGETABLE SALAD COMBINATIONS

#1: Celery (including yellow and green leaves), carrots, and parsley. (Use sparingly to moderately.)

Optional: Celeriac (celery root) when available.
                 Diced cooked parsnip.
                 Diced cooked rabbit.

#2: Lettuce, endive, Jerusalem artichoke.

Optional: Diced, cooked sweet potato.
                 Sunflower seed (roasted or raw).
                 Diced, steamed scallops.

Snacks, Sweets, and Desserts

DATE COCONUT COOKIES

1 c chopped dates   *1/4 t salt*
1 c shredded coconut   *spring water as needed*
1/2 t baking soda   *1 t sunflower oil*
1/3 c artichoke starch

Preheat oven to 375° F. Cover dates with water, bring to boil, and cool. Mix together all dry ingredients and add dates, water, and oil. Drop onto greased cookie sheets. Bake until brown, about 10 to 12 minutes.

DATE COOKIES

2 c pitted dates (moist)   *2 c coconut meal*

Put dates in blender or food processor and grind to a sticky consistency. (Dates that are too dry will not work—see variation.) Shape into balls and roll in the coconut meal. Store in covered container and keep in cool place. For added interest and food value, press whole filberts or chopped chestnuts onto tops of balls.

Variation: To add moisture to dates, add coconut milk (no more than a teaspoon at a time or it will run rather than stick together.

DATE NUT BALLS

2 parts pitted dates　　　　　　　*1 part filberts*
shredded coconut

Put ingredients through food chopper; form into balls and roll in coconut.

DATE PUDDING

1 lb pitted dates, cut fine　　　　*3 T sunflower oil*
1 t baking soda　　　　　　　　*1 1/2 c artichoke flour*
3/4 c boiling water　　　　　　　*nutmeg to taste (optional)*

Preheat oven to 375° F. Mix dates, soda, and boiling water. Stir well and let cool. Mix oil and flour. Stir into date mixture. Add nutmeg. Pour into well-greased baking dish and bake about 45 minutes. Serve with a coconut pineapple topping.

FRUIT PIE FILLING

1/2 c soaked dates (pureed)　　　*1/8 t sea salt*
1 1/4 c water　　　　　　　　　*1 c berries (pureed)*
1 T juice (pineapple, blackberry,　*2 T agar-agar flakes*
* strawberry, or raspberry*　　　*1 c fresh pineapple*

Bring first five ingredients to a boil. Add agar-agar flakes; cook 15 minutes. Cool. Add fresh fruit and pour into filbert pie shell. Top with shredded coconut or finely ground filberts.

See chapter 15, example #8.

PINEAPPLE SORBET

1/2 ripe pineapple

Trim and cut pineapple into small cubes. Place in blender and puree. Pour pureed pineapple into a nine- by nine-inch metal cake pan and freeze for one hour, stirring occasionally. Serve immediately.

STUFFED DATES

Remove pits from dates and stuff with ground sunflower seed. Roll in freshly grated coconut.

　　Variation:　　Stuff with filberts or pineapple chunks.

SUNFLOWER PATTIES

1 c sunflower seeds   *1/3 c water*

Preheat oven to 250° F. Blend sunflower seeds until fine. Slowly mix with water until mixture is moist enough to handle. Form into patties about 1/4 inch thick. Bake on ungreased cookie sheet until brown. Turn and brown other side.

20

MENUS AND RECIPES FOR DAYS 4, 8, 12, ETC.

Food Chart for Days 4, 8, 12, ETC.

Suggested Menus for Days 4, 8, 12, ETC.

Recipes for Days 4, 8, 12, ETC.

Beverages
Dressings, Garnishes, Sauces, and Spreads
Fish, Fowl, and Meat
Grain and Grain Substitutes
Salads and Side Dishes
Snacks, Sweets, and Desserts
Soups

See also recipe section in "Changing Your Eating Habits" and "Understanding the Formula."

FOOD CHART FOR DAYS 4, 8, 12, ETC.

Food Families: 3, 11, 20, 25, 36, 41, 45, 48, 49, 53, 54, 56, 59, 75, 100, 103, 121, 123, 124, 125, 130.

Animal Protein: 100-Swordfish. 103-Flounder, halibut, sole, turbot. 121-Duck (eggs), goose (eggs). 123-Ruffed grouse (partridge). 124-Chicken (eggs), pheasant, quail. 125-Guinea fowl. 130-Squirrel.

Vegetables: 11-Asparagus, chives, garlic, leek, onion, shallot. 36-Broccoli, Brussels sprouts, cabbage, cauliflower, Chinese cabbage, collards, kale, kohlrabi, mustard greens, radish, rutabaga, turnip, watercress. 41-Alfalfa, all beans, all peas, peanut, soybean. 54-Okra.

Fruit: 25-Fig. 45-Grapefruit, kumquat, lemon, lime, muscat, orange, pummelo, tangelo, tangerine. 48-Mango. 56-Kiwi (Chinese gooseberry). 59-Papaya.

Seeds and Nuts: 41-Peanut, soynut. 48-Cashew nut, pistachio nut. 75-Sesame seed.

Fats and Oils: Fats from any of the above. 41-Peanut oil, soy oil. 75-Sesame oil.

Other: 25-Breadfruit flour. 41-Carbo flour, lima bean flour, peanut flour, soy flour. 75-Sesame seed meal, tahini.

Sweeteners: 41-Clover honey, sage honey.

Herbs and Spices: 11-Garlic, chives. 20-Vanilla beans. 36-Horseradish, mustard.

Beverages: Juices, soups, and teas from any of the above. 3-Shavegrass. 49-Mate tea. 53-Basswood. 54-Althea root, hibiscus (roselle).

SUGGESTED MENUS FOR DAYS 4, 8, 12, ETC.

Breakfast	Lunch	Dinner
Cashew nuts and figs or mango	Vegetable salad (cabbage, kale, radish, egg, or chicken) Sesame seed and oil Papaya	Filet of sole (onions and peanut oil) Asparagus with peanut oil Lima bean and split pea pudding
Grapefruit Carob pancakes	Peanut crackers Peanut butter Fruit salad	Roast chicken Asparagus Vegetable salad Orange sherbet (with pistachio or cashew nuts)
Oranges Peanut butter waffles	Carob cookies Vegetable salad with chicken or egg	Roast duck Steamed okra Cole slaw Mangoes and cashews
Onion omelet Fruit shake	Egg salad with alfalfa sprouts Peanut crackers Radishes Tangerines or oranges	Lentil soup Baked flounder Vegetable salad Asparagus Protein cake

WARNING: Only the first suggestion follows the proper rotation plan. The three additional suggestions are for those people who are easing into rotation.

RECIPES FOR DAYS 4, 8, 12, ETC.

Beverages

BANANA CAROB SHAKE

2 T. soy milk*
1 large banana (Day 2**)
1 pint water

1-2 pinches powdered vanilla bean
1 t carob powder

Mix above ingredients in blender at high speed. (**Use formula.)

* See soy milk recipes below.

CAROB SHAKE

1 quart soy milk
1 T honey
1 T soy or peanut oil
3 T carob powder

Combine all ingredients except oil and blend until smooth in electric blender.
Slowly add oil and continue blending. Heat if desired.

FRUIT SHAKE

2 T soya milk powder
1 pint water

4-6 figs, chopped

Blend first at low speed, then at high speed.

HOMEMADE SOY MILK

This delicious milk contains about 3.7% protein (compared to 3.3% for dairy milk) and takes only about 20 minutes to prepare. Using soybeans bought at $.29 per pound, it will cost roughly $.11 a quart, or less than one third the price of milk. This "boiling water-grind" technique, developed at Cornell University, is quicker and easier than traditional methods, and it inactivates the soy enzyme lipoxygenase, yielding a milk flavored more like that of dairy milk.

The necessary utensils are found in most kitchens. A stainless steel or glass blender is ideal. If you use a plastic blender, use the hottest water available to grind the beans, but then mix with boiling water.

1 1/4 c dry soybeans, *washed and drained 4 to 5 times* (this improves the flavor) and soaked in 4 to 6 c water at room temperature for about 10 hours, then drained and rinsed well 4 to 5 times
12 c hot water

1. Run 12 cups water into large teapot or kettle and bring to a boil. Place a deep, six- to eight-quart pot in sink, set a largecolander in mouth of pot, and line the colander with a large moistened cloth (extra large dish towel) to strain the ground bean-water mixture. Divide the soaked beans into three equal portions.

2. Preheat a glass bowl by slowly pouring in two to three cups boiling water. Allow water to stand for one minute, then discard. In the blender combine one portion of beans with two cups *boiling* water from kettle and puree at high speed for one minute, or until very smooth. Pour puree into the cloth lining the colander. Puree the remaining two portions of beans with two cups boiling water each and pour into sack. Rinse out blender with one-quarter cup boiling water to get the last bit out.

3. Twist mouth of sack to close. Using a glass jar or potato masher, press sack repeatedly against bottom of colander to extract as much soy milk as possible. Shake solids (okara) into one corner of the sack, tighten sack, and press again. If you are very economical, open the mouth of the sack wide in colander, stir okara briefly, then pour two and one-half cups boiling water over okara. Close sack and press again. (Okara may be added to burgers, etc.) Transfer pot containing soy milk to stove.

4. Bring soy milk to a boil over medium-high heat, stirring bottom of cooking pot constantly to prevent sticking. When steam, foam, or boiling occurs, reduce heat to medium and simmer for about seven minutes. Remove pot from burner. Heat 30 minutes in a double boiler as an alternate method.

5. Serve soy milk hot if you wish. For a richer, creamier consistency and a flavor more like that of dairy milk, chill by covering and setting pot in circulating cold water for 10 to 15 minutes. The faster it is chilled, the better the milk will taste and the longer it will last (three to six days). If frozen, it will keep indefinitely. One possibility for enhancing flavor is to adding two and one-quarter to four tablespoons of honey and one-quarter teaspoon or less of vanilla to the batch.

SESAME MILK

1/2 c sesame seeds
2 c water
1 T maple syrup (Day 2)*

Blend nuts in electric blender until they form a meal. Gradually add water and maple syrup to form a milky consistency. Add less water if a cream is desired. (*Use formula.)

Dressings, Garnishes, Sauces, and Spreads

FIG NUT SALAD DRESSING

1/2 c boiling water
1/4 c fig butter
grated orange or lemon rind

1/4 c cashew butter
1/8 t sea salt

Pour boiling water over nut butter, fig butter, and salt. Beat with rotary beater, blender, or food processor. Add grated rind to taste. Chill. Delicious on fruit salad, as sandwich filler, or served with pancakes.

HONEY SAUCE FOR PUDDINGS

1 c light honey
2 egg whites

Dash of sea salt
1 t ground vanilla bean

Heat honey. Beat egg white and salt. Then stir in honey in fine stream, continuing to beat until all honey is added. Flavor with powdered vanilla.

ITALIAN DRESSING

1 clove garlic
1 t honey (optional)
1 t mustard

1 T lemon juice
2 T sesame oil
Chopped chives

Pound garlic until smooth. Add mustard and honey. Stir until smooth; add lemon juice drop by drop and beat well. Add oil gradually and follow with sprinkling of chopped chives

ORANGE FLAVORING

Blend dried peel of organic orange until it becomes a powder. Use for flavoring in cakes, cookies, custards, etc.

MAYONNAISE #1 (BLENDER)

1 egg (room temperature)
3/4 t sea salt
1/2 t dry mustard

2 T lemon juice
1 c oil of the day (room
temperature)

Put egg, seasonings, lemon juice, and one-quarter cup of oil into blender and process at blend speed (high speed in a three-speed blender). Immediately remove top and pour in remaining oil in a steady stream. Turn off. If oil remains, stir with spoon and blend a few seconds more. Repeat until oil disappears.

If mayonnaise does not thicken, pour ingredients back into measuring cup or other container, leaving one-quarter cup of mixture in blender. Add another egg. Proceed as above, pouring remaining ingredients in a steady stream.

MAYONNAISE #2

2 egg yolks   1 t sea salt
1 c oil of the day   1 T lemon juice

Beat salt into unbeaten egg yolks. Add oil very slowly, drop by drop at first, until dressing becomes thick and shiny. (If it curdles, add another yolk, beating it in slowly.) After one-half of the oil has been used, add lemon juice.

PEANUT BUTTER

1 c shelled peanuts   1 t peanut oil

Put peanuts and peanut oil in blender. Blend, turning motor off from time to time to prevent overheating, until you have the consistency you want—chunk style, smooth, or soupy. Keep in refrigerator. If you do not like unroasted peanuts, roast them for 20 minutes at 300° F in their shells, and cool before making peanut butter.

If you have a food processor, omit peanut oil.

PEANUT BUTTER, ROASTED

1 c shelled roasted peanuts   1 t peanut oil

Put peanuts and peanut oil in the blender and blend to desired consistency. Store in refrigerator. Substitute other nuts for peanuts if desired.

SEED NUT BUTTER

1 c sesame seeds   1/2 t minced chives or ground
1 T sesame seed oil   vanilla beans (optional)

Grind or blend until fine and smooth. Store in refrigerator.

Variation: Substitute cashews for sesame seed.

SESAME CREAM

Blend: 1 c sesame seeds
1 c warm water (blend smooth)
1 T honey
Dash powdered vanilla beans

Optional: You may add figs or mango for a different flavor.

SESAME NUT CREAM

1 c sesame milk   *6 dried figs, chopped*
1/2 c nut butter

Blend well and serve over breakfast fruit, or as a sweet dressing for salads.

Fish, Fowl, and Meat

CORNISH HEN

Preheat oven to 250° F. Dip cornish hen into beaten egg. Sprinkle generously with sesame seed meal. Place in a greased baking dish with sesame seed oil. Bake three to five hours, depending on crispness desired.

ROAST CHICKEN #1

Rinse chicken under cold water and pat dry. Bake at 325° F for 20 minutes per pound.

ROAST CHICKEN #2

Rub salt and a bit of chives into a frozen fryer (three pounds or larger). Cook in pressure cooker for 30 minutes or less. Remove with great care so it does not fall apart. Fasten legs together with a bit of string. Salt again and add garlic if desired. Broil until browned nicely—just a few minutes. Thicken broth in pressure cooker for gravy, using peanut flour.

SESAME CHICKEN OR GUINEA HEN

Preheat oven to 250° F. Dip chicken into beaten egg. Sprinkle generously with sesame seed meal. (Don't dip into the meal; when sesame meal is wet it doesn't cling to the chicken.) Place in baking dish greased with sesame seed oil. Bake for three to five hours, depending on how crisp you like it. Baked long enough, it becomes as crisp as fried chicken.

Variation: When time does not permit the slow process, preheat oven to 350° F and bake for one hour.

Variation: Liberally coat the chicken first with garlic and then with peanut oil or sesame seed oil. Proceed as above.

STIR FRY CHICKEN

4 T soy or peanut oil
2 c chicken cut into 1" bite-size pieces
1/2 c minced onions
1/2 c carrots, peeled and sliced (Day 3*)
10 asparagus stalks chopped in 1" lengths
1/4 c soy sauce

Heat oil in a wok or skillet until very hot. Add asparagus, carrots, and onion and stir fry until crisp and tender (eight to 10 minutes). Add chicken and stir fry until meat loses its pink color. Remove from heat, add soy sauce, and let it simmer gently a few minutes. (*Use formula.)

Grain and Grain Substitutes

CAROB PANCAKES

3 egg yolks   *1 c peanut starch minus 3 T*
1/4 c water   *3 egg whites*
3 T carob powder

Spoon onto greaseless electric fry pan (380° F). Cook five to 10 minutes, flipping once.

Variation: Grease griddle or fry pan with peanut oil or sesame seed oil.

PEANUT NOODLES

Beat until light:

3 egg yolks   *1 whole egg*

Beat in:

3 T cold water   *1 t sea salt*

Stir in and work with hands:

2 c peanut flour

Divide flour into three parts. Roll out each piece as thin as possible on lightly floured board. Place between two towels until dough is partially dried. Roll up dough as for jelly roll. Cut with sharp knife into strips. Shake out strips and allow to dry before using or storing.

PEANUT WAFFLES

1 c peanut flour
3 eggs, separated and beaten,
  whites very stiff
1/4 c water or less

2 T peanut oil
1/4 t sea salt
2 T honey (optional)

Add flour to beaten yolks, then oil and salt. Stir well and add water very gradually (amount required depends on the humidity). When smooth, fold in beaten whites and bake in thoroughly cleaned waffle iron (to remove any wheat flour residue). Use peanut oil to grease iron if necessary.

Salads and Side Dishes

ALFALFA SPROUTS

Sprouts should never be cooked. Snack on them as they are. Put a handful with your favorite spread. Add to salads, cottage cheese, soup, or stew just before serving. Alfalfa sprouts are excellent for sandwiches—in place of lettuce and a lot cheaper.

ALFALFA SPROUT SALAD

1 T orange or grapefruit juice
2 c alfalfa sprouts
2 T of roasted sesame seeds or cashew nuts

Pour juice over sprouts and mix. Sprinkle nuts or seeds on top.

COLE SLAW

Shred cabbage. Chop up grapefruit and toss with grapefruit juice.

FRUIT SALAD

Combine: Oranges, grapefruit, muscats.
Optional: Add cashews or sesame seeds.
Optional: Add papaya.
Optional: Sweeten with figs.

LEGUMES

One and one-half cups of dried beans will serve six. Split peas, lentils, pinto beans, and blackeyed peas can be cooked without soaking. Other dried legumes should be soaked. Some double in size, lentils more than double, and soybeans increase three times their original size. Wash legumes thoroughly before soaking.

Simmer legumes in the water in which they were soaked to retain nutritive value and develop full natural flavor. Salt, onions, and herbs may be added to the soaking and simmering water to enhance flavor.

Soybeans are an excellent substitute for meat; one-half cup provides 10 units of protein and only 105 calories. The protein in other legumes is incomplete and must be supplemented with eggs, fish, or fowl.

For a variation on string beans, stir in a raw egg when nearly cooked. Salt to taste.

OKRA, BOILED

Drop okra into boiling water, place lid on pan, and cook four to five minutes. Add sea salt and peanut oil and season with lemon juice.

OKRA, FRIED

1 c fresh okra   *1/2 c peanut flour*
1 egg, beaten   *1 c peanut oil*

Cut okra in small one inch cubes. Dip in beaten egg. Roll in flour. Fry in peanut oil.

OKRA (SAUTEED SOUTHERN STYLE)

Cut okra into small pieces about one-quarter inch thick. Roll in beaten egg, then roll in peanut flour. Saute in peanut oil at low heat.

OKRA, STEAMED

Okra is good in soup or cooked with onions. Steam until tender. Season with two tablespoons peanut oil, sea salt, and one teaspoon chives.

SLAW SUPREME

1 head cabbage   *2 T lemon juice*
1/2 c mayonnaise   *4 chopped scallions*

Cut cabbage into thinest shreds possible. Place in large bowl and combine with mayonnaise thinned with lemon juice. Add scallions.

Variation: Use chives, onions, or shallots instead of scallions.

SPLIT PEA/LIMA BEAN PUDDING

1 1/2 c split peas   *6 c water*
1 c dried lima beans   *Sea salt to taste*

Place lima beans in quart container, cover with water, and soak overnight.
Drain off water into four-quart pan, adding enough water to make six cups.
Bring to boil on high heat. Reduce heat to low and add dried peas and
soaked beans. After one hour, stir every 10 or 15 minutes.

If necessary, add enough boiling water to keep beans from thickening and
burning.

Variation: Serve in soup or as a vegetable. Use liquid as stock.
Variation: Cook until water evaporates and serve as pudding. This
              process requires close attention as pudding thickens.

TOFU

1 qt soybean milk
1 1/2 T lemon juice mixed with 1/4 c water

Bring soybean milk to boil, cooking until quite thick. Turn off heat and add
mixture of lemon juice and water. Stir and let set a few minutes until milk
curdles. Pour through cheesecloth. Tie and hang overnight to let liquid drain
into bowl, leaving tofu inside cheesecloth.

Place any tofu not immediately used in a glass jar, cover with water, and
store in refrigerator.

Season with chives and serve on peanut crackers.

Season with horseradish or mustard and serve with alfalfa sprouts and salad.

VEGETABLE SALAD

Combine three of the following: Raw cabbage, watercress, radishes, kale,
mustard greens, and kohlrabi.

Dressing: Sesame cream or peanut oil with chives or mayonnaise.
Optional: Lemon juice.
Optional: Sprouts (alfalfa sprouts are particularly good).
Optional: Sesame seeds.
Optional: Chopped eggs or chopped chives.
Optional: Cold cooked beans or peas.

Snacks, Sweets, and Desserts

CANDIED ORANGE PEEL

Peel of 6 medium oranges   *1/2 c water*
1 c honey

Cut orange peels into sixths. Remove pulp and most of white membrane.
Soak overnight in water (weigh down with plate). Drain and wash. Cover
with cold water and bring to a boil. Repeat two times (to help remove bitter
taste). Boil honey, add water in a saucepan; add peel and boil until
translucent and slightly thick. Drain in colander and spread on greased
cellophane to dry. Makes about two cups.

CAROB ANGEL FOOD CAKE

1 c carob powder   *12 egg whites*

Preheat oven to 300° F. Add carob powder to egg whites and beat until very
light. Bake 20 to 30 minutes.

CAROB COOKIES

3 egg whites   *1/2 c carob powder*

Preheat oven to 300° F. Beat egg whites until very stiff, then fold in carob
powder with spatula. Drop on cookie sheet greased with peanut oil and bake
15 minutes. Add a cashew nut to each cookie before baking if desired.
Honey may be added; however, the cookies are actually sweet with just carob
powder.

   Variation: Add 1 c Spanish peanuts to batter.

CAROB PUDDING

3 1/4 c water or cashew nut milk   *3 T carob*
3 T peanut starch   *Dash of sea salt*
3/4 c honey (optional)

Mix to thicken. Stir while cooking. Serve hot or cold.

FIG NUT BALLS

2 parts dried figs
1 1/3 parts roasted cashew nuts (or peanuts)

Put two parts figs and one part nuts through food chopper; form into balls. Crush remaining nuts. Roll balls in the crushed nuts.

FLOURLESS PIE CRUST

3 egg whites (for a 9" pan)   *Dash of sea salt*
2 t honey

Preheat oven to 300° F. Make a stiff meringue and form as a crust in the pan. Don't use too much because it rises. Bake until brown.

NUT COOKIES

1 c chopped cashew nuts   *1/3 c honey*
  or peanuts   *Sea salt to taste*
1 egg white, unbeaten

Preheat oven to 325° F. Beat together all ingredients and drop by teaspoonfuls onto well-oiled cookie sheet. Bake 15 minutes. Remove from pan while still warm. Add nut meal if needed for thickening.

NUT SQUARES

2 c sesame seeds or ground   *1 egg white*
  cashew nuts   *1 1/2 t sesame seed oil*
1/2 c honey

Preheat oven to 325° F. Combine ingredients over low heat or in top of double boiler. Cool. Shape into balls or roll between layers of greased cellophane and cut into squares. Oil hands before shaping balls. Bake on greased cookie sheet for 30 to 40 minutes. Cool and remove from pan. Add nut meal for body, if needed.

PEANUT BUTTER COOKIES

2/3 c peanut butter
1/2 t sea salt
2 T peanut flour
1/3 c honey

1/2 t vanilla
2 egg whites, beaten until
    slightly stiff

Preheat oven to 325° F. Combine ingredients in order given. Roll into small balls and place on greased cookie sheet. Crisscross with fork and bake for 12 to 15 minutes. Yield: approximately two dozen.

PEANUT CRACKERS

3 c peanut flour
1 c ground sesame seed

3/4 t sea salt
3 T peanut oil

Preheat oven to 250° F. Combine ingredients and add enough boiling water to make stiff dough. Grease cookie sheet with peanut oil and roll dough as thin as possible on sheet. Keep roller wet with water. Bake for 10 minutes, then turn oven up to 350° F for 15 minutes. Cut into squares.

PROTEIN CAKE

7 eggs, separated
1 t vanilla
Pinch sea salt

1/2 lb cashew nuts, ground
    fine
1/3 c honey

Preheat oven to 325° F. Beat egg whites until stiff. Blend honey, vanilla, and salt with egg yolks. Add nuts and mix well. Fold into whites. Place in ungreased angel food pan and bake one hour. Invert and separate.

PROTEIN SNACK

1 egg, well beaten
3/4 c peanut flour
3/4 c sesame seed meal

2 T water
1 T soybean oil
2 T soybean flour

Preheat oven to 350° F. Mix, drop on greased cookie sheet, and press down with fork. Bake about 15 minutes.

SESAME SEED CANDY

2 c sesame seed
1/2 c sesame oil
2 T honey

1/2 t vanilla
1 T peanut butter
1 T carob powder

Place sesame seeds and oil in blender. Run blender with cover on for awhile, then remove cover and push seeds down and under. Add honey and vanilla;

blend until smooth. Divide into three bowls. Add one tablespoon peanut butter to one; one tablespoon carob to another; and leave one plain. Shape.

SHERBET

1 c orange juice or mashed
 papaya
2 egg whites, beaten stiff
 (may be omitted if allergic to eggs)

2 c water
2/3 c honey

Boil water and honey for five minutes. Cool and add fruit juice and put in freezingtray. When firm, remove and mix with stiffly beaten egg whites, beating mixture until light and frothy with electric mixer.

Soups

CHICKEN BROTH

1 1/2 lb chopped chicken
4 c cold water

Put chicken in stock pot. Add water and bring to a boil over medium heat. Continue boiling five minutes. Reduce heat and simmer two to three hours. Be sure to check the pot occasionally to prevent chicken from sticking. Taste the chicken after two hours. If the chicken has no flavor, the broth is done; if it is still flavorful, simmer a maximum of one more hour. When broth is fully cooked, strain it through cheese cloth and cool. Cover and refrigerate overnight. Remove hardened fat from the top of broth. Broth may be refrigerated up to five days and frozen up to two months. Yields two cups.

CHICKEN GUMBO SOUP

One 4-4 1/2 lb stewing chicken, cut up
Add: 2 c water and 1/2 t sea salt

Cook until tender, about two hours. Remove chicken from bones and cube. Skim fat from broth.

Return chicken to broth and add:

4 c okra, thinly sliced
1 t honey (optional)
2 t sea salt

1/2 c chopped onion
1/8 t chives

Cover and simmer one-half hour or until okra is tender. Serves eight.

CHICKEN SOUP (CROCK POT)

1 chicken, quartered   *3-4 cloves garlic*
1 medium onion

Place ingredients into crock pot and cook on high for one hour. Reduce to low heat and cook until chicken is fork tender about five hours). Debone chicken. Put bones back in crock pot and fill the pot with boiling water. Cook for two to 12 hours (the longer the better for strong soup stock).

Optional: Add two tablespoons lemon juice.

Optional: Add one-half teaspoon mustard seeds.

Serve with diced chicken, cooked beans, and/or peas.

Variation: Serve with uncooked seed sprouts.

LENTIL SOUP

1 1/4 c lentils   *4 1/2 c water*
10 leeks (optional)   *1/3 t salt*

Bring water to a boil and add chopped leeks and lentils. Simmer one hour or until done, adding water as needed.

SPLIT PEA OR LENTIL SOUP

1-1 1/2 c lentils or   *1 quart water*
 split peas   *sea salt to taste*
1 diced onion

Place water in large saucepan. Add lentils or dried peas (depending on thickness desired) and onion. Cook slowly one to two hours. Add boiling water when necessary.

APPENDIX A

LIST #1
FOOD FAMILIES
ALPHABETICAL

APPENDIX A

LIST #1
FOOD FAMILIES (ALPHABETICAL)

A

81	abalone
80	absinthe
41	acacia (gum)
46	acerola
79	acorn squash
1	agar agar
12	agave
98	albacore
41	alfalfa
1	Algae Family
63	allspice
40b	almond
11	*Aloe vera*
54	althea root
30	amaranth
12	Amaryllis Family
94	amberjack
86	American eel
117	*Amphibians*
85	anchovy
65	angelica
65	anise
38	annatto
136	antelope
40a	apple
73	apple mint
40b	apricot
47	arrowroot, Brazilian (tapioca)
9	arrowroot *(Colocasia)*
17	arrowroot, East Indian *(Curcuma)*
19	Arrowroot Family
13	arrowroot, Figi *(Tacca)*
4	arrowroot, Florida *(Zamia)*
19	arrowroot *(Maranta* starch)
16	arrowroot *(Musa)*

18	arrowroot, Queensland
80	artichoke flour
80	artichoke (globe)
80	artichoke, Jerusalem
9	Arum Family
11	asparagus
2	*Aspergillus*
34	avocado
41	azuki beans

B

2	baker's yeast
6	bamboo shoots
16	banana
16	Banana Family
46	Barbados cherry
6	barley
73	basil
114	bass (black)
113	bass (yellow)
53	basswood
34	bay leaf
41	bean
132	bear
66	bearberry
24	Beech Family
137	beef
28	beet
74	bell pepper
73	bergamot
121	birds
23	Birch Family
38	Bixa Family
114	black bass
40c	blackberry
41	black beans
41	black-eyed peas
21	black pepper
80	black salsify

41	fenugreek	6	Grass Family
78	fetticus	61	grenadine
25	fig	6	grits
13	Fiji arrowroot	74	ground cherry
23	filbert	7	groundnut
34	filé	91	grouper
65	finocchio	123	grouse (ruffed)
104	fishes (fresh water)	63	guava
83	fishes (salt water)	125	guinea fowl
44	Flax Family	41	gum acacia
44	flaxseed	41	gum tragacanth
65	Florence fennel		
4	Florida arrowroot		**H**
103	flounder		
80	French endive	87	haddock
116	freshwater drum	87	hake
117	frog (frog legs)	103	halibut
2	Fungi Family	101	harvest fish
		23	hazelnut
	G	22	heartnut
		66	Heath Family
41	garbanzo bean	54	hibiscus
27	garden sorrel	22	hickory nut
11	garlic	134	hog
79	gherkin	49	Holly Family
5	gin	6	hominy
17	ginger	79	honeydew
17	Ginger Family	77	Honeysuckle Family
64	ginseng	25	hop
64	Ginseng Family	73	horehound
80	globe artichoke	133	horse
6	gluten flour	36	horseradish
137	goat	3	horsetail
137	goat's milk	3	Horsetail Family
79	golden nugget squash	79	Hubbard squash
80	goldenrod	66	huckleberry
31	golden seal	73	hyssop
121	goose		
39	gooseberry		**I**
28	Goosefoot Family		
65	gotu kola	15	Iris Family
79	Gourd Family	1	Irish moss
6	graham flour		
58	grenadilla		**J**
52	grape		
52	Grape Family	8	Japanese persimmon
45	grapefruit	80	Jerusalem artichoke
52	grapeseed oil	41	jicama

O

P

Y

Z

APPENDIX B

LIST #2
FOOD FAMILIES
NUMERICAL

APPENDIX B

LIST #2 FOOD FAMILIES (NUMERICAL)

PLANT

1 - Algae Family
     agar agar
     carrageen (Irish moss)
  * dulse
     kelp (seaweed)

2 - Fungi Family
     baker's yeast
     brewer's or nutritional
      yeast
     citric acid (*Aspergillus*)
     mold (in certain cheeses)
     morel
     mushroom
     puffball
     truffle

3 - Horsetail Family,
     Equisetaceae
  *   shavegrass (horsetail)

4 - Cycad Family, *Cycadaceae*
     Florida arrowroot (*Zamia*)

5 - Conifer Family, *Coniferae*
  *   juniper (gin)
     pine nut (pinon, pinyon)

6 - Grass Family, *Graminaea*
     bamboo shoots
     barley
       malt
       maltose
     corn (mature)
       corn meal
       corn oil
       cornstarch
       corn sugar
       hominy grits
       popcorn
     lemon grass
       citronella
     millet
     milo
     oat
       oatmeal
     rice
       rice flour
       rice syrup
     rye
       rye flour
     sorghum grain
       syrup
     spelt
     sugar cane
       cane sugar
       molasses
     teff
     triticale
     wheat
       bran
       bulgur
       flour
       gluten
       graham
       patent
       semolina
       whole wheat
       wheat germ
     wild rice

7 - Sedge Family, *Cyperaceae*
     Chinese water chestnut
     chufa (groundnut)

* One or more plant parts (leaf, root, seed, etc.) used as beverage.

8 -   Palm Family, *Palmacaeae*
      coconut
         coconut meal
         coconut oil
      date
         date sugar
      palm cabbage
      sago starch (*Metroxylon*)

9 -   Arum Family, *Araceae*
      ceriman (*Monstera*)
      dasheen (*Colocasia*)
         arrowroot
      malanga (*Xanthosoma*)
      taro (*Colocasia*)
         arrowroot
         poi
      yautia (*Xanthosoma*)

10 - Pineapple Family,
      Bromeliaceae
      pineapple

11 - Lily Family, *Lillaceae*
      Aloe vera
      asparagus
      chives
      garlic
      leek
      onion
      ramp
   * sarsaparilla
      shallot
      yucca (soap plant)

12 - Amaryllis Family,
      Amaryllidaceae
      agave
         mescal
         pulque
         tequila

13 - Tacca Family, *Taccaceae*
      Fiji arrowroot (*Tacca*)

14 - Yam Family, *Dioscoreaceae*
      Chinese potato (yam)
      ñame (yampi)

15 - Iris Family, *Iridaceae*
      orris root (scent)
      saffron (Crocus)

16 - Banana Family, *Muscaeae*
      arrowroot (Musa)
      banana
      plantain

17 - Ginger Family,
      Zingiberaceae
      cardamom
      East Indian arrowroot
         (*Curcuma*)
      ginger
      tumeric

18 - Canna Family, *Cannaceae*
      Queensland arrowroot

19 - Arrowroot Family,
      Marantaceae
      arrowroot (*Maranta starch*)

20 - Orchid Family, *Orchidaceae*
      vanilla

21 - Pepper Family, *Piperaceae*
      peppercorn (*Piper*)
         black pepper
         white pepper

22 - Walnut Family,
      Juglandaceae
      black walnut
      butternut
      English walnut
      heartnut
      hickory nut
      pecan

23 - Birch Family, *Betulaceae*
      filbert (hazelnut)

oil of birch
   (wintergreen)
   (some wintergreen flavor is
   methyl salicylate)

24 - Beech Family, *Fagaceae*
   chestnut
   chinquapin

25 - Mulberry Family, *Moraceae*
   breadfruit
   fig
  * hop
   mulberry

26 - Protea Family, *Proteaceae*
   macademia
     (Queensland nut)

27 - Buckwheat Family,
   Polygonaceae
   buckwheat
   garden sorrel
   rhubarb
   sea grape

28 - Goosefoot Family,
   Chenopodiaceae
   beet
   lamb's quarters
   quinoa
   spinach
   sugar beet
   swiss chard
   tampala

29 - Carpetweed Family,
   Aizoaceae
   New Zealand spinach

30 - Purslane Family,
   Portulacaceae
   amaranth
   pigweed (purslane)

31 - Buttercup Family,
   Ranunculaceae

* golden seal

32 - Custard-Apple Family
   Annonaceae
   cherimoya
   custard-apple
   papaw (paw-paw)

33 - Nutmeg Family,
   Myristicaceae
   nutmeg
   mace

34 - Laurel Family, *Lauraceae*
   avocado
   bay leaf
   cassia bark
   cinnamon
  * sassafras
     file (powder)

35 - Poppy Family,
   Papaveraceae
   poppyseed

36 - Mustard Family, *Cruciferae*
   broccoli
   Brussels sprouts
   cabbage
   canola oil
   cardoon
   cauliflower
   Chinese cabbage
   collards
   colza shoots
   couve tronshuda
   curley cress
   daicon
   horseradish
   kale
   kohlrabi
   mustard greens
     mustard seed/powder
   radish
   rapeseed (oil)
   rutabaga (swede)
   turnip
     turnip greens

upland cress
watercress

37 - Caper Family,
Capparidaceae
caper

38 - Bixa Family, *Bixaceae*
annatto
(natural yellow dye)

39 - Saxifrage Family,
Saxifragaceae
currant
gooseberry

40 - Rose Family, *Rosaceae*
a. pomes
apple
crabapple
loquat
pear
pectin
quince
rosehips
b. stone fruits
almond
apricot
cherry
nectarine
peach
plum (prune)
sloe
c. berries
blackberry
boysenberry
dewberry
loganberry
raspberry
black raspberry
purple raspberry
strawberry
wineberry
d. herb
burnet
(cucumber flavor)

41 - Legume Family,
Leguminoseae
alfalfa (sprouts)
anasazi beans
black beans
black-eyed peas (cowpea)
carob
carob syrup
fava beans
fenugreek
garbanzo beans (chickpea)
green beans (string)
gum acacia
jicama
kidney beans
kudzu
lentil
licorice
lima beans
mung beans (sprouts)
navy beans
pea
peanut
peanut oil
red clover
senna
soy bean
lecithin
soy flour
soy grits
soy milk
soy oil
tamarind
tonka bean
coumarin

42 - Oxalis Family, *Oxalidaceae*
carambola
oxalis

43 - Nasturtium Family,
Tropaeoloceae
nasturtium

44 - Flax Family, *Linaceae*
flaxseed
linseed oil

45 -   Rue (Citrus) Family,
       Ruaceae
       citron
       grapefruit
       kumquat
       lemon
       lime
       murcot
       orange
       pummelo
       tangelo
       tangerine

46 -   Malpighia Family,
       Malpighiaceae
       acerola (Barbados cherry)

47 -   Spurge Family,
       Euphorbiaceae
       cassava or yuca (*Manihot*)
          cassava meal (manioc)
          tapioca
          (Brazilian arrowroot)
       castor bean
          castor oil

48 -   Cashew Family,
       Anacardiaceae
       cashew
       mango
       pistachio

49 -   Holly Family, *Aquifoliaceae*
       matè (yerba matè)

50 -   Maple Family, *Aceraceae*
       maple sugar
       maple syrup

51 -   Soapberry Family,
       Sapindaceae
       litchi (lychee)

52 -   Grape Family, *Vitaceae*
       grape
          brandy
          champagne

cream of tartar
dried "currant"
muscadine
raisin
wine
wine vinegar

53 -   Linden Family, *Tiliceae*
*   basswood (linden)

54 -   Mallow Family, *Malvaceae*
*   althea root
       cottonseed oil
*   hibiscus (roselle)
       okra

55 -   Sterculia Family,
       Sterculiaceae
       chocolate (cacao)
*   cocoa
          cocoa butter
       cola nut

56 -   Dillenia Family,
       Dilleniaceae
       Chinese gooseberry (kiwi)

57 -   Tea Family, *Theaceae*
*   tea

58 -   Passion Flower Family,
       Passifloraceae
       granadilla
          (passion fruit)

59 -   Papaya Family, *Caricaceae*
       papaya

60 -   Cactus Family, *Cactaceae*
       prickly pear

61 -   Pomegranate Family,
       Puniceae
       grenadine
       pomegranate

62 - Sapucaya Family,
    Lecythidaceae
    Brazil nut
    sapucaya nut
      (paradise nut)

63 - Myrtle Family, *Myrtaceae*
    all spice (*Pimenta*)
    clove
*   eucalyptus
    guava

64 - Ginseng Family, *Araliaceae*
*   American ginseng
*   Chinese ginseng

65 - Carrot Family, *Umbelliferae*
    angelica
    anise
    caraway
    carrot
    celeriac (celery root)
    celery
*   celery seed and leaf
    chervil
    coriander
    cumin
    dill
      dill seed
    fennel
      finocchio
      Florence fennel
*   gotu kola
*   lovage
*   parsley
    parsnip
    sweet cecily

66 - Heath Family, *Ericaceae*
*   bearberry
*   blueberry
    cranberry
*   huckleberry

67 - Sapodilla Family,
    Sapotaceae
    chicle (chewing gum)

68 - Ebony Family, *Ebonaceae*
    American persimmon
    kaki (Japanese persimmon)

69 - Olive Family, *Oleaceae*
    olive (green olive)
    olive oil

70 - Morning Glory Family,
    Concolculacea
    camote
    sweet potato

71 - Borage Family, *Boraginceae*
    borage (oil)
*   comfrey leaf and root

72 - Verbena Family,
    Verbenaceae
*   lemon verbena

73 - Mint Family (Herbs),
    Labiatae
    apple mint
    basil
    bergamot
*   catnip
*   chia seed
    clary
*   dittany
*   horehound
*   hyssop
    lavender
    lemon balm
    marjoram
    oregano
*   pennyroyal
*   peppermint
    rosemary
    sage
*   spearmint
    summer savory
    thyme
    winter savory

74 - Potato Family, *Solanaceae*
    eggplant

ground cherry
pepino (melon pear)
pepper (*Capsicum*)
   bell, sweet
   cayenne
   chili pepper
   green pepper
   hot pepper
   paprika
pimiento
potato
tobacco
tomatillo
tomato
tree tomato

75 - Pedalium Family,
     Pedaliceae
   sesame seed
     sesame oil
     tahini

76 - Madder Family, *Rubiceae*
  * coffee
   woodruff

77 - Honeysuckle Family,
     Caprifoliaceae
   elderberry

78 - Valerian Family,
     Valerianceae
   corn salad (fetticus)

79 - Gourd Family,
     Cucurbitaceae
   chayote
   Chinese preserving melon
   cucumber
   gherkin
   melons
     cantaloupe
     casaba
     crenshaw
     honeydew
     Persionmelon

muskmelon
watermelon
pumpkin
   pumpkin seed
squashes
   acorn
   buttercup
   butternut
   Boston marrow
   caserta
   cocozelle
   crookneck
   cushaw
   golden nugget
   Hubbard varieties
   patty pan
   straightneck
   turban
   vegetable spaghetti
   yellow
   zucchini

80 - Composite Family,
     Compositae
  * boneset
  * burdock root
   cardoon
  * chamomile
  * chicory
   coltsfoot
   costmary
   dandelion
   endive
   escarole
   globe artichoke
  * goldenrod
  * Jerusalem artichoke
   artichoke flour
   lettuce
     Boston Bibb
     celtuce
     iceberg
     leaf
     romaine
pyrethrum
safflower oil
salsify (oyster plant)
santolina (herb)

scolymus
(Spanish oyster plant)
scorzonera (black salsify)
southernwood
stevia rebaudiana
sunflower seed
    sunflower oil
tansy (herb)
tarragon
witloof chicory
    (French endive)
wormwood (absinthe)
* yarrow

ANIMAL

81 -   SEAFOOD

81 -   Mollusks
        abalone
        clam
        cockle
        mussel
        Moyster
        scallop
        snail
        squid

82 - Crustaceans
        crab
        crayfish
        lobster
        prawn
        shrimp

83 - FISHES (SALTWATER)

   84 -   Herring Family
           menhaden
           pilchard (sardine)
           sea herring

   85 -   Anchovy Family
           anchovy

   86 -   Eel Family
           American eel

87 -   Codfish Family
        cod (scrod)
        cusk
        haddock
        hake
        pollack
        whiting

88 -   Sea Catfish Family
        ocean catfish

89 -   Mullet Family
        mullet

90 -   Silverside Family
        silverside (whitebait)

91 -   Seabass Family
        grouper
            sea bass

92 -   Tilefish Family
        tilefish

93 -   Bluefish Family
        bluefish

94 -   Jack Family
        amberjack
        pompano
        yellow jack

95 -   Dolphin Family
        dolphin

96 -   Croaker Family
        croaker
        drum
        sea trout
        silver perch
        spot
        weakfish (spotted sea
        trout)

97 -   Porgy Family
        northern scup (porgy)

98 - Mackerel Family
albacore
bonito
mackerel
skipjack
tuna

99 - Marlin Family
marlin
sailfish

100 - Swordfish Family
swordfish

101 - Harvestfish Family
butterfish
harvestfish

102 - Scorpionfish Family
rosefish (ocean perch)

103A - Flounder Family
dab
flounder
halibut
plaice
sole
turbot

103B - Snapper Family
red snapper

103C - Requien Family
shark

104 - FISHES (FRESHWATER)

104 - Sturgeon Family
sturgeon (caviar)

105 - Herring Family
shad (roe)

106 - Salmon Family
salmon species
trout species

107 - Whitefish Family
whitefish

108 - Smelt Family
smelt

109 - Pike Family
muskellunge
pickerel
pike

110 - Sucker Family
buffalofish
sucker

111 - Minnow Family
carp
chub

112 - Catfish Family
lake catfish species

113 - Bass Family
white perch
yellow bass

114 - Sunfish Family
black bass species
crappie
sunfish species
pumpkinseed

115 - Perch Family
sauger
walleye
yellow perch

116 - Croaker Family
freshwater drum

117 - AMPHIBIANS

117 - Frog Family
frog (frog legs)

118 -   <u>REPTILES</u>

119 -   Snake Family
         rattlesnake

120 -   Turtle Family
         terpapin
         turtle species

121 -   <u>BIRDS</u>

121 -   Duck Family
         duck
           duck eggs
         goose
           goose eggs

122 -   Dove Family
         dove
         pigeon (squab)

123 -   Grouse Family
         ruffed grouse
           (partridge)

124 -   Pheasant Family
         chicken
           chicken eggs
         cornish hen
         peafowl
         pheasant
         quail

125 -   Guinea Fowl Family
         guinea fowl
           guinea fowl eggs

126 -   Turkey Family
         turkey
           turkey eggs

127 -   <u>MAMMALS</u>

128 -   Opossum Family
         opossum

129 -   Hare Family
         rabbit

130 -   Squirrel Family
         squirrel

131 -   Whale Family
         whale

132 -   Bear Family
         bear

133 -   Horse Family
         horse

134 -   Swine Family
         hog (pork)
         bacon
         ham
         lard
         pork gelatin
         sausage
         scrapple

135 -   Deer Family
         caribou
         deer (venison)
         elk
         moose
         reindeer

136 -   Pronghorn Family
         antelope

137 -   Bovine Family
         beef
         beef by-products
         butter
         cheese
         cow's milk products
         dried milk
         gelatin
         ice cream
         lactose
         oleomargarine
         rennin (rennet)
         sausage
         suet

yogurt

goat's milk yogurt

veal

sheep (domestic)

buffalo (bison)

lamb

goat (kid)

mutton

goat's milk

Rocky Mountain sheep

goat's cheese

* One or more plant parts (leaf, root, seed, etc.) used as beverage.

APPENDIX C

DAILY FOOD CHARTS

FOOD CHART FOR DAYS 1, 5, 9, ETC.

Food Families: 2, 6, 22, 34, 35, 40a, 42, 46, 52, 61, 62, 73, 74, 82, 87, 88, 105, 112, 137.

Animal Protein: 82-Crab, crayfish, lobster, prawn, shrimp. 87-Cod, haddock. 88-Ocean catfish. 105-Herring, sardine. 112-Catfish species. 137-Beef (butter, cheese, kefir, milk, veal, yogurt), buffalo, goat, sheep (lamb, mutton).

Vegetables: 2-Mushroom, truffle. 6-Corn, bamboo shoots. 74-Eggplant, sweet pepper, potato, tomato.

Fruit: 34-Avocado. 40a-Apple, crabapple, loquat, pear, quince. 42-Carambola. 46-Acerola. 52-Dried currants, grape, raisin. 61-Pomegranate.

Seeds & Nuts: 22-Hickory nut, pecan, walnut. 62-Brazil nut.

Fats and Oils: 6-Corn oil, rice oil. 22-Walnut oil. 34-Avocado oil. 137-Butter and any fat from above.

Other: 2-Yeast. 6-Barley, bulgur, cornmeal, corn starch, millet, oats, oat flour, rice, rice flour, rye, rye flour, spelt, teff, wheat, wheat flour. 52-Cream of tartar. 74-Potato meal, potato starch.

Sweeteners: 6-Grain syrups: barley, corn, malt, molasses and sorghum. 52-Raisin.

Herbs and Spices: 6-Lemon grass. 34-Bay leaf, cassia, cinnamon. 35-Poppyseed. 73-Applemint, basil, mint, lemon balm, marjoram, oregano, peppermint, rosemary, sage, spearmint, summer savory, thyme, winter savory.

Beverages: Juice, soup, and tea from any of the above. 73-Tea from catnip, chia seed, dittany, horehound, hyssop, pennyroyal. 137-Milk.

FOOD CHART FOR DAYS 2, 6, 10, ETC.

Food Families: 4, 9, 13, 14, 16, 17, 18, 19, 24, 26, 28, 30,
31, 32, 40b, 40d, 47, 50, 63, 64, 66, 69, 71,
72, 79, 98, 107, 109, 111, 117, 120, 122, 126.

Animal Protein: 98-Tuna, mackerel. 107-Whitefish. 109-Pike.
111-Carp, chub. 117-Frogs legs. 120-Turtle.
122-Dove, pigeon (squab). 126-Turkey, turkey eggs.

Vegetables: 9-Malanga, poi, taro. 14-Ñame, yam. 28-Beet,
chard, spinach. 47-Yuca. 69-Olive. 71-Comfrey,
79-Cucumber, pumpkin, squash, zucchini.

Fruit: 16-Banana, plantain. 32-Cherimoya, custard
apple, pawpaw. 40b-Apricot, cherry, peach,
plum. 63-Guava. 66-Bearberry, blueberry,
cranberry, huckleberry. 79-Cantaloupe,
melon, watermelon.

Seeds and Nuts: 24-Chestnut. 26-Macadamia. 40b-Almond.
79-Pumpkin seed.

Oils: Fats from any of the above. 40b-Apricot oil, almond
oil. 69-Olive oil.

Other: 4, 9, 13, 16, 17, 18, 19, 28-Quinoa. 30- Amaranth.
47-Arrowroot starch, poi, tapioca starch.

Sweeteners: 50-Maple syrup.

Herbs and Spices: 17-Ginger, turmeric. 40d-Burnet. 63-Allspice, clove.
71-Comfrey. 72-Lemon verbena.

Beverages: Juices, soups, and teas from any of the above.
31-Golden seal. 64-American ginseng, Chinese
ginseng. 71-Comfrey.

FOOD CHART FOR DAYS 3, 7, 11, ETC.

Food Families: 1, 7, 8, 10, 23, 27, 33, 39, 40c, 51, 65, 68, 70, 80, 81, 91, 96, 102, 106, 113, 114, 115, 129, 134, 135.

Animal Protein: 81-Abalone, clam, cockle, mussel, oyster, scallop, snail, squid. 91, 96, 102, 106, 113, 114, 115-All bass, all perch, all trout, croaker, grouper, salmon, sauger, walleye. 129-Rabbit. 134-Swine (bacon, ham, pork). 135-Caribou, deer (venison), elk, moose, reindeer.

Vegetables: 7-Chinese water chestnut. 65-Carrot, celeriac (celery root), celery, parsley, parsnip. 70-Sweet potato, camote. 80-Artichoke, dandelion, endive, Jerusalem artichoke, lettuce.

Fruits: 8-Date, coconut. 10-Pineapple. 27-Rhubarb. 39-Currant, gooseberry. 40c-Blackberry, raspberry, strawberry. 51-Litchi. 60-Prickly pear. 68-Persimmon.

Seeds and Nuts: 8-Coconut. 23-Filbert (hazelnut). 80-Sunflower seeds.

Fats and Oils: Fats from any of the above. 80-Safflower oil, sunflower oil.

Other: 1-Agar-agar. 8-Sago starch or pearls. 27-Buckwheat. 80-Artichoke flour, sunflower seed meal.

Sweeteners: Date sugar.

Herbs and Spices: 1-Kelp (seaweed). 33-Nutmeg. 65-Anise, caraway, celery seed, chervil, coriander, cumin, dill, fennel. 80-Santolina, tansy, tarragon.

Beverages: Juices, soups, and teas from any of the above. 80-Tea from boneset, burdock root, chamomile, chicory, goldenrod, yarrow.

FOOD CHART FOR DAYS 4, 8, 12, ETC.

Food Families: 3, 11, 20, 25, 36, 41, 45, 48, 49, 53, 54, 56, 59, 75, 100, 103, 121, 123, 124, 125, 130.

Animal Protein: 100-Swordfish. 103-Flounder, halibut, sole, turbot. 121-Duck (eggs), goose (eggs). 123-Ruffed grouse (partridge). 124-Chicken (eggs), pheasant, quail. 125-Guinea fowl. 130-Squirrel.

Vegetables: 11-Asparagus, chives, garlic, leek, onion, shallot. 36-Broccoli, Brussels sprouts, cabbage, cauliflower, Chinese cabbage, collards, kale, kohlrabi, mustard greens, radish, rutabaga, turnip, watercress. 41-Alfalfa, all beans, all peas, peanut, soybean. 54-Okra.

Fruit: 25-Fig. 45-Grapefruit, kumquat, lemon, lime, muscat, orange, pummelo, tangelo, tangerine. 48-Mango. 56-Kiwi (Chinese gooseberry). 59-Papaya.

Seeds and Nuts: 41-Peanut, soynut. 48-Cashew nut, pistachio nut. 75-Sesame seed.

Fats and Oils: Fats from any of the above. 41-Peanut oil, soy oil. 75-Sesame oil.

Other: 25-Breadfruit flour. 41-Carbo flour, lima bean flour, peanut flour, soy flour. 75-Sesame seed meal, tahini.

Sweeteners: 41-Clover honey, sage honey.

Herbs and Spices: 11-Garlic, chives. 20-Vanilla beans. 36-Horseradish, mustard.

Beverages: Juices, soups, and teas from any of the above. 3-Shavegrass. 49-Mate tea. 53-Basswood. 54-Althea root, hibiscus (roselle).

APPENDIX D

ALKALINE/ACID FORMING FOOD CHART

FOOD EFFECT ON BODY CHEMISTRY BALANCE:
A SERVICE OF THE ELISA/ACT FAMILY

For the Health of It, Eat to the Left.

HIGH	ALKALINITY	LOW	CATEGORY	LOW	ACIDITY	HIGH
BAKING SODA, UMEBOSHI PLUMS, SALT	SPICES, GRAIN BEVERAGES, MINERAL WATER, SOY SAUCE, SEA SALT; APPLE CIDER VINEGAR, MU TEA, SAKE, FRUIT WINE, GREEN TEA, GINSENG	SULFITE, ALGAE, SUCANAT, MOLASSESS, UMEBOSHI VINEGAR	OTHER ITEMS	MAPLE SYRUP, HONEY, ASPARTAME, COFFEE, BROWN RICE VINEGAR, BALSAMIC VINEGAR	BENZOATE, YEAST, TAPIOCA, VANILLA, ALCOHOL, BLACK TEA; PSYCHOTROPICS, ANTIBIOTICS, SACCHARIN	HOPS/MALT, PUDDING, SUGAR, COCOA, WHITE VINEGAR, JAM/JELLY
	HUMAN		DAIRY / PROCESSED, COW, GOAT, SHEEP, HUMAN	CREAM (COW), AGED CHEESE, GOAT CHEESE, SHEEP CHEESE	COW MILK, AGED CHEESES, GOAT MILK, YOGURT; CASEIN, 30-DAY CHEESES, SOY MILK, COTTAGE CHEESE	PROC. CHEESE, ICE CREAM
			FISH, MEAT, FOWL, GAME, WILD FISH, SHELL FISH, MOLLUSKS	EGGS, GELATIN/ORGAN MEATS, WILD DUCK, WILD VENISON, FISH, CRAB	HERRING, LAMB, GOOSE, TURKEY, SHELL FISH, EEL; VEAL, PORK, CHICKEN, PICKLED HERRING, CRUSTACEA	'FRIED FOODS', MEAT/FLESH, CARP, BONITA FLAKES, LOBSTER, OYSTER
WAKAME, PUMPKIN, BURDOCK, CURRY, LOTUS	POPPY SEED, CINNAMON, CHESTNUT, PEPPER, GINGER; PRIMROSE OIL, SPROUTS, SESAME SEED, ALMOND, COD LIVER OIL	AVOCADO OIL, LINSEED OIL, COCONUT OIL, OLIVE OIL, SEEDS (MOST)	NUTS, SEEDS, OILS, ROOTS, SPROUTS	SESAME OIL, GRAPE SEED OIL, SUNFLOWER OIL, PINE NUT OIL, CANOLA OIL	ALMOND OIL, SESAME OIL, CASHEW OIL, SAFFLOWER OIL, TOFU; PISTACHIO, CHESTNUT, LARD, PECAN, TROPICAL OILS	COTTONSEED MEAL, HAZELNUT, WALNUT, BRAZIL, HYDROGENATED OIL
	OATS, 'GRAIN COFFEE', QUINOA		GRAINS, CEREAL, GRASS	TRITICALE, MILLET, KASHA (CRACKED BW), AMARANTH, BROWN RICE	BUCKWHEAT (WHOLE), WHEAT, SPELT/TEFF, FARINA/SEMOLINA, WHITE RICE; MAIZE, GROATS BUCKWHEAT, CORN, RYE, OAT BRAN	BARLEY
LENTILS, YAM, NORI/KOMBU, DAIKON, BRASSICA, HIJIKI, SWEET POTATO	KHOLRABI, PARSNIP, GARLIC, KALE/SPINACH, ENDIVE, MUSTARD GREEN, TARO, BROCCOLI; FUNGI, MUSHROOM, CAULIFLOWER, RUTABAGA, SALSIFY, NIGHTSHADE, PUMPKIN, COLLARD GREEN	BRUSSEL SPROUT, BEET, CHIVE, OKRA, TURNIP GREEN, SQUASH, LETTUCE, GINGER	VEGETABLES, LEGUMES, PULSES, BEANS, SPICES	SPINACH, FAVA BEANS, KIDNEY BEANS, STRING/WAX BEANS, CURRY, CHUTNEY, RHUBARB	TOFU, PINTO BEANS, WHITE BEANS, NAVY/RED BEANS, AZUKI BEANS, LIMA BEANS, CHARD; GREEN PEA, PEANUT, SNOW PEA, CHICK PEA, CARROTS, LEGUMES, NUTMEG	SOYBEAN, CAROB, SOY MILK
NECTARINE, PERSIMMON, RASPBERRY, WATERMELON, TANGERINE	CANTELOUPE, HONEYDEW, CITRUS, OLIVE, DEWBERRY, LOGANBERRY, MANGO; PEAR, PINEAPPLE, APPLE, BLACKBERRY, CHERRY, PEACH, AVOCADO	APRICOT, BANANA, BLUEBERRY, CURRANT, RAISIN, GRAPE, STRAWBERRY, CREOLE TOMATO	FRUITS	GUAVA, PICKLED FRUIT, PINEAPPLE (DRY), FIGS, PERSIMMON JUICE, AVOCADO, DATES	PLUM, PRUNE, RHUBARB, TOMATOES; CRANBERRY, POMEGRANATE	

Prepared by Dr. Russell Jaffe for Serammune Physicians Lab, 1890 Preston White Drive, Suite 200, Reston, Va. 22091 | (703) 758-0610/(800) 553-5472]
from sources including Food & Nutrition Encyclopedia; Nutrition Applied Personally, by M. Walczak; Acid & Alkaline by H. Aihara.
Food growth, transport, storage, processing, preparation, combination, & assimilation influence effect intensity. [rev 10.91]

APPENDIX E

PRODUCTS, COMPANIES, AND ORGANIZATIONS

Organizations

American Academy of Environmental Medicine (AAEM), P.O. Box 16106, Denver, CO 80216. (303) 622-9755. Fax (303) 622-4224. (See master list for information.)

American Environmental Health Foundation, 8345 Walnut Hill Lane, Suite 200, Dallas, TX 75231. (214) 361-9515. (See master list for information.)

Environmental Health Center-Dallas, 8345 Walnut Hill Lane, Suite 205, Dallas, TX 75231. (214) 368-4132. Fax (214) 691-8432. (See master list for information.)

Practical Allergy Research Foundation, P.O. Box 60, Buffalo, NY 14223-0600. (716) 875-5578. Fax (716) 875-5399.

Pharmacies

If your local drug store cannot find you a dye-free, preservative-free,hard-to-locate nutrient or medication, check with the *Abrams Royal Pharmacy* or *The Apothecary*. (See master list.)

Detoxification Centers in the United States

American Environmental Health Foundation (AEHF). William Rea, M.D., Director. 8345 Walnut Hill Lane, Suite 200, Dallas, TX 75231. (214) 361-9515.

Center for Environmental Medicine. Allan Leiberman, M.D., Director. 7510 North Forest Drive, North Charleston, SC 29420. (803) 572-1600.

Environmental Detoxification Unit. David Buscher, M.D., Director. 1370 116 Avenue N.E., Suite 102, Bellevue, WA 98004-0288. (206) 453-0288.

Enviro-Med Clinic. Jeffrey White, M.D., Director. 3715 Azelle Street, Tampa, FL 33609. (813) 876-5442.

Health Med Clinic. G. Megan Shield, M.D., Director. 314 North Harper, Los Angeles, CA 90048. (213) 655-5928.

Detoxification Centers in Europe

Airedale Allergy Center. Jonathan Maberly, M.D., Director. High Hall, Steeton Nr. Keighley, West Yorkshire, BD20-6SB, England (0535) 56013.

Breakspear Hospital. Jean Monro, M.D., Director. High Street, Abbots Langley, Harts, WD5 OPU, England. 011-44-923-261333.

Institute of Environmental Diseases. Klaus-Dietrich Runow, M.D., Director. T.M. Kurpark 1, D 3501 Emstal, West Germany. 011-49-5624-8601.

Veramed Allergie-Klinik, Inzell H.P. Fredricksen, M.D., Director. Zivieselsto 2, 8221, West Germany. 011-49-08665-671-0.

Specialized Catalog Companies
(See Master List.)

The chapter "Success Stories" tells of two companies that were started because the owners could not find products they needed for themselves: Dust Free and Janice's.

The growing demand for less-toxic products has increased the number of special products and catalog companies. Unfortunately, because there is such a great increase in the use of toxic chemicals, many interested manufacturers have products safer than commercial products but not safe enough for very sensitive people. *Therefore, you must test every product for yourself. NO PRODUCT IS SAFE FOR EVERYONE.*

Some specialized catalog companies have free consultations to help you decide which products you may be able to tolerate depending on your sensitivity. Some companies have a certain return policy. Before purchasing anything, be sure you know what the policy is. Ask what the cost is for a trial period, if there is one.

You will find a brief description of the specialized catalog companies in the alphabetized list of Products, Companies, Organizations (and Detox Centers). To help you know what to look for in the master list, here is an abbreviated list.

Allergy Relief Shop, American Environmental Health Foundation, Cotton Dreams, The Cotton Place, Deva, Dona Designs, Environmental Health Center-Dallas, For Your Health Products, The Janice Corporation, The Living Source, N.E.E.D.S., Sandra DenBraber, R.N. (Write for their catalogs.)

MASTER LIST

Abrams Royal Pharmacy, 8256 Abrams Road, Dallas, TX 75231. (214) 349-8000. Speak to Bob Scarbrough, R.Ph.

Air filters. (See *Dust Free, AllerMed,* or *N.E.E.D.S.*)

Allergy Relief Shop, 2932 Middlebrook Park, Knoxville, TN 37921. (615) 522-2795. Complete line of products including air and water filters, air exchangers, cotton goods, all cotton mattresses and box springs, bedding, household products, and personal care items.

AllerMed Corporation, 31 Steel Road, Wylie, TX 75098. (214) 442-4898. High efficiency air purifiers for removing dust, pollen, mold spores, chemicals, smoke and other odors from the environment.

American Academy of Environmental Medicine (AAEM), P.O. Box 16106, Denver, CO 80216. (303) 622-9755. Fax (303) 622-4224. A group of physicians, scientists, and other professionals who are concerned about environmental effects on sensitive people. Special concerns are volatile hydrocarbons from solvents, plastics, insecticides, and similar agents. Contact them for the name of an Environmental Medicine (EM) specialist. *Meetings:* annual advanced seminars, basic seminars. Publications: The Archives of the Society, available to members.

American Environmental Health Foundation, 8345 Walnut Hill Lane, Suite 200, Dallas, TX 75231. (214) 361-9515. AEHF is an international referral center for environmental information that provides education and training for students, research scientists, and physicians. They also sell products designed specifically for chemically sensitive persons, i.e., ceramic and stoneware oxygen masks, air and water filters, Genitron, ozonators, radon and formaldehyde test kits, EMF measuring device, vitamin and mineral supplements.

Anderson Dental Lab, P.O. Box 327, 108 West Walnut, Centralia, WA 98531. (206) 736-6788.

The Apothecary, 5415 Cedar Lane, Bethesda, MD 20814. 1-800-869-9159 (301) 530-0800. Fax (301) 493-4671. Speak to Irv Rosenberg, P.D.

B. Gordon's Market, 11560A Rockville Pike, Rockville, MD 20852. (301) 230-0966. This is the first certified organic retail store. Contact the produce buyer and manager, Greg Grove, who can help you promote this certification in your area. He is a member of the Board of Certification in the State of Maryland working with the Department of Agriculture.

Bon-Ami Company, 112 West 9th Street, Kansas City, MO 64105. (816) 842-1230. Write or call to find local distributor.

CDX Peak Flow Meter, CDX Corporation, 2 Charles Street, Providence, RI 02904. 1-800-525-3515.

Cellophane. (See *AEHF*, The Living Source, Erlanders, or N.E.E.D.S.) Check to verify it is still wood derived. Products do change.

Ceramic masks. (See *AEHF* or The Living Source.)

Charcoal face masks. (See Sandra DenBraber.)

Chief Equipment Corporation, 70 West Sixth Avenue, #220, Denver, CO 80204. (303) 825-8169.

Chuck's Seafoods, P.O. Box 5478, Charleston, OR 97420. 1-800-255-4370. For tuna fish and salmon in glass jars.

Coconut soap. (See Rokeach.)

Cotton Dreams, P.O. Box 1261, Sebastian, FL 32958. (305) 589-0172. They sell children's underwear and playwear that is *not* treated with flame-retardant chemicals. Although many of their clothes resemble sleepwear, they cannot be sold as sleepwear because of federal regulations. Free catalog.

The Cotton Place, P.O. Box 59721, Dallas, TX 75229. (214) 243-4149. Their most important product is Naturalguard barrier cloth, which is custom manufactured to rigid specifications. Naturalguard is made from white pima cotton and does not contain the permanent chemical finish found in other barrier cloths. Its very fine weave acts as a barrier, providing some protection against dust, pollen, and other foreign particles often found in pillows, mattresses, and upholstery.
Free catalog. Unused and unlaundered items may be returned for a full refund. They will ship free within the continental United States on orders over $30.

Cotton stockings. (See Lismore Hosiery Company.)

Custom-made face masks. (See DenBraber, Sandra.)

Cycles, P.O. Box 23123, San Jose, CA 95153.

DenBraber, Sandra, R.N., 114 Ray Street, Arlington, TX 76010. (817) 860-9299. Cotton masks with charcoal filter (coconut shell) are contoured to the face. A soft metal nosepiece is enclosed in the cotton, and the elastic is cotton covered. Ties are available. Also available are alternatives (e.g., silk masks) for those sensitive to cotton or charcoal.

Denny Foil. (See Living Source or AEHF.)

Dentist: **Ted Moore, D.D.S.,** 8345 Walnut Hill Lane, Suite 100, Dallas, TX 75231. (214) 363-4021.

Deva, 303 East Main Street, Box F84, Burkittsville, MD 21718. (301) 473-4900. Deva is a catalog company which carries almost totally natural and untreated fabrics. If you tell them you are allergic, they will send samples of sufficient size to test different colors of the same fabric. Ask about their Natural Fibers Directory, a list of more than 90 mail order houses offering natural fiber alternatives. Free catalog.

Dinet and Delfosse, Inc., Prescriptive Druggists, 30 N. Michigan Ave., Room 915, Chicago, IL 60602. (312) 332-1364.

Dona Designs, 825 Northlake Drive, Richardson, Texas 75080. (214) 235-0485. Cotton bedding made of organically grown cotton. She also sells solid wood furniture and pure beeswax.

Dust Free^{TM}, Inc., Manufacturing and Distributing Air Cleaning Systems, P.O. Box 519, Royce City, TX 75089. (214) 635-9565. They market a self-charging electrostatic air filter and air quality control products.
Electronic pest control. (See For Your Health.)

EMF measuring device. (See AEHF or N.E.E.D.S.)

Environmental Health Center-Dallas, 8345 Walnut Hill Lane, Suite 205, Dallas, TX 75231. (214) 368-4132. Fax (214) 691-8432. An innovative medical clinic offering most medical practice services, with an added emphasis on exploring the impact of environmental factors on health and disease processes. The Center is devoted to helping patients achieve and maintain optimal health through diagnosis, treatment, and prevention.

Environmental Purification Systems, P.O. Box 191, Concord, CA 94526. 1-800-829-2129.

Erlander's Natural Products, P.O. Box 106, Altadena, CA 91001. (213) 797-7004. Free catalog.

Face masks. (See AEHF, Martha McMillan, or Sandra DenBraber.)

For Your Health Products, P.O. Box 15096, Chevy Chase, MD 20825. (301) 654-1127. This company has many products for clean air and water, natural light, and an electronic pest control system.

Heaters. (See Inter Central, Inc., formerly Zell-aire.)

Herro Care Water Purification System, 5121 North Central Avenue, Phoenix, AZ 85012. (602) 274-6563.

High Country Air System, P.O. Box 800232, Dallas, TX 75380. (214) 386-9615.

Inter Central, Inc. (formerly *Zell-aire*), Reading, PA 19603. (215) 376-5401 or 372-9579.

The Janice Corporation, P.O. Box 1292, West Caldwell, NJ 07007. 1-800-JANICES (1-800-526-4237). They provide clean, natural products for environmentally ill persons and those concerned with the environment and its impact on humans. Their pure and natural products are made from cotton and other natural materials. When there is consumer demand for a product not available in the marketplace, Janice has it made in her sewing room. Merchandise includes custom-made mattress sets, soap, underwear, sleepwear, blankets, sheets, cotton pillows, and other hard-to-find products.

The Janice Corporation runs by mail and telephone. Unused merchandise may be returned for full refund. For extra speedy service, call (201) 226-7753. Also use this number if your state of health requires individual assistance. Janice is an ecology patient and will try to help. Call the 800 number or write for a free catalog.

Keller Medical Specialists, 42609 Crawford Road, Antioch, IL 60002.
    1-800-843-6226.

Kennedy's Natural Foods, 1051 West Broad Street, Falls Church,
    Virginia 22046. (703) 533-8484. They issue a catalog and ship by
    United Parcel Service. We are very grateful to the Kennedys, who
    also helped us locate special items such as fish nail files for those
    sensitive to emery boards, and the Loofa, a natural plant body
    brush, real sponges, and other nontoxic products so difficult to find.

LaMaur, Inc. (Organicure), P.O. Box 1221, Minneapolis, MN 55440.
    (612) 571-1234.

Lismore Hosiery Company, 334 Grand Street, New York, NY 10002.
    (212) 674-3440. Cotton stockings.

The Living Source, 3500 MacArthur, Waco, TX 76708. (817) 756-6341.
    This company is very conscientious with their counselling.

Livos Plant Chemistry, 1365 Rufina Circle, Santa Fe, MN 87501.
    (505) 438-3448. Their products are all natural but many people
    cannot tolerate them. Test cautiously.

McMillan, Martha, 905 East Buffalo Avenue, Santa Ana, CA 92706.
    (714) 542-3296.

Mattresses. (See Janice's, Dona Designs, or Allergy Relief Shop.)

Medic Alert, P.O. Box 1009, Turlock, CA 95381. 1-800-344-3226.

Miele Vacuum Cleaner. Call 1-800-843-7231.

Moore, Ted, D.D.S., 8345 Walnut Hill Lane, Suite 100, Dallas, TX
    75231. (214) 363-4021.

N.E.E.D.S., 527 Charles Avenue, 12A, Syracuse, NY 13209.
    1-800-634-1380. Fax (315) 488-6315. A national mail order
    catalog for individuals with environmental illness and chemical
    sensitivities. Products include air and water purifiers, swimming
    pool purifiers, ozonators, test kits for formaldehyde, wood derived
    cellophane, etc. Free counseling. Request their catalog.

Neo-Life Company of America, 25000 Industrial Boulevard, Hayward, CA 94545. 1-800-432-5844. Call to find a local representative. If there is no local representative, order through AEHF. (See above.)

Nilfisk of America, Inc., 300 Technology Drive, Malvern, PA 19355. (215) 647-6420.

Organicure. (See LaMaur, Inc.)

OTT Light. (See For Your Health.)

Ozark Water, Warren Clough, 114 Spring Street, Sulphur Springs, AR 72768. 1-800-835-8908.

Ozone generator. (See AEHF or N.E.E.D.S.)

Paints. (See Livos, N.E.E.D.S., Allergy Relief Shop, or The Living Source.)

Paper goods. (See Today's Choice.)

Peak-flow meters. (See CDX Peak Flow Meter or Keller Medical Specialists.)

Practical Allergy Research Foundation (PARF), P.O. Box 60, Buffalo, NY 14223-0060. PARF is a foundation dedicated to research in the field of environmentally-triggered illness. In addition to scientific papers and books, the foundation produces videotapes excellent for educating the public, especially parent groups.

The Pure Water Place, Inc., P.O. Box 6715, Longmont, CO 80501. (303) 776-0056.

Red River Menstrual Pads, P.O. Box 486, Huntsville, Arkansas 72740.

Relaxation tapes (See Synesthetics).

RH of Texas, 8345 Walnut Hill Lane, Suite 204, Dallas, TX 75231. (214) 352-4596.

Rokeach and Sons, Farmingdale, NJ 07727. (201) 938-6131.
    Coconut soap.

Rugs. (See Janice's or Erlanders.)

Safe Haven, Inc., P.O. Box 384, Jacumba, CA 92034. (619) 766-4063. Ask for Mary Alice. Free catalog.

Sanitary pads (See Cycles, Red River Menstrual Pads, or Today's Choice.)

Special Foods, c/o Karen Slimak, 9207 Shotgun Court, Springfield, VA 22153. (703) 644-0991. Karen can make breads for you from exotic foods so that you can have bread every day without breaking your rotation. They are expensive but worth it when you're first beginning the rotation diet and feel the need for bread.

Spring-Clear (See High Country Air System.)

Sprout seeds. (See The Sprout House.)

The Sprout House, 40 Railroad Street, Great Barrington, MA 01230. (413) 528-5200. They sell organic sprouting seed of many varieties and also a kit that teaches you how to sprout your own seeds.

Swimming pool purifier. (See N.E.E.D.S.)

Synesthetics, Inc., Box 254, Cos Cob, CT 06807. Relaxation tapes.

Telephone. Call John Bogriski at (717) 282-5100 to order an old metal telephone with cloth wires.

Thurmond Air Quality Systems, Inc., 2512 Summit Avenue, Suite 305, Plano, TX 75074. (214) 422-4000 or 423-7068.

Today's Choice. Call 1-800-262-0042 to find local source of their paper goods and sanitary pads. Now available in many health food stores and drug stores.

Vacuum cleaner. (See Nilfisk, Miele, or Vita-Vac.)

Vita-Mix. (See Vita-Vac.)

Vita-Vac, 8615 Usher Road, Cleveland, OH 44138. 1-800-848-2649 or (216) 235-4840. Fax (216) 235-3726. Free catalog.

Walnut Acres, Penns Creek, PA 17862. (717) 837-0601. Free catalog.

Water filter. (See RH of Texas, AEHF, Herro, N.E.E.D.S., or Ozark Water.)

Winter Silks, The White Pine Company, Ltd., P.O. Box 301, Middleton, WI 53562. 1-800-621-3229. Free catalog; customer service. If others can't help you, ask for Cindy, ext. 247.

APPENDIX F

RECOMMENDED READING

The following publications and sources are suggested as aids for the person with food and/or chemical allergies who encounters daily problems related to an altered lifestyle. They can also be a source of medical information for spouses, relative, friends, and even doctors.

Newsletters

The Delicate Balance, National Center for Environmental Health Strategies, 1100 Rural Avenue, Voorhees, NJ 08043. (609) 429-5358. If you wish to keep up with current information on products, environmental problems, governmental action, etc., contact this non-profit organization. They make great strides educating the government and promoting changes beneficial to the cause of environmentally-triggered illness.

Mastering Food Allergies (Marjorie Hurt Jones, R.N., Editor). Mast Enterprises, Inc., 2615 North Fourth Street, Suite 616, Coeur d'Alene, ID 83814. Try new recipes using alternative foods. The editor is co-author of *The Yeast Connection Cookbook.* (See below.)

20th Century Living, P.O. Box 354, Forestburg, TX 76239.

Books

Buchholtz, Ilene, Karen Cook, and Theron Randolph, M.D.
An Alternative Measure. Human Ecology Research Foundation,
The Holmstad 1103-F, Tabyan Parkway, Route 31, Batavia, IL
60510. 1984.

Crook, William, M.D. *The Yeast Connection*. Professional Books,
Inc., P.O. Box 3494, 689 Skyline Drive, Jackson, TN 38301. 1989.

Crook, William, M.D. and Marjorie Hurt Jones. *The Yeast Connection*
Cookbook. Professional Books, Inc., P.O. Box 3494, 689 Skyline
Drive, Jackson, TN 38301. 1989.

Composition of Foods: Raw, Processed, and Prepared.
Comprehensive tables of the nutrient contents of various foods.
Order Handbook AH8, Stock #001-000-00768-8 from
Superintendent of Documents, U.S. Government Printing Office,
Washington, DC 20402.

Golos, Natalie, and Frances Golos Golbitz. *Coping with Your
Allergies*. New York: Simon & Schuster, Inc. (Fireside Division).
1986.

Gorman, Carolyn. *Less Toxic Living*. Environmental Health Center,
8345 Walnut Hill Lane, Dallas, TX 75231. 1991.

Hughes, Marija Matech. *Computer Health Hazards*. Hughes Press,
500 23rd Street, N.W., Box B203, Washington, DC 20037. 1990.

Jaffe, Russell M., M.D., Ph.D., et al. *Health Studies Collegium*.
Serammune Physicians Lab, 11100 Sunrise Valley Drive, Reston,
VA 22091. 1991.

Miller, Joseph, M.D. *Relief at Last!*, Springfield, Illinois: Charles C.
Thomas Publishing. 1987.

Randolph, Theron G., M.D., and Ralph W. Moss, Ph.D.
An Alternative Approach to Allergies. New York: Harper and
Row. 1989.

Randolph, Theron G. *Human Ecology and Susceptibility to the Chemical Environment.* Springfield, Ill.: Charles C. Thomas, Comprehensive discussion of sources of chemical contamination of air (indoor and outdoor), ingestants (food and drink), personal contacts (such as cosmetics), and treatment. 1962.

Rapp, Doris J. *Allergies and Your Family.* New York: Sterling Publishing Co., Inc. 1980.

____. *Allergies and the Hyperactive Child.* New York: Sovereign. 1979.

____. *Impossible Child.* Practical Allergy Research Foundation (PARF), P.O. Box 60, Buffalo, NY 14223-0060. 1989.

____. *Is This Your Child?* New York: William Morrow and Company, Inc. 1991.

Rea, William, M.D. *Chemical Sensitivities.* Lewis Publishers, Inc., 1215 Main, Chelsea, MI 48118. 1992.

Rousseau, David, William J. Rea, and Jean Enwright. *Your Home, Your Health and Well-Being.* Hartley and Marks, 3663 West Broadway, Vancouver, B.C., Canada V6R 2B8. 1986.

INDEX

A